Midnight heat . . .

Suddenly his lips crushed down upon hers, but when she felt his body boldly pressed against her, Jeanine was frightened into action.

Splaying her hands against his bare chest she began shoving. But the more she pushed against him, the more forcefully he held her, his kiss hard . . . almost drugging in its intensity.

A bizarre sort of weakness claimed Jeanine's insides, having never been kissed so demandingly, by any man. It was a kiss of fire, stirring strange, surely *primitive* sensations within her. And she feared these feelings more than she feared the man, for she was enjoying this overwhelming, euphoric state she was being drawn into.

As though willed by some unseen force, Jeanine felt herself begin to respond to his kiss. Her hands slipped away from his chest, her arms twining themselves about his neck . . .

Dear Reader:

Since the publication of my first sensual Indian romance in 1983, I have received thousands of letters requesting more. *Savage Splendor* is the third book in a series of romances about Indian ecstasy to be published by The Berkley Publishing Group. Two books are being published a year and the series will be set in as many major tribes across the country as possible.

My goal in each book is to give you carefully researched, authentic details of each tribe's customs, and stories of passion and true romance.

I am very enthusiastic about my Indian series. I hope you will read and enjoy every book!

My Warmest Regards,

Cassie Edwards

Charter Books by Cassie Edwards

SAVAGE SURRENDER
SAVAGE EDEN
SAVAGE SPLENDOR

Cassie Edwards

Savage Splendor

CHARTER BOOKS, NEW YORK

SAVAGE SPLENDOR

A Charter Book/published by arrangement with
the author

PRINTING HISTORY
Charter edition/September 1988

ISBN: 1-55773-094-6

Charter Books are published by The Berkley Publishing Group,
200 Madison Avenue, New York, New York 10016.
The name "Charter" and the "C" logo are trademarks
belonging to Charter Communications, Inc.

PRINTED IN THE UNITED STATES OF AMERICA

10 9 8 7 6 5 4 3 2 1

With admiration I dedicate *Savage Splendor* to my friends *Lee* and *Bill Bell,* creators and producers of *The Bold and the Beautiful,* and to those talented actors and actresses who give life to Lee and Bill's wonderful creation on the television screen.

Also

With sincere warmth I dedicate *Savage Splendor* to Mary Ann James, Abbey, and Pam of the Book Worm in Columbus, Georgia, with whom I have shared many special moments in my writing career. Friends found . . . and savored.

—CASSIE EDWARDS

Oh, is it not enough to be
Here with this beauty over me?
My throat should ache with praise, and I
Should kneel in joy beneath the sky.
O beauty, are you not enough?
Why am I crying after love
With youth, a singing voice, and eyes
To take earth's wonder with surprise?
Why have I put off my pride,
Why am I unsatisfied. . . .
I, for whom the pensive night
Binds her cloudy hair with light . . .
I, for whom all beauty burns
Like incense in a million urns?
O beauty, are you not enough?
Why am I crying after love?

—Sara Teasdale

AUTHOR'S NOTE

In *Savage Splendor* the Chippewa Indians are revisited one last time, transporting the reader to the beautiful hills and woods of Minnesota. The Chippewa were not prominent in history because of their remoteness from the frontier during the Colonial Wars. But they comprise one of the largest tribes on the North American continent and are representative of a general division known as Woodland Indians.

With the appearance of the white man in the changing life of the Chippewa, prehistoric tools were abandoned in favor of the white man's iron and steel. Thus a major transition began to take place in which the Chippewa gradually incorporated into their own lives the tools of the white man, as well as his dress, and his hunting and domestic equipment.

Savage Splendor unfolds with a powerful Chippewa warrior torn between two worlds . . . that of the white man, and that of the red man!

One

Duluth, Minnesota: Early summer, 1901

The large room evoked an open feeling that was enhanced by several lit brass lamps suspended from the ceiling, their wicks turned high. A two-sided fireplace jutted into the parlor; a fire simmering low on the grate emitted soft, shadowy glimmers on the paneled walls. An ebony-wood upright Baldwin piano stood against a far wall.

The divan and matching chairs of the room were plush and thick, their flowered designs bright and cheerful. So many had said they matched the personality of their owner, Jeanine Thaxton, so often described as sparkling . . . vivacious.

A loud, gravelly voice broke through the silence of the room. "So, Jeanine, you prefer this over your Uncle Fred's place, eh?" Fred said, walking around the parlor, puffing on a cigar. ''A ranch house in Duluth? Unique, to say the least.''

Stopping to admire Jeanine's collection of paintings, which included a rare Van Gogh and a Monet, Fred smiled to himself. His niece had done herself proud. She had proven herself to be successful at anything she set her mind to. Not only was she the art curator for the Duluth Art Museum, she also traveled to schools, lecturing to children about Minnesotan culture. Even in the field of publishing, Jeanine had achieved a substantial measure of success. Three published books on art and history could now be found in most libraries across the country, bearing her name.

Jeanine moved to her uncle's side and looked up into his eyes, seeing the color of her own in his . . . the color of growing, fresh green grass. ''Well? You haven't told me. Do *you* approve of my new house, Uncle Fred?'' she asked, always seeking his approval. Yet, even when she didn't get it, going ahead and doing as she pleased anyway.

Orphaned at a young age, Jeanine had only recently broken her ties from her adoptive uncle, Fred Hunter, who had taken her in to raise her. She had purchased a wide and sprawling ranch house from Judith McMahon, who had left Duluth to live with her Indian husband, Strong Hawk.

It was often necessary for Jeanine to prove her independence to her uncle, for he was an overbearing man by nature, often pushing his ideals and opinions on others. To gain her own sense of self, Jeanine had left her uncle's house to live alone, needing a space that he would never allow her to enjoy while she was living with him. He had failed to realize that she was no longer a teenager, but instead, a woman . . . an *independent* woman.

''And if I don't approve?'' Fred said, chewing on his cigar. ''Would you come back home? Live with your Uncle Fred?''

His gaze traveled over her, seeing so much of her late mother in those beautiful features. Just like her mother,

Jeanine was the sort to cause a second glance. In her pink silk, floor-length dress, brocaded with tiny green flowers and silver leaves, and with her hair the color of coal tumbling across her fair shoulders and down to her tiny waist, she was a picture of loveliness. Her green eyes fringed with thick, black lashes, were luminous. Her delicate, oval cheeks were pink; her breasts displayed a deep cleavage where her dress dipped low in front.

Yes, she was the image of her mother and so often made Fred's loss of his sister hurt twofold because of the similarity. In his lifetime he had loved only two women—the wife he had been robbed of all those many years ago, and his sister, who had met an untimely death, way too young.

His sister had died in a boating accident. It had been swift, with no suffering. He didn't ever want to labor over how his beautiful wife had died! He had long ago been able to place it behind him. He had managed to make a life without her.

Annoyed that he should even come close to suggesting that she move back with him, Jeanine turned away from Fred, went to the liquor cabinet, and poured herself a glass of wine. Then, aware that he had followed her and was again at her side, she turned and offered him her most winsome smile, sipping her wine and silently studying him before giving him a set answer.

Though Jeanine was statuesque, her Uncle Fred towered over her. Known to stand way over six feet in his stockinged feet, his boots added another two inches; he could easily be taken for being nearly seven feet tall.

But of course this was an exaggeration in Jeanine's mind, having been in awe of her uncle for as far back as her mind could recollect. He was not just a large man with a powerful build; his voice was also outstanding. When he spoke, it was always in a loud, threatening growl, as though he had taught himself to speak in this authoritative way to throw fear into those who dared defy him and his title of Sheriff of Duluth.

But Jeanine had learned long ago not to fear him in any

way for, while with her, his heart was mellow and his intentions pure. She had become the child he never had. He had been married long before Jeanine had been born, but never spoke of his wife or what had happened to her. His work had become his mistress, his life.

So much about her Uncle Fred drew Jeanine to loving him. His hair was more red than blonde, thick, and with some natural curl. A scattering of tight, stubborn curls lay at his brow. The rest of his hair hugged his neck where he wore it cropped short to just above his collar.

His face was not that of a handsome man, instead rugged and ruddy. His eyebrows were bushy over compelling green eyes. The nose displayed a crook in it, having been broken by an outlaw back in St. Louis, Missouri, their original home.

A shaggy, thick mustache covered part of his upper lip; his teeth were yellow from smoking cigars.

Always dressed in dark suits and white shirts which contrasted with his tanned face, Fred Hunter was sometimes referred to as the devil. Yet most who truly knew him, saw him as fair, honest, and very likeable.

"Well? Are you going to answer me?" Fred growled, unnerved by Jeanine's silence. "If I said I didn't approve of your house, *would* you come back home and live with me? My house is mighty quiet without you. All I seem to hear nowadays is my own voice echoin' back at me."

Not wanting to get caught up in feelings of guilt for having left her uncle alone in his waterfront mansion, Jeanine overlooked his reference to her having done so.

"Uncle Fred, admit it," she teased. "You *do* like my house, don't you? It *is* unique, isn't it?" She placed her wine glass down, then fondly curled her fingers about his hands.

"Do you know the history of this place?" she asked excitedly, sounding more like a girl of twelve, than twenty. "The father of Judith McMahon, the woman who sold this house to me, was originally from Texas. That's why he built this sort of house in Duluth when he moved here.

Judith McMahon is now married to the Chippewa Indian Chief Strong Hawk. Don't you find that fascinating, Uncle Fred?''

Fred's face shadowed into a dark frown. He jerked his hands free from hers and grabbed his cigar from his mouth. ''Injuns nor nothin' about them are fascinatin',''he argued, tossing his half-smoked cigar into the fireplace.

He tightened a fist to his side, glowering as he again looked the room over. ''Wouldn't be surprised if fleas from that damn Injun Strong Hawk ain't crawlin' in the corners of this place. That's all Injuns are good for . . . breedin' fleas in their hair and on their grungv flesh.''

Jeanine paled. ''Uncle Fred,'' she gasped. ''How shameful!''

Yet his behavior toward the Indians did not completely surprise her. This was the only thing lacking in her description of her uncle as being fair. He despised Indians. He saw them as less than human, yet feeling so without reason as far as Jeanine knew. Her uncle reacted as so many others did. They could only remember the bad they had heard about the Indians, not the good.

Jeanine turned with a start when she heard a low chuckle behind her. She stiffened when she discovered someone she despised just entering the room, pausing to stand in the doorway. Her eyes met and held those of Cameron Tyner's, her uncle's deputy and sidekick. The two of them were hardly separable. She felt a slow rage rising inside her, wondering who he thought he was, entering her house unannounced, *uninvited*!

A rush of cold spread through Jeanine as Cameron continued to stare at her with his glinting blue eyes. He had never approached her sexually, but she knew to expect it to happen one day. He had mentally undressed her more than once, she knew. Though muscled and handsome in a rugged sort of way with his blonde hair, deep tan, and tight-fitting jeans and shirt, Jeanine detested him. He was nothing but trouble, shifty in every sense of the word.

She knew that his attraction to her wasn't just a sexual

one. He also admired her position in the community. Somewhere in his devious mind, Cameron saw that marrying her would be an opportunity for him to finally look like an upstanding citizen in the community. He would never realize it took more than appearances to become a man of genteel qualities. It took breeding . . . something which Cameron Tyner knew not the first thing about.

Though Jeanine's uncle had been taken in by Cameron Tyner and his slick ways, she would not allow him to use *her* in any way. To Jeanine, he represented everything bad in a man.

The pistols holstered at Cameron's waist and his shiny cowboy boots with their large spurs hinted of his having come from Texas. Jeanine wished he'd never left! As far as she knew, only her uncle came anywhere close to liking him, and that was because Cameron had proven that he had a quicker draw to the gun than her uncle did. Uncle Fred looked to Cameron as a sort of insurance policy for himself. Cameron had already saved her uncle's life once on the streets of Duluth when a gunman had attempted to gun him down.

"Oh, *there* you are, Cameron!" Fred said, his long strides taking him across the room to pat Cameron on the back. "Took you long enough to settle the horses in." He gestured toward the liquor cabinet. "Just make yourself at home." He chuckled low. "The whiskey's invitin', ain't it?"

A slow, angered blush rose to Jeanine's cheeks. Her uncle was taking liberties in her house, as though it were his own. Perhaps he felt anything that was hers was his, for having taken her in when she had been orphaned. But to invite the scoundrel Cameron Tyner to make himself at home was almost too much for Jeanine to bear.

Fearing she just might say too much once she got started, Jeanine looked away from Cameron and how he strutted so boldly to her liquor cabinet. When his spurs quit jangling, she knew that he was helping himself to *her* whiskey, drinking from one of *her* glasses.

Yet she still did not voice her dislike. Her uncle did not come calling all that often. He was usually too occupied with his duties as sheriff. Jeanine had invited him to visit *this* evening for a reason. She was going to give him the opportunity to accompany her on her journey north to the village of the St. Croix Band of the Chippewa. He could never accuse her later of not being open with him about her decision to do something that provoked a keen anxiousness even inside her own heart, each time she thought about it.

But she knew what to expect when she mentioned the word "Indian" to him again. And when he heard her plans to involve her*self* with Indians, she could even now imagine his outrage.

Uncle Fred lumbered over to Jeanine and stepped in her line of vision. "I hope you don't mind that I took it upon myself to make your invite include Cameron," he said, smiling down at her. "He's been wantin' to see your ranch house ever since you moved in. A part of the Texan in him is homesick, I reckon. You don't mind that he came, do you?"

Jeanine couldn't stay angry at her uncle for long when he gave her such a soft, boyish smile. Sometimes he was like a little boy, with the pains of growing up still ahead of him. "Not at all," she lied.

But sorely needing to get away from Cameron's stares, she swept the hem of her dress up into her arms and walked toward the double French doors that led out to a terrace . . . a terrace that she only recently had added to her house, to better enjoy the view of Duluth and Lake Superior.

"It's such a beautiful evening, Uncle Fred. Let's go out on the terrace and enjoy the sunset," she encouraged, casting Cameron a stern look across her shoulder, then a half glance toward her uncle, also needing privacy to tell him her plan.

She knew that he wouldn't approve, much less offer assistance. And if he didn't give it, she, as usual, would go ahead anyway. But she needed to talk to her uncle about it in full privacy . . . not in the company of the dreaded Cameron Tyner.

It had become a strong drive of hers . . . this urge to talk with Judith McMahon, to learn the customs and rituals of the Chippewa people and to find out, if possible, how Judith had become acquainted with Strong Hawk, and later married him. Jeanine was eager to see if Judith would tell her about the other white women who had married into the Chippewa Indian tribe. She wished to delve into the mysteries of these Indians, not only to lecture about them to the school children of Duluth, but also to write a book about them.

But she must do her research firsthand. She must travel to the Indian village. It was important to her to make her book true to life. She must make her lectures true and compelling. These lectures were a way of giving of herself. To share with those who saw the importance of learning, had grown important to her. And she so loved the children. . . .

Grabbing a shawl from a peg on the wall, Jeanine snuggled it about her shoulders, smiling a silent thank-you to her uncle as he opened the doors that led out to the terrace. A cool breeze lifted her hair from her shoulders as she moved alongside her uncle to stand next to the terrace railing.

"I must admit, I *do* like many things about your house," Fred said, placing his hands on the sturdy wood and leaning his full weight against it. He gave a quick glance across his shoulder toward the French doors and laughed, then eyed Jeanine amusedly. "French doors in a ranch house? And a terrace? Yes, only you would do something like that."

Jeanine folded her arms across her chest, enfolding them within the shawl to protect herself from the cool air dancing down the front of her dress. "I had to have full access to this view," she sighed. "Look at it, Uncle Fred. Isn't it just so peaceful?"

Located on a high bluff, her house overlooked the breadth

of Lake Superior. Her gaze swept around her, capturing the loveliness of the setting. A heron crying from somewhere afar informed all that the day was ending. The sunset filled the entire sky, its reflection a great splash of orange in the waters of Lake Superior, drifting westward. Across the way, huge virgin pines were catching the last rays of the sun in their tops. Nothing was astir, only windblown ripples chasing through the trees.

Just below the terrace, the twisted wood of the trees reached upward, then the hill from which they grew seemed suddenly to plunge away to a steep valley slope. The decline was so steep, leaning over the railing Jeanine still could not see where it began or ended. The terrace had been positioned beautifully over this abyss: it was an almost breathtaking experience merely to stand upon it.

Further on, into the distance below, Jeanine could see Duluth. It was a city that ran along the west end of Lake Superior, on St. Louis Bay, one hundred and fifty-six miles northeast of St. Paul. The first settlers had arrived in the 1850s and it had become a city in 1870. Duluth had grown rapidly after 1880, when the lumbering and iron ore trades had developed. It was now a city of widespread industry and commerce.

"Ah, and smell it," Jeanine said, inhaling, not yet having the courage to begin talking about her plans with her uncle. "The air is always heavy with the smell of pine. I just love it. I just love *Duluth*."

"Yeah, Duluth is alright," her uncle replied in a tolerant tone. "But once I rid it of its vermin outlaws, it's going to be *grand*. One year here as sheriff ain't been nearly enough time to prove my true worth."

His eyes squinted as he peered into the distance. "But most people these days ain't worryin' about critters who walk on two legs," he grumbled. "Most are frettin' over the scare of critters that *fly*. Some say this could be the year of the return of the Rocky Mountain locusts. I hear tell that in 1873 those damn locusts, called grasshoppers by some, nearly wiped out Duluth's wheat crop."

"Why do you think they'll return this year, Uncle Fred?" Jeanine asked, shivering at the thought of the beady-eyed insects.

Fred gripped his hands hard onto the rail. " 'Cause this year a terrible blizzard killed hundreds of farm animals in Minnesota just like it did in seventy-three," he stated flatly. "Things move in cycles. The year of the blizzard could be the year of the locusts, just like before. Who can truly say?"

He eyed Jeanine questioningly, seeing how nervously she was fidgeting with the fringes of her shawl. "But something tells me you've more on your mind than talk of locusts. You seem a might restless. What is it, Jeanine? What've you got up your sleeve? Tell me. Do you have another book on the horizon, or what?"

Jeanine smiled up at him awkwardly. She drew the shawl even more closely about her shoulders when a cooler breeze caused goosebumps to rise on her flesh.

Fred saw her sudden chill. He slipped an arm about her waist and began guiding her back into the house. "Well, before you take your death of cold, we're goin' back inside by the fire," he demanded.

Jeanine was already escorted inside before she had time to object. Swinging away from Fred, she let her shawl flutter from her arms onto a chair, relieved to notice that Cameron had made himself scarce; apparently he had left the house. Now if her uncle exploded over what she was going to tell him, at least it would be in privacy.

Trying to behave nonchalantly, Jeanine took a book from the fireplace mantel and began thumbing through it. "You asked if I'm going to be writing another book," she said softly. "Yes. It *is* time. I don't like having too much time between my projects."

Fred went to the liquor cabinet and poured himself a shot of whiskey. "And what might this one be about?" he asked, drinking the whiskey in one fast gulp.

Jeanine watched as he set the glass down and came beside her, stooping to place another log on the fire. She tensed. "My next book?" she said, replacing the book back on the mantel. She sank down onto the divan, nervously positioning the fullness of the skirt of her dress about her.

Purposely avoiding his eyes, Jeanine continued. "I would like to write about Indians. I believe there is much to be said about the Chippewa of Minnesota. Don't you think a book about their lives would be interesting, Uncle Fred? Don't you think the Chippewa Indians would make an interesting topic of discussion in the classroom? I would so enjoy lecturing about them."

Her uncle's quick intake of breath made Jeanine's back stiffen. Her eyes rose upward slowly, to meet his disbelieving stare. Jeanine's pulse raced when she saw a familiar twitch begin in his right cheek and his eyes darken; he was trying to hold his temper at bay.

"And what would you write about? What would you lecture about?" he said thickly. "An Injun is an Injun."

Jeanine rose from the divan. She twined her hands together behind her back, yet boldly spoke up into her uncle's face. "Uncle Fred, I wish to write of—to lecture about—all of the Chippewa customs, of their pride of heritage. I hope even to write about the white women who have married Chippewa Indians," she blurted. "I want to personally interview Judith McMahon . . . ask about her life with Chief Strong Hawk. I want to ask her about Danette, the woman who was married to Chief Gray Wolf."

Aware of Jeanine's stubborn determination once she set something in her mind, Fred didn't want to come right out and forbid her to do anything. He would first try tact. Then, if that didn't work, he would order her to forget this foolishness of Indians.

He turned on his heel and went to the paintings that graced the far wall. "Why not concentrate on one career at a time?" he said thickly. "You have so much talent in acquiring paintings. These that you have are proof of that."

Jeanine's jaw tightened. Her uncle was doing just as she

had expected. But now that she had finally approached him with the subject of Indians, she was not going to be put off all that easily.

"I enjoy writing as much as I enjoy my career as an art curator and lecturer," she said, moving to his side. She nodded to the paintings where his eyes still seemed glued, though she knew he was only looking at them to avoid eye contact with her. "I enjoy my private collection of paintings as I do my private collection of books. And one day I plan to add another book to my collection, Uncle. With it shall be placed the one that I have written about the Chippewa Indians."

Gently placing a hand to his arm, Jeanine urged him to look at her. "Uncle Fred, I must travel to the Chippewa Indian village to interview Judith McMahon personally. I am determined to write this book; I do feel so strongly about it. It lives with me day and night. It has become a part of me. Such a drive cannot be ignored. Do you understand, Uncle Fred? Do you? Will you even accompany me there?"

Fred glared down at her as he clasped his hands to her shoulders. "Hell, no, I won't take you to a damn Indian village," he snarled, his eyes snapping. "And you ain't goin', either. Do you hear?"

A rush of anger scorched Jeanine's insides. "You're giving me an order, Uncle Fred?" she said, unable to hide the tremor in her voice.

"It amounts to about that. Leastways I'm givin' it a damn good try."

"Well, try as you may, it won't work," Jeanine said, lifting her chin stubbornly. "Now do you go with me to the Indian village, or do I have to go by myself?"

"You wouldn't . . ."

"I *will*."

"Damn it, Jeanine . . ."

"Well? Will you go with me, Uncle Fred?"

"You already know the answer to that, Jeanine," Fred said, dropping his hands from her shoulders.

Frustrated, Jeanine combed her fingers through her hair. "Oh, Uncle Fred, why must you be this way?" she sighed. "Why do you hate the Indians so much?"

Her uncle gave her an icy stare, then stomped to the foyer that led to the front door. Grabbing his Stetson hat from a peg on the wall, he turned and glowered down at Jeanine, who had followed him.

"You forget this damn foolishness, Jeanine," he warned, plopping his hat on his head. "Injuns ain't a pleasant lot to be around."

"How would you even know?" Jeanine softly cried. "Lord, Uncle Fred, you've never even given them a chance. It's all in your head. Why can't you see that?"

Fred rushed from the house, slamming the door behind him.

Jeanine opened the door and went to stand on the porch, watching her Uncle Fred mount his roan; he was talking in a low voice to Cameron who was giving Jeanine occasional glances as he also swung up into his saddle.

Jeanine hugged herself as they rode away, trying to ward off the chill that was attacking her. She had expected this reaction from her uncle, but had hoped for better. She hated going against him, but knew that she must . . . and soon.

Two

The air was pungent with the smell of herbs. Smoke circled over round rocks that lay in the fire. The herbs had been placed there to purify the air as the rocks became heated. The wigwam was dark except for the flames that cast a golden light from the firespace, dug deeply into the ground in the center of the floor. The glow enveloped two figures. One was spread out on bulrush mats, dressed in her finest fringed doeskin dress decorated with porcupine quills. The other was kneeling beside the one lying there, lingering somewhere between life and death.

"*Gee-mah-mah,*" Lone Wolf said, looking down at his mother who was so pale . . . so gaunt. He forced the choking sensation not to invade his throat, for it was not manly to show emotion so openly, not even though his dear mother was dying.

He had been taught the skills of self-restraint from childhood to his present age of twenty-five *zee-gwums*, springs. But it was difficult. Lone Wolf had not yet experienced a loved one's death. And to lose a mother was to lose part of one's self.

Reaching a shaking hand to her son, Little Swan reveled in his closeness, his handsomeness. It was almost the same as looking at Gray Wolf, the man she had loved those many years ago. Even now, the thought of Gray Wolf made her heart sing. But he had chosen another. He had only been in her life for a short while, yet enough time to become with child . . . *his* child.

It hadn't seemed fair that Gray Wolf wouldn't know about this son, yet it had been fairness to Little Swan's husband, now a proud chief, that had led her to keep the secret locked within her heart. And pride! That had also been a reason not to reveal that she had been with child when Gray Wolf had married the white woman with the strange name of Danette. The only thing that Little Swan had regretted about it all was the deceit. She had let her husband, Chief White Cloud, believe the son was his.

"Neen nin-gwis," Little Swan said in a bare whisper, grasping onto Lone Wolf's hand. "My son. My . . . beautiful . . . son."

She blinked her eyes and licked her parched lips, then again looked up at Lone Wolf, idolizing him. Attired in only a brief loincloth, his copper skin gleamed in the glow of the fire, almost golden.

Just as his father's had been, Lone Wolf's cheekbones were high, his nose was long and straight, and his jaw, powerfully set. His hair was midnight black and was worn straight to his shoulders, kept in place by a colorfully beaded headband with a lone eagle's feather thrust into the coil of his hair at the back.

His eyes were not of his father's. Lone Wolf's were so dark, they resembled the blackest of nights, while Gray Wolf's had been green, a characteristic passed down to Gray Wolf from his white mother.

But the wide breadth of Lone Wolf's shoulders, the solidness of his torso and thighs, his muscles knotting and rippling even now as he knelt beside his mother, were evidence of his true father's physique. All this, it was clear, had been passed down from father to son.

And Lone Wolf had learned well the art of dignity. He would one day make a great chief. But, in truth, he should already be chief of the St. Croix Band of Chippewa instead of Strong Hawk, who now claimed the title! Lone Wolf had been the first child born to Chief Gray Wolf! Not Strong Hawk nor Strong Hawk's twin brother, Silver Fox.

Turning her eyes away from Lone Wolf, fearing that he might see the sparkle of tears in their corners, Little Swan was ready to welcome death. She had carried too much inside her heart for too long. And even now that she was finally going to tell her son the full truth, the burden to herself would be no lighter; it had been there too long to go away now.

She had felt her life ebbing away the very instant she had heard of Chief Gray Wolf's death. When he had died, so had Little Swan's silent dreams of one day being held again in his arms, being whispered to . . . being kissed by lips that had melted her, made her forever want him.

To him, those many years ago, their moments together had been frivolous. To her, they had been the moon . . . the stars . . . the Heavens!

But Little Swan had never let him know of his importance to her. And now she would never even be given an opportunity to tell him. Unless their paths were to meet in the hereafter. This, too, was her reason for welcoming death. In the hereafter, surely she and Gray Wolf would once again meet.

"*Gee-mah-mah,* what is it?" Lone Wolf said softly, seeing how she turned her eyes from him but not before he could see the tears nestled in their corners. "Your eyes speak to me of more than sadness this day. Tell me what is troubling you, Mother. Your son is here to comfort you."

Lone Wolf would not say to her that he had seen this same strange expression many times before when she had been studying him in silence. It troubled him then, it troubled him now. But this was the only time he had questioned her. If not now, perhaps never. His mother's sunrises seemed now to be numbered.

Sighing heavily, finding it harder and harder to get her breath as each moment passed, Little Swan slowly turned her eyes back to Lone Wolf. How could she say the words required of her?! Though practiced, over and over again in the wee hours of this morning, she was finding it hard to form the words on her lips. Perhaps she had waited too long.

Yet she knew her true reason for the hesitation. She did not want to lose the respect of her only son. He had been her substitute for Gray Wolf throughout the years. Should he turn away from her, her last breath could be taken at that painful moment of denial.

Her fingers trembling against the strength of Lone Wolf's as he held onto her hand, Little Swan smiled up at him weakly. "My son, there is so much to say to you before our final good-bye," she said in the perfect English both she and Lone Wolf knew so well.

Though their times together had been short, the art of this language had been learned by Little Swan from Gray Wolf. She had been an avid pupil, he the teacher. The time he spent with the loggers in Duluth had taught Gray Wolf many things, sadly for Little Swan, even the art of loving a white woman.

"What is it that you feel must be said, *Gee-mah-mah*?" Lone Wolf asked quietly, crossing his legs beneath him as he settled down beside her. "Lone Wolf listens well. Lone Wolf is a dutiful son."

Little Swan reached out with her free hand and patted Lone Wolf's knee. "No one knows better than your mother what sort of son you are," she murmured. "And what sort of mother do you think I have been?"

"Devoted," Lone Wolf said, his dark eyes softening with feeling. "You have been not only devoted but a true *gee-wee-gee-ah-gun*. No son could ever ask for a better friend than you. You have always been there for me. Always."

Little Swan lowered her eyes, feeling the splash of a tear on her cheek as she could no longer hold back the need to cry. "My love for you is so deep," she softly cried. "Yours for me has always been the same. If what I tell you changes that, I . . ."

Lone Wolf leaned closer to his mother and placed a hand to her cheek. With his thumb he smoothed her falling tears away from her flesh, tensing when he felt the utter coldness of her skin. The wigwam was warm, even too warm. Her coldness meant only one thing. She was slipping away from him much too quickly.

"Mother, you did not complete your words to me," he said thickly. His heart was hammering against his chest, aching so inside because he would not have her for much longer, to draw comfort from her arms . . . her sweetness . . . her words.

He did not want to say a final good-bye. Life would be too empty without her. He had not found a woman to love, to take his mother's place in his life. Until now, none had caused special feelings inside him. Thus far when with a woman, only the basic needs of the flesh had been fulfilled.

But now he must look more sincerely for that specially favored woman to bring sunshine and laughter into, not only his heart, but his wigwam, too. A woman to stay at his side, *ah-pah-nay,* forever!

"*Ay-uh,* yes, now is the time to tell you," Little Swan said, blinking tears from her long lashes. "Please understand, my son. Do not lose respect for your *gee-mah-mah* while she takes her final breaths of life. Your mother would never rest in peace in the hereafter should you turn away from her."

Little Swan tried to inch up from her bed, her eyes desperately wide, then crumpled back down, breathing hard. "My son, my son . . ." she sobbed.

Being witness to his mother's struggles was causing pieces of Lone Wolf's heart to tear away and, not understanding her attempts with words, made his heart pain him even more. He reached for a dampened buckskin cloth and placed it to her brow, washing the cold perspiration away, then lay the cloth aside. He bent to cradle her head in the curve of his arm.

"Never would I love you or respect you less," Lone Wolf said hoarsely. "How could you even think that I could, *Gee-mah-mah?* Do not be afraid to speak openly to me. Tell me now what is troubling you, then your heart will be free of sorrow . . . of pain."

"But yours? What will my words do to your heart? You will carry a burden till now carried only by me," Little Swan said, watching his face, seeing how she had so confused him and hating herself for this.

Lone Wolf's eyebrows lifted while he became filled with wonder as his mother began to explain.

"Lone Wolf, long ago there was another man in my life," she said softly, her eyes almost unblinking as she gazed up into his face. "Before my marriage to Chief White Cloud, my heart belonged to another."

She paused to lick her lips, then continued. "I was in love with Gray Wolf of the neighboring St. Croix Band of the Chippewa, but the love was only one-sided. He fell in love with a white woman. After he became blinded by the woman's white flesh, Gray Wolf no longer hungered for a Chippewa woman as his companion."

Gripping Lone Wolf's hand harder, Little Swan pleaded with her eyes. "My son, this must be told to you," she said in a half cry. "I am dying. You must know all truths now, for I am the only one who can tell you. It is only fair that you know."

"That I know *what*?" Lone Wolf asked softly. "That you loved someone besides Father? Why is it best that I know that? It is possible to love more than one man in a lifetime." He swept a fallen lock of hair from her brow. "*Gee-mah-mah*, do not strain yourself so to confess such a thing to me. It is not important. You have been a good wife to your husband. You have been a good mother. Who you loved in the past is not important."

"Oh, but it is," Little Swan said, desperation revealed

in the higher pitch of her voice. "You do not understand what it is I am trying to tell you."

She reached a finger to Lone Wolf's lips. "*Bee-sahn*, my son," she softly urged. "Be quiet and listen to what else I have to say."

Lone Wolf nodded and cradled her closer, trying to transfer some of his strength to her. He feared that she was putting too much strain on herself by continuing to talk. But it was apparent that nothing would stop her. His mother was driven, it seemed.

"When I loved Gray Wolf, it was not known to him just how much," Little Swan said in a near whisper, choking back a sob. "You see, I was with child by Gray Wolf when we said our last good-bye. This child was you, Lone Wolf."

Lone Wolf stifled a gasp as he looked disbelievingly at his mother. He tensed, yet did not move away from her. He feared that the shock of her knowing how her words had stung his heart would be too great.

But to find out something so unbelievable had made him speechless. The father he had worshipped all these years was not his father? His father was, in truth, the recently departed Chief Gray Wolf of the St. Croix Band of the Chippewa? Lone Wolf had brothers? He knew of Strong Hawk and Silver Fox! He knew that Strong Hawk was now chief of the St. Croix Band of the Chippewa! Should . . . Lone Wolf . . . be chief, instead of Strong Hawk? The sudden confusion tore at his insides! Surely he had heard wrong!

"My son, say something," Little Swan softly pleaded, reaching a hand to his face. "Do not sit there so stiffly. Let me further explain—then condemn if you must. But I pray to the Great Spirit that you will not want to. What I did, I did out of love. You were conceived out of love. I love my husband, but I also loved Gray Wolf. With all my heart I loved him."

"He never knew?" Lone Wolf asked, his glittering dark

eyes showing the intensity of his feelings. "Chief Gray Wolf knew not of his other son?"

"You know that your mother is a proud Chippewa," Little Swan said, lowering her hand away from him. "After knowing of Gray Wolf's love for the white woman, I chose not to tell him of the child. Soon after our last good-bye, White Cloud chose me for his woman. I went to him willingly. When you were born, White Cloud believed you were his son. Soon he became chief. Never could I have told him the truth. He would have been disgraced before his people. So I have kept the secret locked inside my heart until now. And, *gah-ween,* no, Gray Wolf never knew. No one but myself, and now . . . you . . ."

"This truth is hard for me to accept," Lone Wolf said, easing his mother's head from his lap, back to the bulrush mat. He rose to his full height and turned to stand before the fire, his spine stiff, the muscles of his shoulders and legs corded. "I have only one father. Chief White Cloud *is* my father. How could you tell me anything different?"

He turned on his heel and looked down at his mother sorrowfully, seeing the silver rivulets of tears on her cheeks. "Why did you tell me?" he said thickly. "It would have been best had I never known. Why not let me live with a peaceful heart, believing Chief White Cloud *is* my true father! Why, *Gee-mah-mah?* Why?"

Little Swan reached a feeble, trembling hand to Lone Wolf. "My son, my spirit would never have rested peacefully in the hereafter if I didn't confess the truth now, to someone. You are the rightful one to be told. You have the right to know who your true father is. And you should be proud, not dismayed by the knowledge. Chief Gray Wolf was a great man, a wise, *kind* man. And had he known of another son, he would gladly have accepted you."

Seeing the desperation in his mother's eyes, Lone Wolf settled onto his haunches beside her. Resting his full weight on his heels, he again took her hand. "Chief Gray Wolf had sons, Chief White Cloud had none," he grumbled.

"Only Lone Wolf! Only Lone Wolf! And I wasn't even truly his!"

"You will always be Chief White Cloud's son," Little Swan sobbed. "And you must never let him know differently! Knowing the truth would shame him, not only in his heart, but also in the eyes of his people. I could not bear him any more sons or daughters after you were born. My health did not permit it. You are the next chief-in-line. You, Lone Wolf. Only you. How could I have taken away Chief White Cloud's only son to give to Chief Gray Wolf when Chief Gray Wolf only shortly after you were born had two beautiful sons of his own?"

"*Ay-uh*, yes," Lone Wolf said, nodding. "I know of his two sons. Strong Hawk, who is now chief, and Silver Fox, who has chosen to live the life of a white man."

His face shadowed into a frown. "These brothers are also *my* brothers," he grumbled. "And I am the eldest!"

"*Ay-uh*, you are, my son," Little Swan said. "And by birthright, you, not Strong Hawk, should now be chief of the St. Croix Band of the Chippewa."

Lone Wolf slowly nodded his head. "That is so," he said hoarsely. "*Ay-uh*, that is so."

He bent to kiss his mother's cheek. "You must rest now, *Gee-mah-mah*. I will leave you so that you can sleep," he said softly. "You have emptied your heart of the pain you have carried with you since my birth. Now you can rest in peace."

"But you? How do you feel, my son?" Little Swan asked, touching him lightly on his cheek, savoring the smooth feel of it. "Do you respect me less?"

"Neither my love nor my respect for you has changed," Lone Wolf said, leaning his cheek into the palm of her hand. "But Lone Wolf has much to sort out inside his mind and heart. Suddenly everything in my life has changed. I must leave you, to think. This knowing will take much getting used to."

"And how do you feel about your father, the father I

ing his mother's death! He was an Indian torn between two families! He had brothers and cousins he had never known existed! He had a father whose spirit had only recently taken that long journey to the hereafter. Yet he had a father who was still alive, depending on him to be the next chief of his people!

Hurrying away from the wigwam, he knew that it could not carry him away from the truths. And one of these truths was that even now he should be a great chief! He should be the chief of the St. Croix Band of the Chippewa! Though he had promised his mother that he would not do anything to cause shame to his father, Chief White Cloud, Lone Wolf could not remove from his heart this question that now gnawed away at him. Should he challenge Strong Hawk's title as chief? Was it not only fair? Perhaps Strong Hawk should even *die*!

Yet would not the Great Spirit Wenebojo be pleased if he might somehow not only one day unite brothers of the [illegible] es because [illegible]

[illegible] d he ever reveal [illegible] in an easy way? [illegible] of chief could cause [illegible]

[illegible] observe my brother who [illegible] also observe his family,'' he [illegible] sons I must do this. It is known [illegible] married a woman with the white [illegible] ay Wolf choose a white woman over [illegible] see why, and also I must see to help me [illegible] must do with this truth spoken to me by my [illegible] ht.''

[illegible] ld also eventually travel to the city of Duluth [illegible] dy his other brother, Silver Fox, who did not live as [illegible] pewa and who even called himself by a white man's [illegible] me, who wore the clothes of a white man. Lone Wolf must also know the whys of this.

Going to his black stallion, Lone Wolf swung himself into his beautiful saddle and rode across a great stretch of meadow toward the beckoning forest. He was torn with feelings! He felt detached from himself, as though two persons with separate identities were battling inside him.

Three

Jeanine had spent several days preparing for the journey north, studying maps of Minnesota. She had discovered that Chief Strong Hawk's St. Croix Band of Chippewa now made its residence near Rice Lake. Jeanine knew the dangers of traveling alone through the dense forest that far, yet she had made up her mind to study the Chippewa Indians, and she would. Nothing and no one would dissuade her from going.

Carrying the last load of supplies to her buggy, Jeanine tensed. She heard the undeniable sound of horses approaching, and then the gruff voice of her Uncle Fred as he rode up behind her and stopped. The timing was too perfect for him. He had surely spied on her, giving him knowledge of the exact moment of her planned departure! He had surely gone to the art museum and discovered that she had taken a leave of her duties for the length of time needed to go and return from the Chippewa Indian village.

It angered Jeanine terribly to think that her uncle would continue to interfere in her private affairs. Would he ever, ever let go? Would he ever see her as a woman instead of a child needing coddling? She doubted it!

Now he *would* try his damnedest to stop her. He should know her well enough, though, to know that he would have to place her behind bars in his jail to stop her, once she had made up her mind to do something.

In a long-sleeved white blouse, and a heavy riding skirt that reached her ankles, revealing the shine of brown leather boots at her feet, Jeanine went ahead and tossed her satchel into the back of the buggy. With her hands stubbornly set to her hips, she turned and faced her uncle and Cameron Tyner. Her black hair shimmered on her shoulders and on down her back as a soft breeze whispered through it. Her oval face was pink with excitement, her green eyes sparkled.

Cameron stayed quietly in the saddle while Fred dismounted and looped his horse's reins around a hitching post. Fred's gaze traveled over Jeanine, and then her buggy. "And what's this all about?" he said in a low grumble.

Fred's coarse, dark trousers rippled on his muscled legs as he moved to the buggy and let his eyes search further. "Now just where do you think *you're* goin'? To the moon, I suppose? Damn. I've never seen the likes of these supplies in my *life*. And surprise of surprises—it ain't the type used to go and check on someone's fancy artwork."

Turning on his heel, Fred again closely scrutinized Jeanine, seeing her travel attire and the stubborn stance she had taken upon his arrival. "Seems these are the sorts of supplies used when searchin' out *Indians*," Fred said, resting his hands on the pistols holstered at his hips. "Jeanine, I'm tellin' you right out that I ain't about to play no cat-and-mouse games with you. I *know* where you *think* you're goin' and I'm here to damn well *stop* you."

Not wanting to further discuss anything with her uncle

about her decision, Jeanine didn't respond to his heated words. She just stared at him in defiance.

"Don't you have nothin' to say for yourself?" Fred growled, taking a step closer to glare down at her. "Or am I seeing your stubborn side again? My brother sure did raise a feisty one in you. Thank God, I don't have myself to blame for *that*. Your personality was clear *way* before *I* got a hold of you."

"And do you think it would have been different, Uncle Fred, had you raised me from a baby?" Jeanine asked, easing her hands from her hips. "As I see it, I would still have been a determined person because you are. I believe it runs in the family, Uncle Fred. So why fight it? Just let me be. Don't interfere in what I want to do. I don't interfere in your life, do I? You do as you please. I am old enough to do as *I* please. Or do you forget my age?"

"Amen," Fred said, chuckling. Then he again walked to the buggy, sorting through her supplies. "Food . . . water . . . rifles . . . and ammunition. Even a saddle for your *horse*. Is that if you decide to leave the buggy behind?" He gave her a half glance from across his shoulder. "Seems you've prepared yourself for a lengthy journey all for nothin'."

Jeanine went to the brown mare already bridled to her buggy and ran her hand over its thick mane. "I should be gone for several days," she dared to say. "And I assure you . . . it's nothing to worry yourself over. As you said, I have food, water, and the means by which to protect myself. I do believe I've thought of everything, Uncle Fred."

"Not entirely," Fred said in a low grumble.

Jeanine defied him with snapping eyes. "Uncle Fred, say no more—" she began, but was interrupted.

"It's not best for women to take out on their own alone," Fred said dryly. "And, Jeanine, you're no exception. Your feisty ways can get you in a helluva lot of trouble."

"I asked you to accompany me," Jeanine said, her

voice softening. "You refused. So it seems I've been forced to go alone." She smiled up at him sweetly, locking her hands behind her back. "Now don't you have duties in town?" she purred. "As *I* see it, I am no longer a duty."

Fred lifted his hat from his head and took a nervous swipe through his hair with his fingers. "I can't let you do this," he said. "Just get the buggy unloaded. *Now*. I don't have all day to waste with such nonsense as this."

Jeanine's cheeks flushed red with renewed anger. She rose on her tiptoes and spoke hotly into her uncle's face. "You know what you can do with your *orders*," she hissed. "I plan to leave and you can't do anything to stop me."

Fred was taken aback by her insolence, yet he had grown used to it. She didn't do this out of disrespect for him, but out of the need to show her independence. He understood too well how he had tried to hold her back while she had been living with him. But it had only been out of love for her. There was too much crime on the streets for a genteel lady to wander about alone. And ever since she had lived alone, so far from his mansion, he had lived in dread of something terrible happening to her.

While researching for her books on history, she had traveled far and wide. But she had usually traveled by way of train, from city to city. This time she was wanting to travel by horse and buggy and did not have any city in mind for visiting. She wanted to be a part of the wilds of the forest region. She wanted to become involved with *Indians*!

"Jeanine, you're my responsibility," Fred said, placing his hat back on his head. "You'll always be my responsibility, at least until you've spoken words of marriage with a man. This is why I must make demands of you. I must be sure that nothing happens to you. If anything did . . ."

Jeanine's mood lightened when he didn't lash back at her with more angry words, but instead spoke in a soft, almost apologetic tone. She took a step backward, looking up at him with wavering eyes. "I appreciate all that you've done for me," she sighed. Jeanine's shoulders dropped, as she felt a sudden tinge of desolation sweep through her. "But, Uncle Fred, now is the time to let go. You see, I may never even *find* the right man to marry. Would you then, at my age of, let's say, even forty, coddle me as though I were a mere child?"

She gave Cameron a sour glance. She had wanted to tell her uncle that she had more than one reason to want to leave Duluth for a while. Cameron Tyner was the reason. She would be leaving him, and the threat he posed for her, behind. It was always there in his devilish blue eyes . . . that look of possessiveness. When *would* he make his move to try to claim her? How would he approach her with such a claim? Didn't he know by the way she looked at him that she detested . . . loathed him? The fact that he had bedded every loose woman in town was enough for Jeanine to know that she would never allow him to so much as touch her.

But she hadn't told her uncle of her feelings for Cameron because, thus far, her fears had been unfounded. There was no actual proof of his intentions toward her. And until Cameron made an actual move that she could prove, Jeanine would use this means to separate herself from him and his silent, imposing ways.

"Uncle Fred, please go on back to town with your deputy and let me be on my way," she added quickly.

"Not on your life," Fred said flatly, placing his hands on the pistols at his hips.

Jeanine looked away from Cameron, her cheeks stinging from his penetrating stare. She sighed again. "You do persist so," she said, giving her horse and buggy a look of longing, so wanting to be on her way. "Uncle Fred, I—"

A great ball of fire shooting up suddenly into the sky, and an ensuing rumbling explosion stole not only Jeanine's words from her mouth, but also her breath. She jumped as though shot, as her gaze became rivetted downward; she saw from her vantage point on the bluff overlooking Duluth, where her ranch house was positioned, a fire that was raging on the waterfront.

"Good Lord, God a'mighty!" Fred shouted, running to his horse. "It's another damn grain elevator explosion! The last time it happened, at least twenty people were killed!"

He swung himself into the saddle and grabbed his reins. Wheeling the horse around, he glared down at Jeanine. "Now you stay put until I can get back here to talk some more sense into your head, do you hear?" he shouted.

He glowered over at Cameron. "Cameron, you stay *with* her," he ordered. "Don't let 'er outta your sight. I'll be back as quick as I can."

Cameron started to protest, but Fred rode away too quickly. Seething, he gave Jeanine an angry stare. Though he had waited for what had already seemed an eternity for the proper time to be alone with her, this was not the time. He was not a damn watchdog!

Another ball of fire lighting the sky and loud cries coming from the waterfront drew Cameron's thoughts from Jeanine. For now, the *true* excitement lay at the waterfront, and, by damn, he was going to be a *part* of it!

He frowned down at Jeanine. "Now you listen to me," he drawled. "I've got duties in town. I *ain't* stayin' here, lookin' after you. But, listen good to what I have to say, pretty lady. If you make trouble for me by takin' off to that Indian village once my back is turned, I'll come after you. I'm not even going to hint at what I'd do to you after I find and hog-tie you!"

He leaned down closer to Jeanine, his eyes afire. "Once I make you mine, I'm gonna have some control over you. You'll not twist me around your finger like you have your uncle." He chuckled low. "Pretty lady, I'm gonna teach you a thing or two about lots of things. And you're gonna *love* it."

Jeanine blanched. She took a step backward, then stood her ground as anger swelled inside her. "You are wasting your time thinking I would ever let you so much as touch me,'' she hissed. ''My uncle would like to see me married, but he would *never* want to see me married to the likes of you. Your reputation with the ladies precedes you, Cameron. And if one dug deeply enough, I am almost certain that it would be discovered that your past is tarnished by evil deeds. It's written in your eyes, Cameron . . . your wickedness.''

Cameron's jaws tightened, and his hands gripped his horse's reins, so startled was he by what Jeanine had just said. Did she have some way of knowing that the law had chased him out of Texas for cattle rustling, that it had only been by chance that he had ended up in Duluth, involved with the law on the opposite end of the spectrum, acting out the role of deputy, *himself*?

But no. She couldn't know. She would have confided in her uncle. She would use this sort of information about Cameron to be *rid* of him!

''When I think the time is right to make my move to claim you, your uncle won't argue over my decision,'' Cameron chuckled. ''I'm too valuable to him. And, Jeanine, he owes me. He *owes* me.''

Cameron thrust his spurs into the flanks of his horse and thundered away from Jeanine, leaving her speechless. His words and the threat held within them swirled around inside her head, making her grow cold. She now knew that all her fears of Cameron's intentions *were* founded!

Yet her uncle would not want to believe her if she did confide in him. Cameron Tyner had a hold on her uncle that would be hard to break. Her uncle *was* grateful to the man. He owed Cameron Tyner his *life*!

Shaking her head to clear it from the confusion scrambling around inside, Jeanine looked downward at the commotion at the waterfront. Horsedrawn firewagons were on the scene; fire raged upward, into the heavens. If she didn't leave now, she would never have such an opportunity again. She would not let Cameron's threats spoil what she had planned. Thus far he was all words and no action.

He loved playing games with her. Yes, it was a game . . . one that he would lose.

"Let's get out of here, Daisy," she said, speaking to her horse. "It's only you and me for the next week or so. Only you and me . . ."

Climbing into the buggy, she grabbed the reins and flicked them, feeling the thrill of excitement that came with any risky undertaking—with *any* remarkable, exciting experience.

Riding away from the ranch house, Jeanine's hair bounced on her shoulders and down her back in black shimmerings. Her eyes were luminous.

Four

The heavy precipitation of all the months of spring throughout the years had produced a land of dense vegetation, of thick stands of conifers, Douglas firs, various spruces, red cedar, yews and redwoods.

After two full days of traveling, Jeanine had left her buggy behind when it had become impossible for her to travel in it through the thick forest. She had loaded as many of her supplies as possible onto her gentle mare and was now continuing her journey on horseback. The saddle creaked slightly beneath her weight. Her mare snorted steam into the fast falling dusk; its hooves squished in the sodden ground of the rotting leaves beneath the trees.

And when the forest region momentarily thinned out where wild flowers dotted the land in reds and yellows, Jeanine urged her horse into a canter across the meadow. Inhaling, she enjoyed the sweet fragrance of the wild flowers and the fresh air. Her eyes absorbed the tranquility of the setting, watching the grass blowing in oceanlike green waves in the distance.

She was glad to have had a reason to come to this land of incredible beauty, which would eventually lead into Chief Strong Hawk's village of Chippewa. She was feeling surely as those had felt at the beginning of time, when the world was innocent. She had never felt as free.

Yet looking up into the sky, seeing how it was metamorphosing into night, she knew that darkness would quickly fill this land of enchantment. She had hoped to reach Chief Strong Hawk's village before another night claimed her. The nights already spent in the forest on her journey north had been spent listening to the cries of panthers and the howls of wolves.

This land was beautiful, but it was also desolate and dangerous.

In her travel skirt and blouse, boots clamped into stirrups, Jeanine sent her horse into a gallop. The evening sun was no longer flashing its red needles of light through the foliage in the west. A campsite must be found, a fire built.

Drawing the reins in more tightly, Jeanine began guiding her horse alongside a lake of slumberous beauty. Where the lake was more shallow, wild rice swayed gently, thickly green, but not yet heavy-topped with rice as it would be at the time of the "Ricing Moon," in September.

Jeanine smiled to herself. She had already begun her studies of the Chippewa from one small book she had found in the local library. She had learned the importance of rice to their people.

"Ricing Moon," she murmured, seeking the moon through the trees as it was now silvering their tips with its new, lovely light. "I also learned at least *that*." She firmed her jaw. "But I shall know much more when I'm through. My book will disclose all the customs of the Chippewa. Even that of marriage. . . ."

Seeing the perfect spot for a campsite beside this lake that she had discovered, Jeanine dismounted and secured her mare's reins to a low tree limb.

Taking her rifle from its gunsling for safety, she moved through knee-high grass to a cleared spot close to the lake embankment. An uneasiness swam through her when she found cold ashes spread out on the ground. Someone had been there before her. But when . . . and *who* . . .?

Jeanine scattered the ashes with the toe of her boot, then shrugged. This *was* the best spot for her night of rest. The water to the left protected her on that side. The clearing that reached from the lake to the trees gave her space to watch for anything that might try to sneak up on her on the other.

Squinting, Jeanine tried to see Daisy where she had left the mare, tied beneath the trees several yards away from her. Daisy's gentle neighing made Jeanine relax. For a moment she thought Daisy had suddenly disappeared.

Hurrying back to her horse, Jeanine unloaded her night gear and then her satchel. After a fire was built and she had satisfied her hunger with fruit and cheese, she settled in by the fire.

Removing her journal and a pencil from her satchel, she began writing of her day's experiences. But the loud scream of a panther caused goosebumps to crawl across her flesh.

Her eyes wide with fear, Jeanine slowly crept her hand to her rifle. . . .

Lone Wolf rose to his feet from his observation point on the edge of a bluff. The dewy starlight and silver shine of the moon were proof that he had watched the village of the St. Croix Band of the Chippewa long enough. Most were now in their wigwams, settling in for the long night. Their outdoor fires were burning low.

His eyes again searched and found the white man's sort of dwelling that sat among the wigwams. Had his brother, Strong Hawk, humbled himself to agree to such a dwelling made of logs to please his white woman? Was a white woman's love worth even *this*?

Lone Wolf had to learn the mystery of such women! Somehow . . . someday. He felt that when he found out why his true father *and* his brother Strong Hawk had chosen white wives, he will have unraveled the many mysteries of his blood relatives that were tormenting him. But could he acquire such answers? When . . .?

His gaze shifted, again moving from wigwam to wigwam. Songs and voices drifted upward from the tranquil village, strangely touching his heart. Among those voices could be cousins', his brother's, and possibly even that of his brother's white woman. Watching them from afar, acquainting himself in this way, was not enough.

Yet he could not enter the village and introduce himself as a brother to Chief Strong Hawk! At least not yet. Who would believe him? Who would even understand? And he always had his father, Chief White Cloud, to consider. If Chief White Cloud knew the truth of his one and only son, who was truly not his son at all, he would forever be shamed!

No. This was *not* the time to reveal this sort of truth to anyone. It was not the time to openly challenge Strong Hawk.

Torn with want—with need—Lone Wolf went to his black stallion and swung himself up into his saddle. He had spent enough time watching the village of his brother, Strong Hawk. Since his *gee-mah-mah's* death, he had done nothing else. And, except for this discovery of the different sort of dwelling in the Chippewa village, he still knew no more than before.

Just how long could he continue with this silence? It was not his nature not to find answers when the need arose. Always in life, he wanted to know it all. . . .

Wheeling his horse around, he guided it down a steep incline, through tangled underbrush, and around mimosa trees clinging to the side of the hill, their pink blossoms closed for the night. The night air was losing the warmth left there by the sun; sparkles of dew were clinging to the tips of the grass.

Yet Lone Wolf, attired in only a loincloth and moccasins, did not feel the ensuing dampness of night, though it was now pressing in on his bare chest, arms and legs. He had learned well the art of living with the seasons . . . the change of temperature. His body heat changed as well, keeping him immune to the cold . . . to the heat.

He was a strong Chippewa Brave, a future leader of his father's people, the Cedar Falls Band of Chippewa! Strange that he had the capacity, now, of being chief to two bands of Chippewa, to combine them into one powerful faction of Indian!

Two fathers. One son? Lone Wolf! He was the son that should be chief to both bands of Chippewa. Yet now that his mother was dead, he was the only one who knew such a truth. But one day he would share the truth with *many*.

Riding onward, his bare shoulders were proudly squared. His coarse, black hair was blowing in the wind. The eagle feather fluttered in the loop at the back of his hair as though still a part of a bird, alive.

He led his horse into a dense forest of elms and oaks. The huge virgin pines towered over him. Lone Wolf had to move on his proud steed more slowly, working his stallion around the trees and through skin-tangle, ground pine and junipers.

Bending low, avoiding a tree limb, he peered into the distance, his mind now on the white woman who had married his true father, Gray Wolf. In his search for answers, would he be given a chance also to see *her* . . . compare her beauty with his mother's?

"*Ay-uh,*" he whispered. "I *must*."

The darkness of night was now as though it were a shroud, drawing the forest into its veil of black. The sudden harsh scream of a panther from somewhere ahead tore through the branches of the trees, a threat to Lone Wolf's safety.

His hand reached and found his rifle in the gunsling on the right side of his horse. He patted it, then moved his hand to the knife sheathed at his waist.

Five

Having traveled for a while now, Lone Wolf had left the scream of the panther behind. The aroma of smoke wafting through the air touched his nose with alarm. Tensing, he drew his steed to a halt. He dismounted and grabbed his rifle. By foot he guided his horse onward, then stopped abruptly when he saw a golden, pulsing glow from a campfire through the trees just ahead.

And then his keen, penetrating gaze captured something else. A horse. It was grazing only a few footsteps away, its saddle close by on the ground.

Securing his stallion beside this horse, Lone Wolf crept on ahead alone and drew closer to the campfire. His rifle was poised, prepared to fire should he feel threatened by this traveler.

When he reached the point where the forest stopped and a clearing began, leading to Slumber Lake, he stopped and crouched behind a fully-blossomed lilac bush. His eyes widened and his breath became anxious. Sitting beside the campfire was not a white man as expected . . . but, instead, a white woman.

Never had Lone Wolf seen a white woman so alone . . . so far from a white man's community. And why *was* she here? Was she perhaps traveling to Strong Hawk's village? Was she of blood relation to Strong Hawk's white wife? Why else would a white woman be traveling alone in these parts if not to visit another person of her own skin coloring? Thus far there was no white man's community in these parts!

Lone Wolf's pulse raced as he observed the woman more closely. She seemed totally absorbed in whatever she was doing. She seemed to be writing in some sort of book. Squinting, he tried to see her full facial features. But this was impossible from his vantage point, for she was turned so that he could see only her profile. But that was enough to tell him that her features were delicate, that her skin was satiny white. . . .

Lone Wolf's eyes narrowed into two points of hate. She was white. Danette, the woman who had stolen Gray Wolf from his mother, had been white! Seeing this white woman so reminded him of his mother's loss of the man she had dearly loved, and of Lone Wolf's loss because he had been denied his true father. Both losses had been caused by a white woman! And here was a white woman, so alone . . . so vulnerable . . .

Hate ate away at his heart and then a sudden thought came to him, causing him to smile smugly to himself. Couldn't *this* white woman be the answer to many questions laying heavy on Lone Wolf's heart? He could abduct her and take her to his village and observe her. In many ways he could test her! By doing so he could possibly discover why Gray Wolf chose a white woman over Lone Wolf's beautiful mother!

Smiling, Lone Wolf nodded. *Ay-uh,* yes, he would abduct this white woman. He would take her captive and put her through many tests, to see how she compared to a Chippewa woman! It was, perhaps, the best way, or he would never have peace of mind for what his true father had done to Lone Wolf's beautiful, gentle *gee-mah-mah*!

In abducting her, could he not also somehow avenge the pain his mother had felt all those years because of the white woman called Danette?

"*Ay-uh*, she *will* become my captive, at least for a while. . . ." he whispered.

Determined, Lone Wolf stepped beyond the trees and into the clearing. He moved along stealthily, circling around so that he would come upon Jeanine from the rear. But the neighing of his stallion and the other horse neighing in kind made his heart skip a beat and his finger move to his rifle trigger, knowing that the white woman had surely heard also. . . .

Jeanine dropped her pencil when she heard two horses whinnying. She knew that Daisy was no longer the only horse close by in the forest. And where there was a second, there was surely a rider, a . . . *man*?

The shine of her rifle caught her eye where it lay too far from her hand. Her heart thundered wildly as she laid her journal aside and slowly crept to her feet. She took one step toward the rifle but stopped suddenly when she heard the snapping of twigs on the ground behind her. A rush of cold fear spread through her as she slowly turned around. She gasped and her knees grew threateningly weak when she discovered a sparsely-clad Indian standing there, a rifle in his hands, aimed at her. . . .

The fire illuminated Jeanine's face enough for Lone Wolf to now see her fully. He was stunned—even *jolted*—by how fully seeing her grabbed him so. His dark eyes raked over her. He saw so much about her that was uniquely lovely. Though he wanted to feel nothing but loathing for all white women now that he knew that one had wronged his mother, his body betrayed him! His loins were strangely aching. His heart was behaving so oddly in its erratic beats; so mesmerized was he by her compelling eyes and waist-length, dark hair that shimmered in the soft breeze of night.

Then his gaze lowered. Her blouse lay half-unbuttoned across her heaving bosom, revealing the pink curves of her breasts to his wondering eyes. He felt heat rise to his face. Again his body betrayed him—he hungered to touch her!

He forced his eyes to move elsewhere. He saw her tiny waist, then her *height*. She was much taller than any Chippewa women he knew. And not only was she taller, her shoulders were more squared, broader. Did this mean that she was even stronger, too?

He again looked at her face and saw fear in her eyes. She had been foolish to travel alone! This was proof that she had failed in her first test as Lone Wolf saw it. She had proven not to be as *smart* as the Chippewa women!

Jeanine squirmed uneasily beneath the Indian's close scrutiny. Though she had been on her way to an Indian village, to trust that no Indian would harm her along the way was foolish. She was vulnerable to him in every respect. He could even easily rape her, then leave her to die. . . .

"What do you want?" she blurted, her gaze moving from his face to his firearm. "Why do you come in the night threatening me with a rifle? I've done nothing to warrant such treatment." She nodded toward her campfire. "I've stopped to rest for the night. That surely can be no threat to *you*."

Lone Wolf's gaze moved to the journal, recalling the writing he had seen her do. He challenged her set stare with his own. "Why are you here? Why do you write in a book while the heavens are dark?" he demanded, taking a step closer to her.

Jeanine's eyes wavered, then she again met his steady gaze with stubbornness. "That is no concern of yours," she spat. "Now if you will just go on your way, I can return to what I was doing."

Lone Wolf motioned with his rifle in the direction of the waiting horses. "*Mah-bee-szhon,*" he said coldly. "Come.

You go with Lone Wolf. You will return with Lone Wolf to Chippewa village. *Now,* white woman. Do as you are told.''

Jeanine's throat went dry, her face paled. There were no friendly overtures in his words. Instead, they were cold and *commanding*. Was she to be a captive . . .? Surely not! Captives were no longer taken by Indians. She had ventured north to learn more about Indians. Was she going to learn that her uncle had been right all along? That they *were* . . . savages? Or was this one Indian the exception . . . perhaps an Indian outlaw of sorts. . . .?

The color rose slowly in her cheeks as hope awakened inside her. He was Chippewa, for he had said they would be going to a Chippewa village. Could he be taking her to the St. Croix Band of Chippewa?

If so, she knew that she would be welcomed there in a friendly manner where even the chief was married to a white woman. Surely this particular Indian was misguided in his actions by ignorance *or* by the need to prove something to the other Indian Braves of his village. Perhaps he *was* a renegade, one who cared nothing for authority.

Whichever, Jeanine had no choice, it seemed, but to do as he commanded. Hopefully he would soon learn of his wrong judgment!

Lone Wolf took a bold step closer to her. ''You do not listen well,'' he grumbled. ''Go. *Now.*''

He gave Jeanine a shove. She glared up at him, stumbling clumsily over the tail of her skirt as it twisted about her legs. ''You won't get away with this,'' she hissed, angrily flipping her skirt back in place. ''Captives aren't taken by Indians these days. I soon will be free again. You'll see.''

Lone Wolf grabbed her by a wrist and jerked her close to him. He glowered down into her face. ''You will be free only when Lone Wolf *frees* you,'' he said flatly, yet troubled by her soft green eyes and alluring lips so close to him. It would be so easy to kiss her.

Then he was angry at himself for such thoughts. Perhaps

it was *he* who needed testing, as well as *she*. He had to now prove to himself that she did not have powers of magic that seemed to be ensnaring him as though one caught in a giant web. He would not allow her to have power over him in such a way! He would kiss her and feel nothing.

He released her wrist only to place his hand at the nape of her neck, keeping her locked in place as his lips crushed down upon hers.

He had moved so quickly Jeanine's breath was momentarily stolen. Then when she felt his body boldly pressed into hers, she was frightened into action.

Splaying her hands against his bare chest she began shoving. But the more she pushed against him, the more forcefully he held her, his kiss hard . . . almost drugging in its intensity.

A bizarre sort of weakness claimed Jeanine's insides, having never before been kissed so demandingly, by any man. It was a kiss of fire, stirring strange, surely *primitive* sensations within her. This sensation could only be what passion for a man must feel like. And she feared these feelings more than she feared the man, for she was enjoying this overwhelming, euphoric state that she was being drawn into.

As though willed by some unseen force, Jeanine felt herself begin to respond to his kiss. Her hands slipped away from his chest, her arms crept up, twining themselves about his neck. . . .

Suddenly Lone Wolf loosed his lips from hers and jerked her arms away from him. He looked down at her with fire in his eyes, puzzled, the moment of testing himself proving that he had failed. He had enjoyed the taste of her lips, the smell of her hair and skin! Never before had a woman felt so good in his arms! Was it to be for him as it had been for his true father, Gray Wolf, and his brother, Strong Hawk? Was Lone Wolf also doomed to love a white woman?

Lone Wolf had a fleeting thought of forgetting his notion of taking this woman captive. If he turned his back on her now, wouldn't it be as though she had never existed?

But, no. He would overcome this weakness in his character, surely handed down from father to son, brother to brother! He would prove to himself that no white woman could ever be important to him. His only interest was in learning *of* her, to fully compare her with the women of his tribe . . . of *all* tribes! The choice to capture her had been made and would not be turned aside simply because of the foolishness of a kiss!

Jeanine was shaken not by only his kiss and her response to it, but also by the Indian's changing moods. Shivering, she wiped her mouth with the back of a hand in an effort to remove any remembrances of his kiss from her lips. She looked up at him, wondering what mood would strike him next. And while looking so intently at him, she couldn't help but notice how the fire's glow was so golden on the copper sheen of his bare flesh.

There was no denying how his dark, fathomless eyes and his handsome, sculpted features were affecting her, nor the fact that he was scarcely clothed, revealing his broad shoulders, his thin flanks, narrow hips and muscular thighs to her wondering eyes.

And the way he was looking at her. It was as a caress, causing Jeanine's every nerve ending to tingle.

Yet, she knew that she should not be thinking of anything now but survival. She especially shouldn't be thinking about *him*. She did not want to discover firsthand why the white women had married the Chippewa chiefs. She was this Indian's captive . . . nothing more. At least this Indian was going to take her to his village . . . not kill her. Then she would surely be allowed to go on her way.

Lone Wolf kept his eyes on Jeanine as he went to kick dirt into the campfire, causing the flames to die away into only orange, glowing embers. Once all was covered by dirt and cold ashes, Lone Wolf went back to Jeanine and began guiding her away by an elbow.

Jeanine stopped suddenly, and glanced frantically across

her shoulder at her satchel and the journal beside it. Without these she could not record her daily experiences or the interviews with Judith McMahon once she arrived at Strong Hawk's village.

She looked up at Lone Wolf, pleading with her eyes. "I must at least be allowed to take some of my possessions with me," she murmured. "Please? May I?"

Lone Wolf glanced from her to what lay on the ground. He nodded. "Take what you wish," he said flatly. His eyes caught the shine of the moon on the barrel of Jeanine's rifle where it lay among her scattered belongings. He stepped away from her and grabbed the rifle, holding it up for her to see.

"This now *mine*," he growled. "Not yours."

Jeanine frowned at him, then stomped away, placing her journal and pencil inside her satchel. But as she stood and surveyed the rest of her belongings—the coffeepot, the blanket and her bedroll—his voice broke through the darkness, reminding her that he was waiting.

"Enough time has been wasted," Lone Wolf said, motioning with his rifle. "We go to horses. *Now*."

Clutching the satchel to her as though it were a lifeline, Jeanine moved ahead of Lone Wolf until the horses were reached. She stood by mutely while he positioned each of the rifles into their separate gunslings and then placed her saddle on Daisy.

Jeanine froze inside as she watched him tie Daisy's reins into his own, and led Jeanine to his horse instead.

Turning with a start, she looked up at him, her eyes wide. "Can't I ride on my own horse?" she asked. "Why must I ride *yours*?"

She gasped lightly when Lone Wolf ignored her question and placed his hands on her waist suddenly lifting her onto his beautiful black stallion. Before she could again question him, he was behind her on the horse, his arm held possessively about her waist.

"What . . . are . . . you *doing*?" Jeanine dared to ask, her face flaming from having his man's hardness pressed so definably against her backside. "Surely I can be allowed to ride my own horse!"

"You cannot be allowed a means of escape," Lone Wolf grumbled. "And there are many miles to travel. You sleep while Lone Wolf rides."

Jeanine sighed languidly. "Oh, thank you, dear sir, for such a kindness," she said, sarcasm thick in her words.

"Your name?" Lone Wolf said, nudging his horse with his knees, urging it north, in the direction of his village.

"Jeanine," she said coldly, not seeing any reason not to tell him. At least *she* would be civil!

She gave him a mischievous look from across her shoulder. "And you are called Lone Wolf?" she tested. Perhaps if she could find out more about her captor, she could inform her uncle when she returned to Duluth about this Indian who was more savage than human.

"You called yourself Lone Wolf?" she prodded.

"*Ay-uh*, yes," Lone Wolf said, nodding.

"Are you of the St. Croix Band of the Chippewa?" Jeanine then dared to ask.

Lone Wolf frowned as he gave her a sudden, steady stare. "Lone Wolf of the Cedar Falls Chippewa!" he said, as though insulted by her question. Her asking him if he belonged to Strong Hawk's tribe of Chippewa must mean this white woman knew of them. But in what capacity? If she had been on her way to Strong Hawk's village and she did not arrive, would they come searching for her?

If so, perhaps that was best!

It would be a way to force Strong Hawk's hand to become acquainted with Lone Wolf first! They would banter over the white woman's welfare later!

Jeanine looked quickly away from him, stung by his response, and realized that what she had hoped for wasn't to be at all. He was *not* taking her to Chief Strong Hawk's village where white women were welcome. Lord! She now had no idea where he was taking her, or what to expect!

She straightened her back and began struggling in his arms. "Let me go!" she screamed. "Let . . . me . . . go . . . !"

"White woman, save your strength," Lone Wolf growled, holding her more firmly about the waist. "Did I not tell you the journey to my village is long?"

Feeling defeated and bone-weary, Jeanine weakened, temporarily giving in to her fate for now. She would find a way to escape later. She *would*. But for now she must do everything to protect herself. Even traveling on the horse with Lone Wolf was a threat, for his stallion was going much too fast, jostling her about as though she were a mere sack of potatoes.

Needing something to cling to for support, she had no choice but to turn to the Indian. . . .

Lone Wolf tried not to feel the press of the white woman's body against his as she turned sideways to cling to him for support. He lifted his chin and rode with her into the wind. He was proud of his find, his very first white captive.

Now he must make sure *he* wasn't to become the *true* captive, for there was much about her that troubled his heart. . . .

Six

With Cameron Tyner accompanying him in his search for his niece, Fred Hunter rode straight-backed on his roan. His gaze was searching out every bent blade of grass that might have been made by Jeanine's mare. His first break had come after he had found her abandoned buggy; she hadn't hidden it well enough in the brush, away from the road. As Fred saw it, his niece would have headed north on horseback through the forest from this point on . . . for Chief Strong Hawk's village lay north.

Tilting his Stetson hat back from his sweating brow, then smacking dust from his dark breeches, Fred gave Cameron a sour glance. If Cameron's skills at shooting weren't so outstanding, Fred would have booted him out on his ear the minute he had discovered that Cameron had left Jeanine unattended. It was because of Cameron's inability to follow orders that Jeanine was now on the trail, alone.

"God forbid if anything happens to her," Fred suddenly spat.

Cameron's blond eyebrows forked. Then a slow smile lifted his lips. "Oh, you're speakin' of your niece," he said matter-of-factly.

"Who *else*?" Fred snapped. "Damn it all to hell, Cameron, you don't know the first thing about followin' orders."

Deep resentment caused Cameron's smile to fade and his blue eyes to take on a cloudiness. It was all the girl's fault that he was looking so bad in her uncle's eyes. "Seems your niece is the one who needs fussin' over about orders," Cameron said, gripping his horse's reins more tightly, recalling how Jeanine had looked at him so daringly when he had warned her not to take off on her own once his back was turned. She hadn't heeded his warning—not believing that he *would* make her pay for her disobedience . . . her disobedience to *him* . . . *not* her grizzly uncle.

Cameron was counting on the day when he and Jeanine would be alone. She would discover quickly enough that his warning had been a valid one.

"You don't know my niece at all if you think just tellin' her somethin' means she's gonna *do* it," Fred said, squinting his eyes against the bright rays of the afternoon sun. "Damn it, Cameron, that's why I told you to stay behind and keep an eye on her whilst I went and saw to the commotion on the waterfront after the grain elevator explosion."

"How was I supposed to know she was that headstrong?" Cameron asked, shrugging casually.

"I told you enough times. *That's* why," Fred said. He tensed as he caught a sudden whiff of a campfire's deadening ashes in the breeze. "Smell that, Cameron?"

"Yeah. Think I do," Cameron said, his eyes searching through the dense forest ahead. "There's been a fire close by here."

"Exactly," Fred said, leaning over his saddle and peering ahead. His eyes brightened when he saw the shine of water through the trees. "Slumber Lake is through those trees. Let's check it out, Cameron."

Cameron's spurs jangled as he teased his horse's flesh with their sharp points, following Fred's lead through the oak and spruce trees. His hand was resting on the pistol holstered at his right hip. His eyes alert, he urged his horse into a gallop alongside Fred's as they approached a clearing that reached to the lake, already seeing the abandoned campsite.

Fred's face flushed red with anxiety. His gut twisted when he saw the abandoned bedroll, blanket and various other gear that he recognized only too well. He had seen these identical items in Jeanine's buggy. The camp had been made by her . . . and then *abandoned* . . . ?

"God a'mighty," he mumbled, drawing his roan to a shuddering halt. He quickly dismounted and knelt on one knee, testing the gray ash where a coffeepot still stood, half covered with dirt, and more ashes.

Cameron frowned down at Fred. "Are the ashes cold?" he asked. He slowly looked about, and felt an inkling of doubt about Jeanine's safety. Until now it had looked as though she might just be succeeding in her venture north. And why wouldn't she? She was a stubborn, strong-willed tigress!

But Cameron had to confess that his main worry was not for Jeanine, but for himself. If anything *had* happened to her—if another man had claimed her—then Cameron could be robbed of the chance to tame her as he had so often fantasized.

"Cold . . . damn cold . . ." Fred said. He rose to his full height and wiped the ash from his hands onto his breeches. He stood and studied Jeanine's discarded belongings. "It's been a while since she was here. Damn . . ."

"What do you think's happened to her?" Cameron dared to ask, seeing that Fred was shaken by the discovery.

Fred's gaze moved slowly up and locked with Cameron's eyes. "You damn well better pray *nothin's* happened to her," he warned flatly. "You'll answer to *me*, Cameron. Do you understand . . . ?"

Cameron's eyes glinted as Fred turned and sauntered back to his horse.

Fred swung himself up into his saddle and wheeled his roan around to face Cameron. He took a half-smoked cigar from his shirt pocket, thrust it between his lips and lit it. "We'd better find Jeanine safe and sound at Chief Strong Hawk's village, or . . ."

He didn't complete his statement. Instead, he sank the heels of his boots into the flanks of his roan and rode on away from Cameron, puffing hard on his cigar. Little did Cameron know that "wanted" posters bearing his very face had just arrived at the Sheriff's office. If anything happened to Jeanine, Fred would have a *legal* reason to hang the bastard. He had almost lost all usefulness in Fred's eyes.

Yes . . . gratitude went just so far and then it was time to seriously consider other factors. Fred had seen the way Cameron had looked at Jeanine. Now *that* was testing Fred's gratitude a mite *too* far!

Cameron rode up beside Fred. "I still think we should have formed a posse before going to the Injun village," he grumbled.

Fred looked straight ahead. "The last time I entered an Injun's community it was with a posse," he said flatly. "I swore I'd never do that again. If I have a quarrel with a filthy Injun, I'll take care of it myself, in my own way."

"Oh? Was there a lot of blood spilled when you rode with a posse?" Cameron asked, anxious.

Fred's insides grew cold with remembrances. "Yeah, there was blood spilled alright," he said in a strain.

He glanced over at the deputy. "Have you ever seen scalp poles, Cameron?" he asked, an involuntary shudder encasing him.

"No. Cain't say that I have."

"It ain't a pretty sight."

"No. Cain't say that it *would* be."

Fred swallowed hard, again looking ahead, yet seeing nothing but what was forming in his mind's eye. "I'll never forget one scalp pole in particular," he mumbled. "The hair was blowing long and red, as though the sun had kissed it. . . ."

He lowered his eyes, missing his Darla, his wife, oh so much. . . .

Close by, the loud sound of rushing water startled Jeanine awake. She blinked her eyes and stirred against the chest upon which she had been sleeping, then jerked away from Lone Wolf when she realized just where she was and who she was with.

But still, thoughts—flashbacks—came to her, though she was still numb and disoriented from her long time of almost constant travel on horseback. As the horse on which she was traveling galloped onward, Jeanine felt detached, as if in another world.

Yet there was still the roaring sound of rushing water coming to her through the blackness of night, capturing her attention. There were the eyes of Lone Wolf looking down at her where she again clung to his chest, her tangled hair brushing against her face as the wind whipped it about. There was the strength of Lone Wolf's one arm as it held her in placc on the horse.

And it was then that Jeanine realized that in her sleep she had been turned to him and was now totally facing Lone Wolf; she was actually on his lap, her legs straddling his hips, her legs dangling on either side of the horse.

Feeling the intimacy of her position on Lone Wolf's lap, Jeanine struggled to move away from him. But as he had since they had met, he held her against her will, and she already knew the futility of fighting him.

Instead, she sighed heavily and returned her cheek to his chest. She was sorely tired. She had fought sleep as long as was humanly possible. But it had become impossible for her to stay awake and she had now slept a full night in this Indian's arms. She had been this way since she and Lone Wolf had stopped to eat the last time. After drinking a cup of liquid he had offered her, she had soon drifted off into a lethargic sleep. She had been unable to shake herself from the strange euphoria that had enveloped her, surely caused by some sort of potion Lone Wolf had concocted.

Oh, wouldn't he ever get . . . to . . . his village . . . ? Surely then she would regain her senses. And once she did, she . . . would . . . make him . . . pay. . . .

Lone Wolf smiled to himself. He was, ah, so intrigued by the white woman's boldness, for *again* she had tried to free herself from him, knowing too well how impossible it would be. This white woman with the strange name of Jeanine had the bravery of a man! And this bravery could cause Lone Wolf much trouble once they reached his village. She *would* try to escape, if given a chance. He would have to do everything within his power to keep this from happening.

But he did not want to have to keep her drugged, for he wished to observe her while she was fully awake! And he did not wish to have to bind her wrists and ankles. Her skin was too fair. Never would he cause scars on such skin the color of the petals of the fragile serviceberry blossoms that burst forth like cottony clouds in the leafless landscape of spring.

Yet *she* was not as fragile! She was strong. She was willful. Her adventurous nature attested to that. She would not want to be held against her will in *any* capacity. She seemed the sort to fight back until she won.

His only answer was to stay with her constantly until his time of observing her was over, and until he felt that he had avenged the spirit of his dead mother by keeping a white woman captive!

Sensing that she had again fallen asleep, Lone Wolf was glad. It would be easier to enter with her into his village this way. Should she awaken, protesting, it would cause too much of a stir in his community of Chippewa. They weren't used to captives. But being the next chief-in-line, no one would dare question Lone Wolf about why he had chosen to introduce a captive into their village. Yet most would be silently wondering. . . .

Lone Wolf was driven to many wonders of the white woman himself, even more than that which had caused him to abduct her. With her body now pressed hard against his in her drugged sleep, he could feel the outline of her breasts on his chest and he ached to fully touch them. He desired to kiss her again. His insides quivered at the thought of seeing her standing nude before him. Her eyes the color of the greenest grasses invited him to her, to love her.

He emitted a low growl, knowing that what he was thinking was *gee-wah-nah-dis*! He was foolish to let his mind wander so. He did not wish to desire the white woman. He did not want his future to be clouded by *loving* a white woman. It was a weakness in his character to have such forbidden feelings! Now he had *many* reasons to hate his true father, especially for this trait, which he surely had inherited.

Again Jeanine stirred, having heard something similar to a growl emit from deep inside Lone Wolf. She momentarily opened her eyes and looked up at him, but it was more pleasant to have them closed, to drift back to sleep . . . peacefully sleeping. . . .

Lone Wolf steered his stallion up a steep incline. The rush of the waterfall so close on one side of him was proof that he would soon be entering his village. The moon cast a glow on the outline of the towering bluffs which stood majestically above the Cedar Falls River. They rose in the forms of immense cones, domes and ramparts, with spots and clusters of huge cedar trees clinging to their sides.

Only shimmerings of orange glowed on the ground in the distance as the outdoor fires burned low beside the wigwams of his village. It was a melancholy time when everyone but the forest night creatures slept. The cloak of night was momentarily aroused by the mournful complaint of a wolf, as it also was by the startled interrogation of "who? who?" by the winged monarch of the dark, the owl.

Inching his horse along the edge of the bluff, the rush of

the waterfall was almost deafening as it plummeted into the river. Lone Wolf felt an anxiousness that was quite new to him. He was eager to get the white woman to his dwelling. It would be a time of privacy, and hopefully, of learning.

Looking heavenward, he saw how morning was slowly replacing night with streamers of gold along the horizon. Soon his people would be awakening and weaving a new day about them. Lone Wolf would be experiencing a new sort of day, one unfamiliar to him—that which would be shared with a white woman. His pulse raced with the possibilities. . . .

Holding tightly to Jeanine, Lone Wolf urged his steed down a ravine, up another incline, then across a place of brilliant, yellow-faced daisies and summer green meadow that ran like a carpet into his village. Beyond that, the grass gave way to conifers and birches. The river on one side glowed with a soft, deep light, and was still and serene. The frogs hidden there were faintly filling the air with their pleasant croaking. Then the sun appeared, casting its gilding rays over the land, giving life and light.

Breathless, Lone Wolf entered his tranquil village of wigwams with their birchbark coverings and curved roofs. He did not wish for anyone to see his captive just yet. First she must be made aware of the impossibility of escape until he was ready to return her to her way of life. Once she understood this, then Lone Wolf would share her with his people. But only then. . . .

Several dogs stirred from their sleep and bounded out into the open, yapping and snarling at his stallion's hooves, causing the horse to whinny noisily and shake his thick mane.

Lone Wolf kicked at the dogs and rode onward, glad when he finally reached his wigwam. With care he dismounted his horse, Jeanine still sleeping soundly in his arms. Her face was so peaceful . . . so . . . so beautiful. Her lustrous hair tumbled down in waves, hanging loosely, like rich black satin, in the breeze.

Disgruntled at himself for again seeing her loveliness, Lone Wolf lifted his eyes away from the white woman and nudged his deerskin entrance flap aside with a knee and took her inside his dwelling.

Looking about him, Lone Wolf smiled. Pale Dove, his small friend, had kept the fire burning in his fireplace. She had spread new bulrush mats along the floor, and had neatly curled up the blankets on which he usually slept, placing them against the walls.

Not knowing the length of time Lone Wolf had planned to be gone this time, Pale Dove had kept fresh pots of soup simmering over the hot coals of the fire. The aroma of the soup was rich and inviting, causing his stomach to growl. It reminded him of how long it had been since he and the white woman had eaten. They had stopped to feed their hunger only twice on their way to the village. That last time he had placed the rare herb in the white woman's drink. . . .

Lone Wolf's heart soared with love when his eyes came upon a tiny bundle curled fetal-style on the other side of the firespace from where he stood. His fifteen-year-old friend, crippled from birth, clung to him for hope of the future and treated him like the chief he would one day become. She had crept from her wigwam to his, to feel closer to him, and was sleeping now among Lone Wolf's collection of furs.

Pale Dove idolized him, for Lone Wolf had one day saved the life of her father when he had been attacked by a pack of wild dogs. Her family did not mind allowing her to help keep Lone Wolf's dwelling neat and cozy, and to cook for him. And Lone Wolf helped, in exchange, to provide for her family.

Stepping lightly around the fire, Lone Wolf bent over his friend and spoke her name. "Awaken, Pale Dove," he said. He was glad to see her respond quickly as she moved to an elbow to look unblinkingly up at him, then wobbled to her feet when she saw the white woman in his arms.

"Way-nen-dush-win-ah-ow?" Pale Dove asked, her dark eyes wide.

Lone Wolf gently eased Jeanine down onto the furs where Pale Dove had lain. He knelt down as his gaze swept over her, again feeling drawn to her as a man is drawn to a woman. She was even more beautiful in the light of the fire's soft glow. Her delicate cheekbones were so unlike those of the Chippewa women; the pale color of her flesh and her green eyes now hidden beneath the feathering of thick, dark lashes. All these things were making it so hard to hate her! Instead, the sight of her caused a blaze of desire to ignite his heart.

Only his friend's presence could draw him from such a reverie. Her words cut through his consciousness, startling him into rising quickly back to his feet.

"Lone Wolf," Pale Dove whispered, touching him gingerly on the arm. "Why do you place this white woman on furs warmed by Pale Dove's body?"

Turning to Pale Dove, Lone Wolf drew her gently into his arms. "You will have reason to question many things, my special friend," he murmured, caressing the tiny curve of her crooked back through the buckskin material of her blouse. "But do not. What I do is for a purpose, but known only to me."

Pale Dove leaned her face away from him, imploring him with her eyes. "Is she to be your captive?" she asked softly. "Lone Wolf, you have never stolen white women before to bring to your dwelling. Why do you now?"

Lone Wolf framed her thin face between his hands, seeing her frailness. If one looked beyond the limp that was quite noticeable while walking, and her crooked back, most would see a lovely child. Her wide-set eyes were dark. Her face was of a soft copper color, her nose was narrow and slightly tilted at the end.

Long black braids oiled with bear's grease hung glossy and beautiful across her budding breasts, her buckskin blouse and skirt were highly fringed, the moccasins at her feet colorfully beaded.

"Little friend, Lone Wolf will tell you only once that this white woman is, *ay-uh*, to be a captive," he quietly explained. "But for only a little while. Then she will be taken back to the white world community. Do not ask for more answers than this."

Pale Dove cast her eyes downward. "Then Pale Dove cannot ask if you desire this woman *as* a woman?"

"You ask a question even when you do not," Lone Wolf chuckled, lifting her chin with a forefinger. Then his smile faded. "But this question you ask in roundabout way cannot be answered by me. Please do not ask it again, Pale Dove. This white woman is of another culture . . . another life. She is worlds apart from the Chippewa!"

"*Ay-uh,*" Pale Dove murmured, nodding, yet fearing that she heard more in Lone Wolf's words than he had wished her to. He *did* find this white woman attractive. He possibly even *desired* her. Was *this* his true reason for bringing her to his dwelling?

Pale Dove studied him in silence as he again balanced himself on his haunches beside the white woman, even daring to touch her cheek.

Pale Dove jumped, startled, when the white woman flinched and groaned, tossing herself to lie on her side away from Lone Wolf, her eyes still tightly closed in sleep. Pale Dove was glad to be part of such excitement! Being such a close friend to Lone Wolf, surely he would share his experiences with this white woman with *her*. Never had she had the opportunity to be around white people. Surely there was much to learn!

"She must eat. And soon," Lone Wolf said, glancing up at Pale Dove. "You offer her food, Pale Dove. I will watch."

Pale Dove moved to her knees beside Lone Wolf, her hands to her cheeks. "But how does one offer food to one so lost in sleep?" she asked, her eyes wide.

Lone Wolf chuckled low. "One awakens the one who is sleeping," he said. He moved a hand to Jeanine's shoulder and slightly shook it. She tossed again, positioning her face toward him and Lone Wolf took her hand and gently patted it.

"Nee-go-shkos," he said dryly. "White woman, awaken. You are now in Lone Wolf's dwelling. *Nee-go-shkos.*"

Jeanine heard the gentle voice of a man break through her veil of sleep. And there was warmth transferring to her hand. She stirred again, soon realizing that the voice she had heard was Lone Wolf's. The warmth was Lone Wolf's hand holding hers.

Her eyes fluttered open. She found Lone Wolf bending low over her, then her gaze fell upon the Indian child at his side.

Again she looked at Lone Wolf, her eyes meeting his in cold hatred. She jerked her hand away and began shifting away from him. The euphoric state she had been in was ebbing, causing her not only to see more clearly, but also to remember everything. She was a captive. This Indian's captive! And he had *drugged* her. Surely he would do so again if he chose to.

"Get away from me," she hissed. Yet, though she didn't want to, she found herself remembering the ride on his horse with him, her cheek pressed against his powerful chest, his arms about her waist. She even now could recall the wondrous scent of his flesh and feeling the great strength of his arm as it had held her in place against him. She was also remembering the heat of his kiss. . . .

Her eyes followed him as he rose to his feet and went to sit down beside the fire, hurt hovering in the depths of his dark eyes.

Pale Dove ladled some soup into a wooden bowl, then took it to Jeanine. "White woman want food?" she asked softly, offering the bowl to Jeanine. "White woman hungry? Pale Dove offer food to you for my friend Lone Wolf. You take? You eat?"

Jeanine's eyes wavered as she looked up into Pale Dove's frail but lovely features, noticing, too, her crooked back. She had no quarrel with this tiny thing, yet was it a trick of

Lone Wolf's to use Pale Dove? Would the soup also be filled with a strange potion?

Jeanine shook her head. "No. I don't want anything your *friend* has to offer," she said dryly, leaning on an elbow to glare at Lone Wolf.

Pale Dove sank the spoon into the soup and took a taste for herself in an effort to encourage the white woman to follow her lead. It was a trick taught to Pale Dove by her mother many moons ago when Pale Dove had not wished to eat the wild turnips that were so often prepared for dinner.

"Hmm. *O-nee-shee-shin*, good," Pale Dove said, licking her lips. She again offered the bowl to Jeanine.

Jeanine's eyes widened. The young girl had tasted the soup. Surely Lone Wolf wouldn't have let her if he had placed a foreign substance in it. And the more solid food Jeanine got into her stomach, the more the drug that had enslaved her would be diluted. The stronger she would become.

Stubbornly staring at Lone Wolf, Jeanine crept to a sitting position and accepted the hot mixture. "Thank you," she murmured to Pale Dove, then began eating, all the while thinking of escape.

Seven

Jeanine ate heartily, determined to fully regain the strength she had been robbed of when the drug had entered her system. But her eyes began to waver beneath Lone Wolf's constant, steady stare. It was unnerving her. It was not as though he were seeing a white woman for the first time in his life, but as though he were studying her to learn of her.

For these past two days since her abduction, Jeanine had cast aside thoughts of why she had traveled north, to learn of Indians. Her writing career had begun to seem almost inconsequential. But now, it was there, an idea forming, her mind alert, grasping onto every thought, every possibility . . .

When she had thought of writing a book about the Chippewa Indians, she had never imagined there could be entries of an "abduction." Only now did she feel the excitement of this addition to her book.

Jeanine glanced from Lone Wolf to Pale Dove. She had heard and seen his gentleness toward this crippled child.

She felt the threat he posed lessening inside her heart, for surely no man this gentle in nature to one female could be capable of violence to another, no matter that her skin *was* white. And hadn't Lone Wolf held her hand with gentleness . . . even awakened her in the same way?

The opportunity to learn more about the Chippewa than ever before imagined, about an abduction of a white woman, and the reason behind it, intrigued her. That it was herself who was captive overshadowed Jeanine's fear. If she were to show less hostility toward her captor, perhaps he would eventually tell her the reason for the abduction. She would be interviewing him and he would not even be aware of it. She would have to be careful. No Indian would want to be exploited.

Yes . . . she would get all the answers and then find a way to escape.

Dipping the wooden spoon into the soup, she captured a piece of floating wild turnip. Jeanine again returned Lone Wolf's studious stare, yet blushed when, now in a fully awakened state, she saw the scarcity of his clothes. Attired in only a loincloth and moccasins, he did not even seem dressed. In one sweep of her eyes she saw the wide breadth of his shoulders and the muscles of his chest, then lower, the outline of his strong, proud manhood beneath the lightweight material of his buckskin loincloth.

Then her gaze shot upward, seeing how his eyes continued to study her. They seemed to be branding her, causing her to blush anew, to again remember those moments in his arms, his kiss of fire. It would be easy to show less hostility toward this Indian, for, in truth, so much about him had already caused a strange warmth to surge through her. She wanted to fight these strange feelings plaguing her, but how could she, with him so near, so handsome . . . so mysterious?

She hated to reveal to him that he was disturbing her in any way at all. No man had ever caused her to be so awkward. Even the spoon was trembling in her hand. The pit of her stomach was troubling her even more severely. It felt warm and quivery, as though a candle were inside her, flickering.

Thrusting the spoon into her mouth, trying to focus her attention on the tastes, not the feelings being aroused in her, Jeanine sipped the wild turnip and the liquid flavored with venison.

Yet now that her hunger was being fully fed, and her hands occupied by eating, Jeanine could not think of anything but Lone Wolf. As she looked at him, it was as if she were memorizing his every feature. She wanted to believe it was for her journal, not for herself.

She was again sensing the keen penetration of those eyes that were as black as the darkest of nights. His sinewy, gleaming body was the most beautiful color of copper. His lean, long torso and firm abdomen led downward to narrow hips, where his passions were locked within him beneath his loincloth.

She forced her gaze upward, embarrassed by such thoughts that made her pulse race and her stomach flutter. When she found his eyes still upon her, but now filled with a sort of quiet amusement, her eyebrows rose with wonder.

When his gaze traveled downward along her body and stopped, mesmerized, Jeanine followed his eyes, then jumped as though shot when she saw his point of attention. In her dazed state she had forgotten about her half-unbuttoned blouse. She could even see the flesh of her breasts! She had forgotten that she had unbuttoned the blouse to make herself more comfortable that last night by her campfire.

Dropping the spoon, she quickly drew the folds of her blouse together. She then looked up at Lone Wolf, forcing a smile. She would pretend a lighthearted mood. She must remember that she had to be friendly toward him to eventually get the answers she sought.

"It seems that I have arrived to your village in quite a disheveled state," she laughed softly.

She quickly buttoned her blouse, then tensed when Pale Dove rose to her feet and left the wigwam, leaving Jeanine and Lone Wolf totally alone. Jeanine swallowed hard, wondering what to expect next from this Indian of steady stares and few words. This new day with him had just begun and would be long. The morning sun was casting rivulets of gold down through the smoke-escape hole in the ceiling of the wigwam. Birds were awakening in the nearby trees. Songs mingled with the calls of the mockingbird, the robin, and the occasional throaty cry from a cardinal, beautifully filling the air.

"Your strength has returned?" Lone Wolf enquired so suddenly that Jeanine's nerves jumped, though she was glad he had decided to talk again.

"Yes. I am fine," she answered, again reminding herself to keep the sting from her voice: she must pretend to herself that she was not a captive . . . just a guest. She had much information to attain from him. "The soup was quite delicious."

"You would like more?" Lone Wolf asked, moving to her side to pick up the wooden bowl.

"Perhaps later," Jeanine murmured, wishing she could relax. Her every muscle was tight. Her spine was stiff, her neck tense.

Lone Wolf's brows arched, surprised at her sudden gentle tone of voice. Until now she had behaved as a panther, ready to spring upon its prey. But he liked her change in mood, her decision to accept her captivity. He did not wish to keep her captive for too long. Once he fully understood why his brother and true father had chosen to marry white women, he would let her go.

Yet, did he not already know? This white woman he held captive had stirred wild passions within him. He was battling these feelings as though he were on the warpath with the Sioux! He had to prove to himself that he was stronger than his brother and father. He would not need the arms of this white woman to quell the hunger eating away at his insides. He would get answers from her, then return her to her way of life, just as he would return to his.

But first he must fully test her to see how white women

could adapt to an Indian's life. In knowing that, perhaps he *could* understand his brother better, and even the father Lone Wolf had never known.

Jeanine was becoming unnerved. Again Lone Wolf was silent. She watched him pick up a blanket, then turn and eye her with another stare.

She squirmed, then set her jaw tightly. "Why do you persist in looking at me in such a way?" she blurted. "It is as though . . . as though I am continually on display."

When he didn't answer her, her eyes snapped back at him angrily. She was finding that it was not easy to behave civilly toward him after all. "What am I to expect from you now? You have brought me here for a purpose, haven't you?" she said, her voice trailing off at the end of her questioning.

Her gaze settled on the blanket that he had draped over his arm. "You don't intend to force me to lie with you on the blanket, do you?" she gasped, her cheeks growing hot with a blush.

She looked directly into his eyes. "Talk to me, damn it," she hissed. "What *are* your intentions toward me? Do you plan to take advantage of me . . . ?"

A soft smile touched Lone Wolf's lips. In a way he was glad to see the anger return in the white woman's eyes and to hear it in her words. He had been right about her. She was full of fight! She was full of spirit! She was similar to a wild horse that was hard to tame!

But this made her even more attractive to Lone Wolf though he also felt even more threatened by her, afraid he would be the one to lose the battle. The battle of the heart. . . .

"The blanket is for you to wrap around yourself after your bath in the river," Lone Wolf said, bending to a knee, placing the blanket on Jeanine's lap. "You will go and bathe before the people of my village rise from their heavy sleep. You will go now. Lone Wolf will take you."

Jeanine was at first embarrassed by her accusations about his intentions, then paled and gasped when she realized that what he was offering her could be even more embarrassing. In fact, it could even lead to what she had just feared. To bathe, she would have to undress! And if he accompanied her to the river, he would be a witness to her undressing. And once undressed, he could . . .

She looked from the blanket back to Lone Wolf, disbelieving. "A bath?" she said in an almost whisper. "You intend for me to take a bath? And in . . . your . . . presence . . . ?"

"*Ay-uh*, yes, you are to bathe, and, yes, Lone Wolf will be close by," Lone Wolf nodded. He rose to his full height and towered over Jeanine. "Lone Wolf will not observe you while bathing. You will be offered this sort of privacy."

"Well, I refuse to be forced to bathe under any circumstances," Jeanine said hotly. She moved to her feet, then almost tumbled back down to the floor when she discovered that full strength had not returned to her legs after all.

Lone Wolf stooped and placed his hands on Jeanine's waist, urging her fully back to her feet. "You will get strength back when you exercise your muscles by walking to the river," he said flatly. Was she going to fail even this test? To have to bathe in the out-of-doors, without modern conveniences, as the Chippewa women were accustomed to? Would she even fail the test of swimming when forced to enter the river? She would probably fail many tests at once!

"We go. *Now*," he quickly added.

Jeanine trembled as he placed an arm about her waist and began forcing her toward the closed entrance flap. She wanted to fight him, but she didn't for more than one reason. She was weak. He was strong. He was determined. And no matter what his motive was in demanding that she take a bath, she was very aware of his manliness. She was even secretly reveling beneath his touch, yet hating herself for feeling anything for him. She wished for only one thing from him. She wanted information for her book and her lectures. Nothing more! She couldn't want his lips to possess her. She couldn't! Nor could she wish to be totally in his arms! Such wants—such cravings—were wrong and could only get her in deeper trouble than that in which she had already found herself.

The brisk air of morning, blowing down from Canada which bordered so close to Minnesota this far north, splashed onto Jeanine's face as she was led outside. She looked up quickly. "You expect me to go into the water when it is so cold?" she questioned weakly. "Why do you insist that I take a bath? Do I look so . . . so unclean to you?"

"All Chippewa bathe daily," Lone Wolf said, casually shrugging. His eyes locked with hers. "Do not the white men and women bathe daily? Your skin is as white as alabaster. Surely bathing is required to keep it that way."

His eyes sparkled with a smile. "And have you not missed bathing while traveling with Lone Wolf through the forest? There are smudges on your face that one finds on a child after a day of playing in a dusty ravine," he added.

Sighing heavily, Jeanine shook her head in frustration. "Yes, most bathe daily," she said dryly. "But it is done in the privacy of our homes. Never in a river." Her eyes sparkled with renewed anger. "And most take baths when they *choose* to. Not when they are told to."

A chill coursed through her as another brisk breeze reached through her clothes, touching her all over. "And we white people bathe where there is *warmth*," she continued to argue, clutching the blanket more closely about her. "I will catch my death of cold bathing in the out-of-doors."

Lone Wolf smiled smugly to himself. She *had* failed this one test. It was now proven to him that Chippewa women were stronger in mind, for one had to will oneself to accept this rugged life.

"Do not fret so, white woman. You will be warm while bathing," Lone Wolf grumbled, tightening his hold about her waist as he guided her on through his village. "Lone Wolf takes you to a place in the water where it is warm, as though the spirit of the sun lingers even when the sun hides beyond the far horizon. You will not even want to leave the water, it will so warm you."

He wanted to tell her that one of the true tests had been in her reaction to being ordered to the river. He had known from the beginning that she would find the water warm after entering it.

Ay-uh, she would fail in all her tests! He would prove that his true father and his brother had been wrong to take white wives! Ah, how good it was to know that in some small way he was avenging his beloved mother by at least finding out this truth of white women!

"I doubt any river could be warm," Jeanine scoffed, now looking about her, seeing what she had missed upon her arrival to the village drugged, in the wee hours of the morning.

The Indians' dwellings were not at all what she had expected. She had expected to see tepees, not these birchbark-covered huts. There were many, with only a little space between each. They faced where the sun was now quickly rising in the sky, positioned in a semi-circle, their backs to the forest, their entrances opening to the wide spaces of a magnificent river.

The rush of water reminded Jeanine of what she had heard the previous night. And then she saw what was causing the great sound. Lone Wolf was leading her toward a huge waterfall where on each side were monstrous, clinging cedar trees. Their aroma wafted through the air, sweet and fresh.

Then she recalled Lone Wolf telling her the name of his band of Indians . . . the Cedar Falls Band of the Chippewa, and now knew why they had chosen such a name.

Lone Wolf hurried his pace, half-lifting, half-carrying her from the ground with his firm grip about her waist, Jeanine again was reminded of what he had planned for her. And the closer they came to the water, the more she dreaded it. Though Lone Wolf had promised her privacy while bathing, she doubted his word. She had never been nude in the presence of a man. How could she be now?

"Why do you insist on accompanying me while I am

forced to bathe?'' Jeanine suddenly blurted, wincing as he guided her away from the river, into a thick stand of grass where briars reached out and pierced her skirt, and then the flesh of her legs. ''Couldn't your small friend have showed me? Why must you?''

As she was again pierced by more briars, she emitted a soft cry of pain and yanked away from him. ''And how can I take a bath when you guide me through these hellish briars?'' she stormed, clutching the blanket to her chest. ''Where are you taking me? We are no longer at the river. Have you changed your mind?''

''The water that is warm is only a bird's cry away through the forest,'' Lone Wolf said, gesturing with his free hand. ''White woman, you must learn the art of patience. Come. We go. Perhaps the water will soften your words as well as your mood.''

''Quit calling me white woman,'' Jeanine said between clenched teeth. ''My name is Jeanine.'' She jerked free from him and stood with a hand on a hip. She glared up at him, realizing that her legs were no longer wobbly, nor her knees weak. ''And I refuse to go any farther with you.''

''You will go with Lone Wolf,'' Lone Wolf grumbled. ''You will go *now*.''

''Only if you will return to the village and let me bathe alone,'' Jeanine argued.

''That is impossible,'' Lone Wolf said flatly, his face darkening into a frown.

Frustration soared through Jeanine. ''But, why?'' she cried softly. ''I need full privacy, Lone Wolf.''

''That is impossible,'' he again stated. ''I must accompany you. I cannot give you the opportunity . . . to . . . escape.''

The muscles of Lone Wolf's shoulders and legs corded as he watched the coloring in Jeanine's face change. First it paled to the color of snow, and then blushed the color of a bright, red sunrise.

He did not wait for her renewed onslaught of anger. Instead, he took two long steps toward her and whisked her up high in his arms and began carrying her. He stalked through the forest, ignoring her as she pummeled his chest with her fists, uttering unintelligible words.

When he came to the water's edge, only then did he release her from his arms.

"You . . . you . . . are a monster!" Jeanine screamed, again hitting his chest with a fist, forgetting her book and her research. "You cannot continue holding me captive. Why would you even *want* to?"

Lone Wolf withstood her words and her eyes, which had grown dark green with anger. Instead he took the blanket from her arms and tossed it aside, then began unbuttoning her blouse.

"No!" Jeanine softly cried, struggling.

"You will bathe, then we will return to my dwelling," he said flatly. He was tired of bantering with her. If she would not do as he told her willingly, he would do it for her. He had given her the chance to agree to his wishes. He would have afforded her privacy to bathe had she not become so unwilling to cooperate. Now, he would have to force her, for he could never let her believe she was the one in charge while with him.

Yet did she not already have partial control over him? His loins were becoming alive, desire for her fully blossoming inside him as he swept her blouse open, baring her breasts to his hungry eyes.

Though Jeanine's gasp pervaded the stillness of the morning and her hands were pushing against his powerful chest, Lone Wolf could not help but move a hand to touch the wondrous, dark peak of one of her breasts, feeling it grow hard against his fingers at his mere touch.

Jeanine dropped her hands away from him, frozen to the spot on which she stood. She looked up at Lone Wolf wonderingly, scarcely breathing now that his hand was cupping her breast, his thumb circling her hardened nipple. His touch was draining all fight from her. His midnight-dark eyes so boldly returning her gaze were mesmerizing her. She no longer had the desire to battle him. She no longer denied just how much she wanted him. Though she had fought her feelings, she had wanted him from almost that first moment their eyes met.

But could this be real? Was she dreaming? The splash of desire raging through her was so sudden! It was like wildfire, heating her insides to an inferno. And yet shouldn't she be afraid? Hadn't he again called her his captive? Wasn't he, as most called him . . . a savage?

But when he twined his fingers through her hair and drew her lips to his, crushing her breasts against his powerful chest, all protests died within her. As though some unseen force was willing her to, she crept wantonly into his arms and not only returned his kiss, but clung to him as though he had always been there . . . her lover. . . .

Eight

Lone Wolf's kiss was reviving the weakness in Jeanine's knees; the sensual feel of his hard chest pressed against her breasts caused her insides to melt. She returned his kiss with ardor, twining her arms about his neck, her mind awash with passion never before known to her.

She had often wondered if she would ever find a man who could send her into such a tailspin of rapture. But never would she have thought that the man who would possess such skills could be an Indian. She was even forgetting that she was Lone Wolf's captive. At this moment, she just welcomed being with him.

Jeanine became startled when Lone Wolf suddenly jerked himself free and walked away from her. He stopped only a few footsteps away to turn and look at her without a word of explanation as to why he had done so. The heat of his gaze was scorching. There was a look of possession in his dark, stormy eyes as he folded his arms across his chest and firmly set his jaw.

At first Jeanine just stared back at him, still rendered speechless first by his display of passion and now his abruptness to leave her. Then, when a soft breeze caressed her bare breasts she became aware of how brazen she had been. She had not only permitted Lone Wolf to loosen the buttons of her blouse, she had let him touch her breasts!

Feeling the fool, Jeanine jerked her blouse closed. "I don't know what got into me," she said, her voice breaking in her shame. "I've never behaved so . . . so . . . wantonly before. Never . . . never shall I again."

Lone Wolf's heart was beating fiercely against his ribs, echoing as though distant thunder in his ears. Again his body . . . his mind . . . had betrayed him! He had wanted to fully fight this urge to kiss and hold the white woman. He had not wanted the feel of her breasts to reach clean into his soul, to allow his hunger to overpower his determination to ignore that she was beautiful and enticing. He did not wish to be weak like his true father! A lovely Chippewa maiden was who he would desire . . . who he wanted to bear him his children! He did not wish to fail his beautiful mother by giving in to these desirous longings for the white woman! It would be hard to know that he had failed his mother in such a way . . . that he could even understand why his true father could choose a white woman over a Chippewa wife!

But this second kiss from lips that tasted as soft and sweet as rose petals proved that he would never wish to kiss another. It was not the color of her skin that made the difference—it was the *woman*. It was the touch. It was the kiss! Jeanine's kiss had aroused in him an intense passion. Lone Wolf knew that no matter what he might do to prove to himself that he could step away from his need of her, he would eventually have to have her . . . fully have her. It was most surely his destiny that she be his.

Lone Wolf would keep Jeanine with him for several days, not only to observe, but also to love. And he knew that she would love him in return. He had felt her respond to his kiss, to his discovery of the soft sweetness of her breasts. Again she would respond.

Looking toward the horizon, he saw the orange disc of the sun rising higher into the sky. Lone Wolf gestured with a hand toward the river, turning to Jeanine. "You have come to the river for morning bath, so take bath," he said firmly.

Jeanine's spine stiffened. She took a step backward, still clutching the blouse to cover her breasts. "No," she blurted. "I won't."

She could not let him see any part of her anatomy again. There were too many feelings being exchanged between her and this Indian. She had felt the desire in his kiss . . . in his embrace. If she again let him become passionate with her, she could expect more than mere kisses and touches. He would seduce her. And, she feared, she would let him. When in his arms she thought of nothing but him. And she knew that was wrong.

Yes, her research would have to be delayed. She would find her answers elsewhere.

Yet, could she ever put Lone Wolf totally from her mind? Running from him would not be the answer. He was now a part of her, as sure as the sky was blue this lovely morning! Ah, she had to distance herself from the temptation of his arms.

Yes, she must escape!

"Do you force me to take a bath because you find me so filthy that you cannot tolerate me? Aren't you afraid that my filth may have rubbed off on you when you kissed me?" she asked, glaring up at him.

Lone Wolf chuckled. His dark eyes gleamed as he placed his thumbs to the waistband of his loincloth and began slowly lowering it across his hips.

Gasping, placing her hands to her throat in shock, Jeanine turned quickly on her heel and put her back to him. "What do you think you're doing?" she said in a shallow whisper, barely loud enough for him to hear. Her pulse was racing, her face hot with embarrassment. She knew that, should she have watched only a moment longer, he would have bared himself fully before her eyes.

When Lone Wolf did not answer, Jeanine grew tense. She scarcely breathed, listening. She was afraid he was going to step in front of her, to force her to look at him in his total nudity.

Then she jumped nervously when she heard a splash of water beside her.

Slowly she turned her gaze toward the river where a circle of ripples revealed to her where Lone Wolf had entered the water. Looking over her shoulder, she saw his loincloth and moccasins, beside them, his colorfully beaded headband and feather lay on the ground.

She had been right. He had undressed completely.

Again she looked toward the river. Lone Wolf's head broke through the surface and he was raising his arms in expert strokes as he swam toward her. His fathomless, dark eyes were watching her, a smile soft on his lips.

"The water is warm as promised!" Lone Wolf shouted, now stopping to tread water. "*Mah-bee-szhon*. Come. *Gee-mee-nwayn-dum*. Enjoy. After your long journey the water will relax you. Your weariness will be taken away from you by the spirits of the water! Come. Swim."

Jeanine was finding it hard to stay angry with Lone Wolf. He now seemed genuinely friendly, yet that word "captive" plagued her heart as though it were a piercing knife. Surely any Indian . . . any man . . . who made a woman a captive did so for only one purpose.

She glanced down at him. She feared revealing to him that she trusted him the least bit. Hoping that getting this chore behind her would bring her closer to escape now that she saw that was her only recourse, she sighed desolately and moved toward the water. She wanted to get this over with.

Lone Wolf's eyes widened. "You do not remove your clothes?" he shouted. "Lone Wolf will look away so you may do so. Lone Wolf gives privacy you request."

"If I am forced to bathe *or* swim for whatever reason, I

shall do so with my clothes on,'' Jeanine said sourly, bending to at least remove her boots. She frowned at Lone Wolf as she jerked first one boot from her foot, then the other. ''Though you have chosen to remove your clothes, if you want to call that scanty thing that you wear clothing, I am not inclined to follow your lead. I can swim quite well with *my* clothes *on.*''

Sighing heavily, she raised her hands over her head and pushed herself forward. As she made contact with the water, she felt its warmth. It was as though she had plunged her body into the depths of a heated bath!

It was a strange phenomenon, but a welcome one. Most rivers this far north were cold, so cold, one could last but a few minutes if forced to enter.

She had read of the hot springs discovered many years ago in Wyoming. Surely this river in which she was swimming was also fed by such a hot spring. She reveled in the warmth she felt through her clothes, caressing her flesh. She could already feel her tensed muscles loosening and was glad that Lone Wolf had forced this upon her.

Rising back to the surface, she felt around with her feet for the bottom. Finding no solid ground, she skillfully treaded water as she combed her fingers through her wet and tangled hair, momentarily blinded by the water in her eyes.

But as her vision cleared she became awed by the color of the water. Now that she was farther out where it wasn't so shallow, she could see that it was crystal clear. The reflection from the river floor gave it a delicate blue tint in some sections, almost silver in others.

Her gaze moved farther now that she was away from the dense trees of the forest that lined the river. In the distance she could see more great forests of lodgepole pine, spruce and Douglas fir. She could even see occasional valleys covered by thick growth of grass and great splashes of flowers, intermingling colors of yellows, reds, white, and orange set against the green of the surrounding forests and the blue of the sky.

She reveled in the thrilling sensation she felt for being a part of this primitive setting. The force of illimitable freedom she felt was overwhelming, her body and mind entering a new element. She felt almost as free as the wind.

Jeanine was brought back to reality when Lone Wolf disrupted her line of vision. She was anything but free. For the moment, she was his. She was Lone Wolf's captive. . . .

Remembering this, she gave him a sour stare then swung around and began swimming away from him. Her arms felt like liquid in the warm water. She swam onward, with no destination, enjoying the moment of weightlessness.

But again Lone Wolf was there, swimming beside her. "White woman swims as skillfully as a fish," he said, smiling over at her. He was puzzled over his gladness that she could swim so well. He had wanted proof that her skills were inferior to those of the Chippewa women. How could he be pleased to find she was not failing in all tests?

He reached out and gently curled the fingers of his right hand about Jeanine's wrist, stopping her. He then drew her close to him. "What was your destination when Lone Wolf found you in forest so far from white man's community?" he asked, his smile fading along with his lighthearted mood. He wanted to ask her if she knew Strong Hawk. Did she know Strong Hawk's wife? If she did, she could tell him so much that he hungered to know! But he could not reveal this need to her without arousing her own questions of him. . . .

"That is none of your business," Jeanine said, trying to quell the nervous tremor in her voice. She was too aware of his nearness and how, if she looked downward, she could see his manhood through the translucent water. She had already been introduced to feelings she wanted to deny. Even now she felt waves of passion sweeping through her. His eyes! They were two points of fire! And his handsomeness. It nearly took her breath away!

She was aware of having given him the wrong answer to his question when he strengthened the hold on her wrist.

Gentle before, he was now rough. This Indian was so complex—what were his thoughts?

"You come to the land of the Chippewa? Why?" he demanded.

Jeanine stiffened beneath his hold. Should she tell him why she was truly in the forest? What would his reaction be? Would he accuse her of wanting to exploit the Indians?

"Why do you hold me captive?" she dared to ask, still evading his question.

"Lone Wolf asks questions, not white woman!" he grumbled.

"I owe you no answers," Jeanine murmured, trying to keep her emotions from running wild. Until now she could not confess to feeling anything special for a man. But she had never met Lone Wolf. When with him, her heart relayed messages to her brain which spoke of a need so intense she knew it would be a struggle to deny herself of pleasures her body demanded. He was the first, ever, to cause such feelings inside her.

"You are a stubborn white woman," Lone Wolf growled, releasing his hold on her.

He began swimming toward the shore, leaving Jeanine gaping after him. She had never expected him to give up on his questioning of her so easily. But she already knew not to second-guess this man. He seemed to run hot, then cold. And she understood, for she was guilty of behaving the same way.

Jeanine's breath was momentarily stolen when Lone Wolf pulled himself up out of the water, his buttocks revealed to her in a copper sheen. She was mesmerized by his nakedness, thinking this part of him beautiful.

Then she turned her head away in shame, amazed that she was exhibiting such bizarre behavior. She was fast becoming a stranger to herself, one filled with questions about many things. These feelings for Lone Wolf seemed to dominate everything else!

She purposely waited long enough to be sure that he was dressed, then she spun around in the water and began swimming to the shore. When she reached the embankment, she groped around trying to grasp onto something solid so she could pull herself up. Despite her efforts she felt her fingers slip on the mud, sending her sprawling back into the water.

Pushing to the surface, she coughed and choked, having swallowed a good amount of water in her surprise backward plunge. She brushed wet strands of hair back from her eyes, then saw the hand being offered her.

Meeting his gaze, she smiled weakly and accepted Lone Wolf's friendly gesture. When their hands made contact, her stomach churned wildly as it had done before when their flesh had touched.

As if by command, she continued looking up into his dark, mystical eyes as he drew her fully from the water. When he didn't let her go, but instead slipped his hands downward to curve his fingers about her buttocks, melding her body to his hard frame, she suddenly realized that her clothes were not the shield she thought them to be. Wet and clinging, they made it possible for her to feel every outline of his body against hers. Even the part of him that had risen in his renewed passion for her.

Splaying her fingers against his chest, Jeanine slowly shook her head back and forth. "No," she murmured, her lips quivering. "Please . . . don't. . . ."

But she didn't draw her head away when he lowered his lips to hers. Instead she confessed to herself that she welcomed his kiss.

He at first tested her with gentle, teasing kisses. He swept a hand upward to twine his fingers through her hair, and increased the pressure of his mouth on hers. Jeanine quickly became heady with rapture, enthusiastically returning his kiss. When he pressed his hard maleness more fully against her, she thought she might faint from the keen pleasure spiraling inside her head.

Again he abruptly parted from her, leaving her shaken, even numb. She gently ran her tongue over her lips, still tasting, even savoring him. Her body was hot from his having awakened her so. The sweet pain between her thighs was a sensation she had never before experienced. It was as though her heart were there, unmercifully pounding.

"First you want me, then you don't," she said, almost choking on the words. Again she could not believe it was she saying such a thing to a man, to *him*, an Indian, her captor. . . .

His silence unnerved her. But she was aware of his eyes avoiding hers. It was as though he were trying to prevent her from reading his feelings, bared in their depths.

Yet, as she silently studied him, she saw that it was for another reason that he was not looking into her eyes. She could almost feel his gaze burning along her body as his eyes slowly traveled its length.

She looked down to see why, and gasped. Her wet skirt and blouse clung to her like a second skin, displaying all her curves and crevices. Even the dark, bold outline of her nipples were well-defined beneath the wetness of her white blouse. It was as if she were standing there nude!

Her face flushed red with embarrassment, Jeanine moved to grab the Indian blanket and wrapped it snugly about her shoulders. Then she slipped into her boots, breathless, as she felt Lone Wolf watching her.

But she did not hear his footsteps as he walked toward her. He moved with the soft steps of a cat, it seemed. She flinched when the blanket was brushed from her shoulders and Lone Wolf's hands were there, taking its place. She scarcely breathed as she was forced to her feet, to look into his eyes.

"White woman, you must understand something that I only moments ago recognized," Lone Wolf said thickly. "It is plain now to Lone Wolf. You were in the forest for Lone Wolf to find, as does a shooting star suddenly appear in the heavens, also most surely for a purpose. Do you not see why I hold you captive? I seek answers to questions troubling me. You were surely sent by the Great Spirit, for Lone Wolf in his time of need. Soon you can return to your people. But for now, you are mine."

Jeanine felt powerless beneath the command of his eyes and his words of Great Spirits. She did not reply and he said no more. He draped the blanket back around her shoulders, quickly dressed, then in silence they walked back in the direction of his village. Jeanine trembled, aware of Lone Wolf's arm held possessively about her waist. More and more she felt drawn into feelings for him . . . the mystique of him that made him different than other men she had known.

She recalled his having just said that he would return her to her people . . . *soon*. Was he to use, then . . . discard her? Could he truly discard her? She had felt too much in his kiss. She had heard too much in his words!

They walked on past the plunging waterfall. In its leap the water was dashing into sprays that completely hid the lower part of the fall. The narrow gorge in which it was encased enhanced the full effect of the great height of the fall. The roar of the water was deafening.

Soon they entered Lone Wolf's village, now alive with morning activities. Jeanine's spine stiffened when she became the target of scrutinizing eyes. Everything and everyone around her became hushed. Even the dogs only sniffed silently at her feet. . . .

Nine

Humiliated, having felt as though on display while walking through Lone Wolf's village of curious onlookers, Jeanine very much welcomed being inside Lone Wolf's wigwam, away from the crowd of people and sniffing dogs. She was becoming aware quite quickly that Lone Wolf was not a renegade as she had first suspected. He drew too many admiring glances from the other Indians. He was treated with too much respect. It was as though he were being singled out by the Chippewa as a person of greatness.

Would Jeanine ever know why? Lone Wolf was such a secret person!

Trembling from the intense chill of the morning, Jeanine stepped up to the firespace and huddled close. Drawing as much warmth into her flesh as the fire afforded, she ignored Lone Wolf as he came to stand beside her.

But when he took the blanket from her shoulders where it hung down to fit snugly against the curves of her breasts, she turned with a start, breathless when she saw the way Lone Wolf was looking at her. It seemed he was apologizing to her without even saying the words. She then recalled how he had wanted them to go to the river before the people of this village awakened. He had surely wanted to return sooner for the same reason.

This was the reason for the silent apology, and she was glad that he at least cared that the stares of the Chippewa had caused her some discomfort. If she and Lone Wolf had not gotten so caught up in feelings for one another, they would have arrived at his dwelling much sooner. As it was, even now, these feelings were again being exchanged between them, as electric as lightning in a thunderous storm.

"The people of this village do not see white women often," Lone Wolf said thickly. "You are like a rare jewel, so lovely it poses a threat to all women of the village. This is why they looked at you in such a way."

"It was a bit unsettling," Jeanine said, laughing awkwardly. She wanted to say that she was still unnerved, but for different reasons. She was very aware of how her wet skirt and blouse still clung to her, and how Lone Wolf's eyes were discovering this anew now that the blanket was no longer there to hide her.

She shifted her own eyes, so aware of his lean and bronzed body. She had been carried to heights of ecstasy while held within his muscled arms. With just a kiss she had become a part of his world . . . a part of *him*. Should he ever fully take her, surely she would be lost to him forever.

Jeanine felt threatened by such thoughts; she was a person who treasured her freedom. No ties. Nothing. Could she give this up so easily for a man? Not only a man, but an Indian? Surely giving up such freedoms to someone whose customs and ideals were so different from her own could imprison her in many ways.

Yet she knew how foolish she was to let her mind wander so. Here she was a true captive, unable to leave the Chippewa Indian village on her own, at all. How could she even think of spending her entire future with a man who would take her captive?

Instead of silently hungering for Lone wolf, she should loathe him!

Forcing her eyes away, Jeanine placed her back to him and hugged herself with her arms. She was at least glad that she was finally feeling the warmth of the fire.

Or was this delicious heat spiraling within her because of the sensual feelings aroused by Lone Wolf's nearness?

No. She did not want him to be the cause of anything that made her feel good. She just wanted to escape! To be with him only meant confusion. And she had traveled north for a purpose, now wanting to write a book about the Chippewa more than ever before. Someone as intriguing as Lone Wolf would surely provide good material for a book. But she would have to find out other answers and information in another Indian village.

Yet didn't she already understand why Judith McMahon had married a Chippewa Brave? If any others were like Lone Wolf, they had the art to make a woman senseless with desire with merely a look from their fathomless, dark eyes. And once captured within their arms, surely all became hopeless!

Jeanine was adamant about not letting that happen to her, prepared to escape at the first opportunity. With renewed strength, surely she could find the other Chippewa village.

"All people of this village will grow accustomed to seeing you," Lone Wolf said, placing a hand to Jeanine's shoulder. He urged her around so their eyes could again meet.

"You are still determined to keep me here, against my will?" Jeanine fumed, her cheeks growing hot with anger. "Don't you know the wrong in doing that? My uncle is a sheriff. Should he come looking for me and find that I am being held captive, you will be arrested and placed in jail, and your people could suffer. My Uncle Fred despises

Indians. He would enjoy causing your people problems. Surely you don't want this, Lone Wolf. Let me leave. It would be so simple, to let . . . me . . . just . . . leave. And not later. *Now.*"

"It is not your place to worry about the Chippewa," Lone Wolf said flatly. "You do not need to worry even about yourself. You will not be harmed. You will be set free. But only when Lone Wolf says. Then I will even escort you safely back to the city you have left."

He dropped the blanket to the bulrush mats at his feet and cupped her chin with his free hand. "You see, Lone Wolf does not wish harm to come to you," he said hoarsely. "Lone Wolf only wishes to observe you, a white woman." He would not confess his need to test her. "That is all. Then you will be free to go."

"Observe . . . me . . . ? What on earth *for*?" Jeanine said, not wanting to feel pleasure in his touch as his thumb now traveled sensually beneath her chin in a soft caress. "Why *me*?"

"Why do I wish to observe you? That I cannot tell you. Why *you*? Because you were there, in the forest, for Lone Wolf to find," was all that Lone Wolf would say. Though he still suspected that she knew Strong Hawk and his wife, and that she could tell him so much that he hungered to know, he was not ready to reveal the truths of his family just yet. She would not understand if he did decide to challenge Strong Hawk for the title of chief! She did not understand anything about how the Chippewa thought . . . lived . . .

"Now Lone Wolf will say no more about this," he grumbled. You have had bath. Now is time for hair grooming."

Jeanine jerked away from him, her eyes wide with surprise. "Hair grooming?" she gasped. "Lord, what *next*? It's as though you are preparing me for some sort of . . . of . . . ritual. Are you? What *are* your true plans for me? Should I expect to even be shown to your family, as though on display again?"

"*Gah-ween*, no," Lone Wolf said, frowning. "None of that which you speak will happen. As for my family, all that is left is my father, the great chief of this band of Chippewa, and he is not at all well. You will not meet him."

Jeanine's mouth want agape, jarred clean to the toes by the sudden discovery of whose presence she was in. Lone Wolf had just confessed to being the son of a Chippewa chief! One day he would be chief!

Firming her jaw, her eyes flashing, Jeanine did not appreciate Lone Wolf using his standing in the Indian community to justify his right to take her captive. She was more determined than ever to be set free.

"Then why do you first force me to bathe, then groom my *hair*?" Jeanine said hotly. "What sort of grooming do you plan? All I need is a hairbrush. I could make myself quite presentable, thank you."

"Each day in the life of the Chippewa everything is done in order," Lone Wolf said flatly, walking to the closed entrance flap. He paused and turned, giving Jeanine another lingering stare. "A bath is first, hair grooming is second." His gaze traveled over her. "You remove your clothes. I will return with replacement."

Jeanine gaped after him as he hurried from the wigwam, then jumped with alarm as he suddenly stuck his head back inside it.

"Do not try to escape," he grumbled. "You will not get far. And should you try, when you are brought back to my village, you would then be bound by ankles and wrists to ensure this time with you that I request."

Jeanine took a shaky step backward, stunned by this declaration. She didn't have time to reply, for again, he was gone, leaving her to wonder about this man who spoke gently one minute, then spoke of binding her as a true prisoner, the next. First she felt safe enough with him, and then in the next breath, she sorely feared him.

Her heart hammering inside her chest, Jeanine glanced down at her wet blouse and her soiled, ripped skirt, and then further to her boots. He had ordered her to undress. She knew that she had no other choice but to comply. She did not want him to remove her clothes himself, for she knew there were more dangers than not in him undressing her. Though there was a part of her that feared him, there was no denying this want festering inside her. She was torn—two people, it seemed.

Glancing quickly toward the closed entrance flap, Jeanine decided it was best to get undressed before Lone Wolf returned. She still had the blanket to hide her body. Upon his return she at least wanted to be covered, ready to change into whatever sort of garment he was going to force upon her.

In her mind's eye she was remembering Pale Dove's skirt and blouse made of buckskin. They had been lovely with their beads and fringe. Jeanine would not dislike exchanging her drab attire for something as attractive. And if what Lone Wolf said was true, it would only be for a short while. As quickly as time passed, she would again be in Duluth, as though this time with Lone Wolf and the Chippewa were only a dream, a figment of her imagination. Hopefully it wouldn't turn into a nightmare before she was set free to return to her usual way of life.

Scurrying, Jeanine jerked her clothes off. Wrapping the blanket about her shoulders, she settled on the floor beside the fire and began struggling with her boots. Having become damp inside from her wet feet, they were clinging like leeches. She struggled. She softly cursed. And when she was finally able to jerk one of the boots off, she was thrown backward, causing the blanket to fall away from her in the plunge.

Angry, she tossed one boot and then the second on the other side of the fire. Before she had a chance to draw the blanket back around her, Lone Wolf was suddenly there, his dark eyes traveling over her nudity, stopping where hair made a dark triangle of tight curls between the juncture of her thighs.

Aghast, Jeanine scrambled from the blanket. Breathing

hard, she again wrapped it about her, her eyes now held by the command in Lone Wolf's. She paid no attention to what he had brought her, so fearing his having seen her completely nude.

Her heart pounded so fiercely she was beginning to feel light-headed, yet deep down inside, where her desires were formed, she knew that it was not totally fear that was causing her head to spin crazily. It was her own hunger to have him hold her . . . again kiss her. And she knew that even letting her mind wander so was sinful.

But it was the first time, ever, for her to want this with a man. Surely it could not be so wrong. This was a drive known to man and woman since the beginning of time. Could she help it if it was at this moment that she had become aware of such feelings? She was in love. Surely this was what it felt like to be in love. But she would fight it! She would fight it!

Lone Wolf's insides were afire, having again seen enough of her creamy skin to ignite his desire. The muscles of his shoulders corded as he watched her quickly cover herself, breaking this spell that had momentarily begun to weave between them. He had seen the flame of desire leap into her eyes when she had discovered him watching her. But this was a need they both were fighting. She for her reasons . . . he, for his.

Walking farther into the dwelling, Lone Wolf bent to a knee and offered what he held in his arms. "Yours," he said, lowering his eyes. He would not tell her that these were his mother's clothes. To borrow from other squaws would have raised too many questions that Lone Wolf did not want to answer.

Jeanine clasped her fingers to the blanket with one hand to keep it snug about her, then let Lone Wolf drape the buckskin skirt and blouse over her other arm, which she extended from the cover of the blanket. The feel of buckskin was that of butterfly wings, satiny soft. The light of the fire was captured in the beads sewn onto the blouse, as well as those sewn onto the moccasins Lone Wolf was now placing at her feet.

And then Jeanine's mouth opened in a soft gasp when she saw the hairbrush and mirror that he also so gently placed at her feet.

Rising to his full height, Lone Wolf towered over her. He folded his arms across his bare chest and smiled down at her. "You use the white man's brush. Then I will place bear grease in your hair and plait it. You will soon look Chippewa, except for the pale coloring of your skin. That will make it more acceptable to my people when you mingle with them while at my side."

Jeanine blanched. "Bear grease?" she said in a faint whisper. Then she spoke more loudly. "You will plait my hair? You wish that I look Chippewa? Why? You said that I would be your captive for only a short while. Do you lie?"

"You question everything that I do," Lone Wolf growled. "You just listen. Understand? Now you dress. Lone Wolf's patience runs thin."

"Oh!" Jeanine said, exasperated. She moved with haste to her feet, then became numb, realizing how Lone Wolf's eyes were still watching her. Did he intend to even watch her dress? How could she be expected to? Yet again she felt that she had no other choice but to do as told. Even if it meant stripping herself of all her dignity to please him!

Turning her back to him, Jeanine struggled to keep the blanket up around her with one hand while she slipped the blouse over her head with her other. But it was no use. It was too clumsy. The blanket kept slipping, an inch at a time, lower down her back, until she felt the warmth of the fire on the bare flesh of her buttocks. Once again a part of her that had never been looked upon by anyone but her mother was fully revealed to a man . . . not only a man, but the one who so stirred desire inside her!

Stomping a foot, Jeanine gave up and let the blanket ripple to the floor, to lay at her feet. With an anxious heartbeat she hurried on with the chore of dressing herself.

She sighed with relief when finally even the moccasins were slipped on and she could turn to face Lone Wolf, her chin stubbornly lifted.

"Well?" she said, placing her hands on her hips. "Are you happy? So far I have done everything you have ordered." She glanced down at the hairbrush, then back up at him. "And I shall even brush my hair. But never will I let you place bear grease in my hair! Never!"

With a smile, Lone Wolf bent to a knee and picked up the hairbrush and mirror. "Pale Dove's," he said, handing them toward Jeanine. "She has love of white woman's mirror and brush given to her when trading with white man. It pleases her to see herself in the mirror. She likes the feel of the brush as it is drawn through her hair."

He rose back to his feet and forced the mirror and hairbrush into Jeanine's hands. "But she always grooms her hair with bear grease," he said, his smile fading. "And so shall *you*."

Jeanine heard the force, the command in his voice. She saw the set of his jaw and the sudden coldness in his eyes. She would be doing whatever he ordered her to do, though the thought of bear grease in her hair made a sickness ripple in the pit of her stomach. Would she smell as badly as bear grease surely smelled?

Her gaze moved upward, seeing how Lone Wolf's hair so keenly shone. He most surely had applied bear grease to his hair, yet he didn't smell unpleasant. In fact, when so close to him, she had smelled something quite spicy and sweet, as though his skin had picked up the scent of the river . . . the forest . . . the wild flowers. . . .

"Yes. You will apply bear grease to my hair," she said faintly, hating to have to back down, to agree with him.

"And then you will join me in the forest," Lone Wolf said, going to the opposite side of his wigwam, where his bow and quiver of arrows awaited him.

Jeanine swirled around, her eyes wide. "The forest?" she gulped. "Why? We just came from the forest. Why must we return?"

Lone Wolf picked up his bow, constructed from the branch of an ash tree, the cord made from deerskin. The arrows had been crafted from the bough of an oak, tipped with flint and winged with feathers. He checked the tautness of its cord. "This time we enter forest for different reason," he said flatly, still not wanting to tell her why he tested her first one way and then another. "I have neglected the hunt. I must go today to replenish my food supply. You go with me."

"You want me to accompany you while you go hunting?" Jeanine asked, paling.

"*Ay-uh*, yes," Lone Wolf nodded. "Chippewa woman and man go separate ways through the day, doing separate chores. But you will go with me. We will work together as one."

His lips lifted into a smile as he slowly turned his eyes back to her. "White woman, you are too cunning to leave alone for even one minute," he said. "You will accompany me while I perform my duties as Chippewa Brave."

Jeanine was numb, fearing such a hunt. But she had come this far to learn the ways of the Chippewa, hadn't she? She just hadn't thought she would experience what it was to *be* a Chippewa!

She smiled back at Lone Wolf meekly and began slowly pulling the brush through her hair. . . .

Ten

With his boots clamped into stirrups, his fingers curled tightly about his horse's reins and a cigar hanging from the corner of his mouth, Fred Hunter's insides tightened. He was now guiding his horse alongside another lake edged with tall, swaying rice plants.

"Rice Lake," he grumbled, giving Cameron Tyner an uneasy glance. "This is the lake the Injuns call 'Water of Mystical Powers' because it's not fed by any larger body of water, rising mysteriously from deep inside the earth." He nodded. "Across the lake. That's the Injun village we've been lookin' for."

Cameron spat over his right shoulder, then peered across the body of water. "The village seems peaceful enough to me," he said, yet cautiously rested his hand on a holstered pistol. "We ain't got no true quarrel with the Injuns. We've come for Jeanine. That's all."

Fred drew his reins taut, stopping his horse. He jerked the cigar from his lips. "If she's even *there*," he said sourly. "We ain't seen no more signs of her on the trail since we left Slumber Lake behind us. It don't look good, Cameron."

"I'm sure she's just fine," Cameron scoffed. "No Injun in his right mind would abduct a white girl these days."

"Then how do you account for her abandoned gear?" Fred worried. He tried to capture movement in the village of dome-roofed wigwams that were colored orange by the setting sun. But he couldn't see clearly enough. Fog was now shimmering up from Rice Lake and reaching into the village like spreading, white cotton.

"Maybe she got frightened off by a bear?" Cameron calculated.

"Do bears kick dirt on campfires to kill the blaze?" Fred spat.

"No. Cain't say that I ever heard of one that did that."

"Then, Cameron, we have to figure that somethin' walkin' on two legs instead of four is behind my niece's disappearance."

"Yeah. Guess you're right."

"There's only one way to find out," Fred said, his insides cold with the thought of meeting a savage face to face again. In Duluth he avoided all contact with stray Injuns dressed and acting like whites. But here . . . ? He was being forced to meet the Injuns on their own turf and it made an uneasy itch begin at the base of his spine.

Fred slapped his horse with his reins and rode on around the end of the lake with Cameron trailing along behind him. Flashes of the past were appearing in Fred's mind, recalling another Indian village . . . another time, long ago. He had gone there, searching for his wife, Darla.

When word had reached him that Darla had been taken captive by Indians, he knew even then never to expect to see her alive again. The discovered red, shimmering hair on the scalp pole had proved him right. After raiding the Indian camp, her mutilated body had been found.

Even now Fred had the urge to retch when thinking about it. The fact that it had been the Sioux who had committed such a savage act didn't make Fred feel any better about Chippewa. To him one Injun was as bad as the next, and he was going to find it hard to speak a civil tongue to any of them. But for Jeanine, he must. . . .

Tensing as he reached the very edge of the village, Fred swallowed hard and continued on his way. Fires burned before each wigwam; the aroma of cooked meat wafted through the air, reaching Fred's nose. In the twilight of early evening, children were playing, dogs were barking. Men were sitting outside their dwellings, some carving, others peacefully smoking their pipes. Women were mingling about, absorbed in their various activities of tanning hides, or tending outdoor fires.

Most looked up and gave Fred and Cameron quiet stares, stopping their chores for the moment to watch the strangers working their way through the village. Fred's pulse raced, knowing that his sheriff's badge was catching the shine of the fires, illuminating it in a golden hue, surely a threat to the Indians who might know of its meaning.

Fred and Cameron exchanged nervous, frowning glances. Fred then looked past everything and everyone and saw the one different style of dwelling in this village of Indians. It was a log cabin built beneath a cover of thickly-leafed elm trees at the far edge of the village. Glass windows sparkled at the front, and smoke spiraled lazily from the immense stone fireplace chimney on one side.

Fred was not at all surprised to find such a house. No white woman could ever get used to living in such small quarters of a wigwam. He smiled smugly to himself. He *had* found the right village. He had found Judith McMahon and Chief Strong Hawk!

He traveled on through the village, stiff-backed, then finally drew his horse up in front of the cabin. He slowly dismounted and whipped his reins about a hitching rail, glowering over at Cameron.

"You stay outside and keep a watch on things," he flatly ordered. "If you see anything cockeyed at *all*, you come for me. Do you hear, Cameron?"

"Yeah, I got'cha," Cameron said, nodding, his hand still resting on his pistol.

"You'd better hope Jeanine's alive and well," Fred warned, then turned on his heel and lumbered to the cabin door.

He hesitated a moment, trying to calm his trembling fingers, then rapped his knuckles against the door. He waited, nervous.

When the door swung open, he looked down upon a face of pink radiance, so shatteringly pretty, with her sky blue eyes and cute, upturned nose, he couldn't help but take a shaky step backward.

He had found Judith McMahon, alright. He had heard her described by the local folk who still gossiped about her marriage to the damn Injun. He looked at her waist-length, golden hair, disbelieving that anyone as pretty as she could have married a filthy Injun.

Yet she had . . . and she was even dressed as an Injun squaw, herself. His gaze swept over her, seeing how the ankle-length buckskin dress with its decoration of beads clung to her voluptuous figure. Strands of colorful beads hung about her neck, laying where her dress parted at the bodice, revealing the upper lobes of her satiny, large breasts. She wore fancy moccasins on her feet.

"Yes? May I help you?" Judith asked cautiously, puzzled by this stranger suddenly at her door.

Her gaze searched over the man and found the sheriff's badge on his suit jacket, making her grow tense. So far the law had stayed out of their lives. Why would they appear *now* . . . ? Unless something had happened to Strong Hawk's brother, Silver Fox, Giles?

Everyone who knew Giles at all knew of his recent problems with the family business, the Thomas Lumber Company. He had even mentioned possible bankruptcy. His state of mind worried the entire family. That was the reason for his mother, Danette, making residence with him, to keep an eye on him. . . .

"Is something wrong, Sir?" Judith added. "Have you brought news from Duluth? Is that why you are here?"

Fred coughed nervously into a cupped fist, then regained his composure. He removed his Stetson hat and circled it around, between his fingers. ''Beg your pardon, Ma'am,'' he said thickly. ''Sometimes I forget my manners. But let me introduce myself. I'm Sheriff Fred Hunter, from Duluth.'' He motioned with a nod of his head toward Cameron. ''And that's my deputy, Cameron Tyner.''

He shifted his feet nervously. ''May I have a word with you, Ma'am?'' he said further. He looked past her, over her shoulder. ''May I speak with your husband Chief Strong Hawk?''

''Sir, why have you come all the way from Duluth to speak to my husband and me?'' Judith persisted, standing her ground. She looked past Fred, at Cameron who was still waiting on his horse. Her shoulders became squared, readying herself for anything unpleasant that might be said, or that might happen, in the next few moments.

''It's about my niece,'' Fred said, frustrated by her stubborn stance. ''She seems either lost in these parts, or . . .''

He stopped, afraid to even breathe the word ''captive.''

''Or, *what* . . . ?'' Judith said blandly.

Color rose in Fred's cheeks, anger fusing with frustration inside him. He wanted answers and he damn well wasn't getting them. ''She's *missing*,'' he growled as he leaned down into Judith's face. ''I've come to see if she just might have—somehow—managed to come, or was *brought* here.''

Judith paled. She knew the implication of his words without his coming right out and accusing the Chippewa of possibly abducting his niece. She grabbed the edge of the door and attempted to close it, but Fred's booted foot moved too quickly, placing it where the door could not close against it.

''Sir . . . !'' Judith hissed.

''My niece, Jeanine Thaxton. She said that she was comin' this way,'' Fred said, forcing the door back open with a stern shove. ''She said she wanted to come and talk with *you*. You *are* Judith, aren't you?''

"Yes . . . I'm Judith," she said in a bare whisper, quickly recognizing the name Jeanine Thaxton. Jeanine had purchased Judith's house in Duluth shortly after Judith's father had died. Yet Judith could not help but let fear ebb its way into her heart, wishing Strong Hawk would hurry back to the cabin. He would know how to handle this overbearing man. No matter what his reasons, he had no right to barge into her house.

"Why did your niece want to talk to me?" she asked. "Was it something to do with the house I sold her? Is something the matter?"

"That's not important," Fred growled. "What is . . . is she here?"

"No . . ." Judith murmured. She realized that she had answered Fred Hunter much too quietly, as he forced his way into the house, his eyes searching eagerly about. . . .

Judith swung around and rushed after Fred, looking nervously toward the cradle that sat across the room in front of the fireplace where a fire burned low on the grate. "What do you think you're *doing*?" she gasped, now more concerned over her tiny, one-month-old son, Flying Eagle, than anyone else. She went to stand protectively over the cradle, placing her back to it.

"I've come to find my niece and by damn that's what I intend to do," Fred snapped. "Is she here, or ain't she?"

"No. She's not and hasn't been," Judith said dryly. "Your niece must be lost. Why not leave my house? Go to the council house. You will find Strong Hawk there. Perhaps he can get some of his Braves together to go search for your niece. Sir, she is *not* here."

Fred turned with a start and stared down at Judith, bitter at her suggestion that he even ask anything of an Injun. Again while looking down at her gentle loveliness he was amazed that she had chosen to live such a life . . . wasting away in the wilderness, living the life of a savage . . . with a savage. . . .

He stretched his neck and looked down into the baby cradle. His insides rippled cold when he saw a tiny Indian baby. The way she was protecting it, it was surely hers.

Again he looked her square in the eye. "Weren't white men good enough for you?" he tormented. "You had to go and marry a damn Injun . . . even have a damn *papoose* . . . ?"

"Who is this who enters my dwelling and questions my wife about husband and child?" a voice deep and commanding said suddenly from across the room.

Fred's spine stiffened at the sound of the deep male voice behind him, flavored with a tinge of accent . . . an *Injun's*. Instinct drew his hand to a pistol. Clasping onto it, he turned around slowly and saw Strong Hawk standing in the shadows of the opened door.

As Strong Hawk stepped into the room, Fred felt the same old hate enter his heart that plagued him whenever he was near an Indian. His gaze swept over Strong Hawk. He damn well looked the role of chief. His cheekbones were high and pronounced. His nose was long and commanding. He displayed quite well the wide-muscled strength of his shoulders and chest.

Strong Hawk was wearing a buckskin shirt that was beautifully embroidered and painted in curious hieroglyphics the charts of his life. His leggings were of deerskin, fitting tightly to the legs, extending from the feet to the hips, and fastened to a belt which was passed around the waist. There was a band worked with porcupine quills of richest dyes passing down the seam on the outer part of the leg, and fringed also the whole length of the leg.

His moccasins were of buckskin and covered in almost every part with the beautiful embroidery of porcupine quills. The headband that held his coarse, shoulder-length black hair in place was also as highly-embroidered, where at the back, in the loop of his hair, he wore his prized yellow feather, handed down to him by his great-grandfather, Chief Yellow Feather.

"Again I ask you. Why are you here, troubling my wife?" Strong Hawk asked. He stepped to Judith's side and placed an arm possessively about her waist. "You did not come alone. Another man waits outside. Tell me.

What is your name?'' His gaze swept to the badge, then moved back to the stranger's face. ''And you wear a badge. Why do you come into my village, troubling my people?''

Judith snuggled into Strong Hawk's embrace. Her heart soared with pride to have him so close, at her side. She looked worshippingly up at him, even still captivated by his handsomeness. At times she could hardly distinguish between his eyes and the night, both so dark.

''Strong Hawk, he's come from Duluth,'' she said softly. ''His name is Fred Hunter, sheriff of Duluth. He's come searching for his niece . . . the lady who purchased my house there. She was headed this way but now no one can find her.''

She frowned at Fred, wondering again why Jeanine wanted to talk with her. But that should be no true concern here. The fact that she was missing, was. ''Tell Mr. Hunter that she hasn't been here, Strong Hawk,'' she quietly urged.

''There has been no one here that is a stranger to my people except *you*,'' Strong Hawk said flatly. His eyes were fathomless as he glared at Fred's hand resting on his pistol.

''Then where in the hell *is* she?'' Fred grumbled. He eased his hand away from his gun to knead his brow. He believed Strong Hawk and Judith. He truly had no reason not to. And they did appear to be a truthful sort though it cut like a knife to admit this to himself. He didn't want to trust an Injun. *Any* Injun. . . .

''She may be lost, Strong Hawk,'' Judith said, pleading with her eyes up at her husband. ''I remember the one time I got lost. I almost didn't . . . make it. . . .''

Strong Hawk looked down at Judith with heavy lashes. ''*Ay-uh*, yes. I also remember,'' he said thickly.

He stepped away from Judith and took a step closer to Fred. ''Strong Hawk offers you assistance in searching for your niece,'' he said firmly. ''We leave. Soon. Together. We search side by side, white man.''

Fred was taken aback by Strong Hawk's abruptness . . . his offer . . . his *kindness*. His eyes wavered. He had never expected this from an Injun. But could he be trusted? Could he actually ride beside an Injun, no matter the reason? The seed of his hate for all Indians lay deeply inside him.

Yet, he did have to consider Jeanine's safety. If she wasn't with this band of Indians, couldn't she be with another? This Indian, Chief Strong Hawk, surely knew where to look. He would surely know which Indians would abduct a white woman.

"I appreciate your kindness," Fred managed to say, unable to actually say the words "thank you." He gasped, then his face turned crimson when Strong Hawk clasped his fingers onto his shoulders.

"We will find her," Strong Hawk tried to reassure him. "*Wenebojo* will make it so."

"*Wenebojo*?" Fred said, idly scratching his brow.

"I will instruct my men," Strong Hawk said flatly, moving away from Fred. "We shall leave. Soon."

Fred nodded. "I do appreciate your help," he commented dryly. He hoped his trust wasn't being misplaced. But as he saw it, he had no choice but to trust!

Strong Hawk nodded, then looked toward the cradle. "Before I leave, to search in the forest, I first must see my son," he said, pride thick in his words. He went over to the cradle, placing an arm about Judith's waist. Together they gazed down at their child, remembering in each of their minds and hearts their own trials and tribulations of the forest. It seemed so long ago, yet in truth, it wasn't. . . .

Eleven

Kingfishers were chittering back and forth across the river in fussy irritability. The noon sunlight stabbing downward from a sky of pale blue dappled the river with shimmering light. The birchbark canoe slid through the water as though it were weightless, yet its hollowed-out cottonwood bulk was, in truth, large and cumbersome as Jeanine could judge.

But Lone Wolf drove it forward effortlessly with his paddle rhythmically dipping in and out of the crystal clear abyss. His masterful strokes were taking them farther and farther away from Lone Wolf's village, though he had already claimed several rabbits and squirrels from his morning hunt.

Lone Wolf had chosen to travel by canoe this day instead of by horseback. Jeanine was again his passenger, but this time she was sitting on spread furs, where even at her feet lay furs on which to place her moccasined feet. If she would let herself, she could feel queenly today, for that was the way Lone Wolf was treating her.

Her being with him as captive was reason enough for her not to be able to accept any of his kindnesses with ease. Being a captive, even for a short while as he said, was wrong. Yet she could not help but confess to herself that she was enjoying every passing moment in his company. These were times that would stay with her, forever, and not because she was being forced to be with him, but because she was with him!

Her gaze settled on his bronzed, muscled shoulders as he sat with his back to her, paddling from the middle of the canoe. Again she felt herself being swept up by sensual feelings for him. Her skin tingled with awareness when recalling how it had felt to be in his arms, how her body had turned to liquid each time his eyes had touched her. She still could not understand why it was different with him than all other men she had met. Was it the mystique of his being Indian?

But no matter the reason, the timing was wrong. She was his captive. A full surrender to him would be wrong. She could not allow it to happen. She expected this to be part of his plan for her, to be fully his, whenever he chose to approach her in that way, again. Until now, something had stopped him just at the moment she had expected him to seduce her. She wondered *what* . . . ?

Her gaze again went to the slain animals in the canoe. Barely a trace of blood could be seen on their fur. Lone Wolf had used a bow and arrow for their capture instead of a gun, explaining that an arrow left a much cleaner wound, and that an arrow was more exact.

He had then said that he knew where he might find a bear, not only for food, but for its magnificent pelt. He had said he had found this particular bear's winter home and had gone there many times since the bear's hibernation months had passed, but with no success in finding it. Always when out on a new hunt, he went to this same spot, hoping luck would one day be with him. He wanted this bear because it had proven to be as cunning as he. And Lone Wolf had to be the victor!

The thought of being on a hunt for a bear sent goosebumps along Jeanine's flesh. She spied the rifle resting against the side of the canoe beside Lone Wolf's leg. Hopefully, if he went searching for a bear he would also take his rifle. Jeanine did not trust the bow and arrow as much as Lone Wolf did!

Suddenly thirsty, Jeanine went to her knees to the bottom of the canoe. She bent over the sides and cupped her hands into the water, then stopped and gazed at the reflection staring back at her from the mirror of the water. She hardly recognized herself! She had forgotten that Lone Wolf had braided her hair . . . had even applied bear grease to it, to make it shine.

And then her gaze moved downward, seeing the beautiful blouse and its trimming of beads. It was so soft it had been easy to forget that she was even wearing it.

Feeling a sudden change in the direction of the canoe, Jeanine turned her head. Lone Wolf was guiding the canoe quickly toward shore where a pine forest was split by this curving river. The beach was pebbled. Cattails with their waving green leaves stood as though sentinels. Silky down was spilling from some of their long brown spikes, blowing in the wind resembling puffs of smoke from a chimney, while others were still brown and firm.

Jeanine rushed a drink to her mouth from her cupped hands then repositioned herself on the seat of the canoe, just as Lone Wolf swept the vessel to shore and jumped into the water, dragging it, to beach it.

Breathless, not knowing what to expect next, still in awe of Lone Wolf having brought her with him on this hunt, Jeanine watched his every move. The powerful muscles of his legs corded as he stepped up from the beach into taller grass, searching with his eyes, seeming barely to breathe. When he moved stealthily past the pines, now walking beneath stately elms and oak trees, Jeanine was beginning to panic, thinking that he was going to abandon her, to continue on this hunt alone.

Then her gaze moved to where his bow and arrow and

rifle still rested in the canoe. He would surely not go far without means to protect himself. Even so, she moved on her knees to the rifle and grabbed it. She crept on from the canoe and emitted a low cry of pain when a sharp rock reached through the soft sole of her moccasin, into her tender foot.

She moved onward, into the knee-high swaying grasses and stopped suddenly as Lone Wolf turned and looked her way. When his gaze captured the rifle in her possession she saw a coldness enter the depths of his dark eyes. Even his hands clenched into fists at his sides.

Then Jeanine understood why. She was white. He was Indian. She had a weapon. He did not!

A strange sort of thrill coursed through her veins. For only an instant she had known what most who were captors would think, suddenly finding herself armed, the true captor not!

But she did not feel all that threatened by Lone Wolf. And she could never . . . never . . . do anything that would harm him. Her feelings ran too deep. And God help her for this!

Seeing that he hadn't moved a muscle, still watching her so threateningly, Jeanine took a step backward and dropped the rifle. "I brought the rifle from the canoe for protection," she said, laughing awkwardly.

He still did not move. Jeanine looked from the rifle, back to him, now understanding his hesitancy. She gestured with a hand toward him. "Protection from that bear you have more than once mentioned, Lone Wolf. Nothing else."

When she had spoken the words "nothing else," there had been a tone of apology in the way she had spoken them. Should she be apologizing to him? Incredible! She was surely daft to let him continue affecting her in such a way. But it was as though she were someone else, alien to everything she had ever felt or done.

She was eager to be released, to at least feel free to return not only to the life she had always known, but also to be the person she had always been. Only then could she sort out these feelings inside her. Only then . . .

Her pulse racing, she further watched Lone Wolf as he moved in cautious steps toward her. And when he came to her side, his dark gaze held her still, while he stooped and took the rifle in hand.

"A rifle is a dangerous weapon," he growled. "It is only used when ready to *kill*." He tossed it farther away from Jeanine's reach. "Lone Wolf kills. Not white woman! Do you understand?"

"But, Lone Wolf . . ." Jeanine stammered, almost feeling his body heat as he towered over her. "I only brought it from the canoe because you did not take it with you for protection. I felt perhaps you or I might need it. You have spoken of a bear more than once today."

Her spine stiffened as she began looking cautiously about her. "Is this the spot?" she murmured. "Is this where you have seen the bear's place of hibernation? Would he even return to it, now that the weather frees him to wander as he pleases?"

Lone Wolf nodded. His gaze finally left Jeanine and moved from tree to tree. "*Ay-uh*, yes," he said flatly. "There are signs on the trees. Do you not see the wide scratches from its claws?"

His gaze moved upward and stopped at a large hole in a powerfully huge elm tree, sufficiently large enough to admit a bear. "Up there. That is the bear's dwelling. The bear must still come and go. The claw marks are fresh, possibly even made today. Lone Wolf will see if he is there now."

Lone Wolf began running toward his canoe. Jeanine grew cold with fear, wondering why. But before she could question him he had already returned with his bow and arrow. Scarcely breathing, she watched him climb the tree that grew near the elm and extended up near the hole. And fearing that he might scare the bear from the hole in her direction, she hurriedly searched for the rifle and found it. Surely he could not fell the bear with only an arrow!

Lone Wolf moved out on a limb that reached to the elm tree, then cautiously peeked inside the hole. His shoulders slumped in disappointment. The bear was not there. It was surely also out hunting for food.

Disgruntled, he slid back down to the base of the tree and walked heavy-footed back to Jeanine. His gaze caught the shine of the rifle in her hands. And just as he was about to take it from her, a sound of breaking twigs and an ensuing sudden roar that filled the woods behind Lone Wolf made him turn with a start. His spine stiffened when he saw that not more than ten yards from where he stood the grizzly bear was lumbering toward him on its hind legs.

For a split second Lone Wolf and the bear eyed each other, then with a thunderous heartbeat, Lone Wolf raised his bow and arrow, with thoughts to aim for the bear's throat. . . .

Jeanine's eyes were wide as she watched the bear. It was a cinnamon bear, called thus because its color was reddish-brown. And it was huge, yet surely looking even bigger because of its long, coarse hair.

Her gaze went quickly to Lone Wolf. It seemed to be taking him forever to notch his arrow onto the bow cord. She felt he didn't have that long. If the bear dropped to its four feet, it could be upon Lone Wolf before Lone Wolf even had the chance for another eye blink.

Her stomach churning, her fingers trembling, Jeanine raised the rifle and aimed. But when she fired, the bullet missed the bear and crashed into the trunk of a tree. She bit her lower lip in frustration, but sighed with relief when the bear jolted with fright, dropped to its feet, and turned and fled.

Lowering the rifle to her side, Jeanine smiled up at Lone Wolf meekly as he turned and totally faced her. But her smile faded when she saw fire in his eyes. She took a step backward and almost stumbled over a fallen limb when he moved toward her, anger etched across his bronzed, handsome face.

"You shoot rifle?" he hissed. "You frighten bear away? Why did you do this?"

Jeanine fumbled around to find the right words, stunned by his reaction to her trying to help him. He should be thanking, not scolding her. "Lone Wolf, the bear was so near," she murmured. "I . . . I . . . didn't think you were going to shoot him soon enough. I feared for your life, Lone Wolf. And now you are angry with me? Why?"

"The arrow is swift!" he argued. "It is deadly! If you had not interfered, the bear would be mine!"

"But you were so slow. . . ." Jeanine softly pleaded.

"Lone Wolf not slow," he stormed. "Lone Wolf deliberate!"

Lone Wolf dropped his bow and arrow to the ground, then jerked the rifle away from Jeanine. Frowning at her, he tossed it to the ground. When he saw the sparkle of tears in the corners of her eyes and how she trembled, he became drawn into a softer, sympathetic mood. Thinking that to her he was almost as gruff as the bear, so wounded was she in her appearance, he was touched by her show of emotion. Until now, she had only shown him her strong and stubborn side. And he was glad to see that within her there were weaknesses. And it was this newly found weakness, this vulnerability he was now witnessing, that was feeding his desire for her!

Without another thought of having lost the bear and her being the cause, Lone Wolf took Jeanine's hands in his. Their wondering eyes met and held. "You tremble so," he said thickly. His loins ached, wanting her so. "Lone Wolf was too harsh? Is that the cause of your trembling? Or is it fear of the bear?"

Jeanine swallowed hard. Her insides melted as his touch . . . his eyes . . . again so mesmerized her. He had lost his anger and was now behaving more gently toward her. It was this gentleness that was the danger to her heart. Though she didn't want to, she was being caught up in him again.

"I tremble for many reasons," she said, her voice

foreign to her in its strange huskiness. She could feel color rising to her cheeks. Had he heard the change in her voice . . . such a change brought on by unleashed passion?

"These reasons are?" Lone Wolf said thickly, his heart pounding erratically, seeing so much in her eyes, hearing so much in her voice.

"I mustn't tell you," Jeanine said, casting her eyes downward. "Let us just please return to your village."

Lone Wolf did not like the way in which she hid her eyes beneath the dark droop of lashes on her cheeks. He wanted to see desire in her eyes. There was a madness in him now. How fiercely he wanted her!

Placing a forefinger to her chin he lifted it and urged her eyes once again to meet the command of his. "You do not truly want to return to my village just yet," he said hoarsely. "White woman, we have much left undone between us. Let us no longer fight this that we feel for each other. You want Lone Wolf. Lone Wolf wants you. Can you deny such feelings? I can no longer deny that which *I* feel, though I do know that it is not best for me, the next chief-in-line, for my band of Chippewa. It is not best that the white skin of a woman blind Lone Wolf! But it has . . . but it has. . . ."

His words rang true inside Jeanine's heart. How could this be, that they both felt this attraction, both knowing the complications it would create?

What he said reached her consciousness. Again he had mentioned that he was the next chief-in-line, that his father was now chief. Though she had from the beginning thought he might be a renegade, his dignity . . . his pride . . . had been there, worn outwardly, for everyone to see, a physical thing, it seemed, as well as mental. She should have known that he was not an ordinary Indian! She should have known . . . !

"It isn't right," she suddenly spoke. "You. Me. Our feelings. None of it, Lone Wolf."

Then her eyes moved past him, into the forest. "And the bear. It might return," she murmured. Her gaze again met Lone Wolf's wondering eyes. "Let us leave. Now. Please?"

"We are safe from the bear," Lone Wolf said, squeezing her hands for reassurance. "Bears seldom attack human beings unless they are fearing for their young. This bear today must have a cub nearby. We became a threat."

"But won't it return? Are we not still a threat?" Jeanine softly questioned.

"I am sure the gunfire frightened both the cub and its mother far away," Lone Wolf said. "They will not return to this place, ever. The smell of gunpowder and humans will remain in their hearts."

"You are no longer angry with me because of this?" Jeanine dared to ask. "You so wanted that bear."

"*Gah-ween*, no, I am no longer angry," Lone Wolf said gently. "Lone Wolf is glad."

Jeanine's eyes widened. "Glad? You . . . are . . . glad . . . ?" she softly gasped. "You may never get the chance to capture the bear again. And it is my fault, Lone Wolf."

"Had Lone Wolf killed the bear and had duties of preparing bear for return to village, then moments like this with you would be delayed," he said huskily. "And Lone Wolf can wait no longer. Lone Wolf . . . needs . . . you. Lone Wolf needs you now."

Sunshine laced through the overhead branches where they stood and fell on Jeanine's upturned face in pools of golden light. She scarcely breathed. She did not protest when Lone Wolf reached his hands to her hair and began unbraiding it.

"I was wrong," he said thickly. "Your hair should be free. It is more beautiful free. As *you* are beautiful."

With deft fingers he finished unbraiding her hair until it spilled out across her fair shoulders, then tumbled down her back. He lifted the buckskin blouse over her head, revealing to him her ripe, curving breasts.

A tremor coursed through Jeanine's body when Lone Wolf bent his head and his lips touched hers in a gentle and lingering kiss. While his hands molded her breasts, the wondrous excitement stirring within her was so keen she felt as though she might swoon. The press of his lips was warm and soft, yet demanding. Then with practiced skill, he tantalized her closed lips with his tongue and urged them apart, then trembled himself, as he found the honey dew taste of her responding in kind as her tongue twined with his.

Jeanine's breasts responded, swelling within his hands. The nipples hardened into his thumbs as each caressed her dark tips. He pressed his pulsating hardness against her abdomen as she moved more into his embrace, while her arms clung about his neck. He lowered his hands and began easing her skirt from around her waist, stiffening when she emitted a soft sort of protest against his lips.

But though she protested he continued to undress her, knowing the protest was not sincere, for she still leaned too fully into him for her to want anything else, but this that he had begun.

There was a stirring of fire within Jeanine. So blinded by passion, she closed her eyes to the fact that she was being seduced. She knew that she would allow it. She hungered for the full knowledge of what she had thus far missed as a woman. And she had never felt so alive. Being with him, discovering these feelings that were new to her, made her realize just how much she did love him. Would always love him.

An incredible sweetness swept through her when again his fingers caressed her breasts and then moved to her back, making a slow, sensuous descent along her spine. And then she barely drew in her breath when his hand crept around and found her warm and secret place, where, trembling, she let him part her thighs and caress the damp valley that, until Lone Wolf, had never before known the touch of a man.

Lone Wolf drew his lips from hers. His eyes were heated, dark pools as he looked down at her, watching her as he slowly tested the entrance where her patch of soft, curly hair protected the core of her womanhood.

And when he searched with a finger and found her womanhood still intact, Lone Wolf smiled to himself. He had hoped that he would be the first. He did not want to believe that she would easily give herself to any man. His heart soared, realizing that she had chosen him.

Wanting to teach her everything about their union, Lone Wolf took one of Jeanine's hands and guided it to his proud shaft. Jeanine gasped with shock as he forced her hand upon his hardness which was so boldly outlined, now, through the flimsy material of his loincloth. Feeling his largeness, she understood the full meaning of his intentions. Breathtakingly aware of his strong hands on her body, Jeanine realized that she was wantonly nude with him. She blushed and tried to inch away.

But he would not allow it. He held her, and her hand firmly in place. His eyes were dark with desire as he commanded her to again look up at him. His fingers were tightly enmeshed with hers against his throbbing desire. "Do you not feel its life?" He said huskily. "It is aroused because of you. Are you not as much aroused?"

His fingers on the soft mound of hair that lay at the juncture of her thighs, where he was now so sensually caressing her, moved more intently. "My hand feels your wetness. This speaks to me words that do not come from your mouth. Let us make love, beautiful one. Lone Wolf will be gentle, for he knows you have never been with a man in such a way before."

Before she could utter a protest, Lone Wolf was again tormenting Jeanine with a kiss. Her lips parted this time without coaxing. She let his tongue probe. Gently at first he explored, then withdrew to kiss her fully with fire, all the while easing her to the ground. The long, waving grass bending beneath Jeanine's weight became a bed of desire, soft as a feather mattress against her bare flesh.

Lone Wolf moved his lips to kiss the hollow of her throat, almost tasting Jeanine's heartbeat it was beating so profoundly against his lips. His hands searched out the silken curves and crevices of her flesh. Her body quivered beneath his caresses as does a bow cord quiver after releasing its arrow.

In one swift movement he removed his loincloth, then moved over her, his hard body touching hers, pressing along its full length. His hands went to her buttocks where he fit his fingers around her, to lift and mold her slender, sweet body more fully against him. The pulsing crest of his passion crept closer as he parted her thighs, then with a slow thrust of his pelvis he entered her.

Jeanine's eyes widened as the momentary pain robbed her of her breath. But when the pain changed into something sweet, and his strokes reached more deeply inside her, she opened as a flower to him. Her hips responded in a rhythmic movement, so natural, it was not as though something new to her.

She clung and rocked with him, disbelieving this person she had become. A languorous ecstasy began to weave throughout her, first through her veins, and then her heart.

She sighed with pleasure as his mouth once again claimed her lips in a heated kiss. Her legs locked about his waist and drew him further into her. Having never felt anything as delicious as the feelings he was awakening inside her, she wanted to feel all of him. Her breasts ached against the hard press of his chest. But it was a wondrous sort of ache, one that she wished would never leave.

He withdrew his lips and nibbled on the tender lobes of her ear, his breath hot as he spoke against her cheek. "You are *neen-nee-dah-ee-een*," he whispered. "*Gee-zah-gi-ee-nah*? Lone Wolf will never love another. Only *geen*. Only you."

Jeanine did not know all that he had said to her, but the way in which he said it had been enough. And she had understood well enough when he had said that he would never love another. Oh, that he should, would break her heart! Jeanine could never love another. Never. And it no longer pained her to know that such a love existed between them. It was too sweet not to be right.

"Oh, how I love you, my handsome Chippewa Brave," she whispered against his cheek. "I wanted you, but I did not want to. Now I want you forever."

"It is the same with Lone Wolf," he said, raising up so that their eyes could meet and hold, both hazed over with wonder at this newly found love between them.

Ay-uh, he wanted to ask Jeanine to stay with him, to be his woman, and not as captive! Until now no woman had caused special feelings inside his heart. Thus far when with a woman, only the basic needs of the flesh had been fulfilled.

But now he had found this special woman to bring sunshine and laughter into his heart. But what about his wigwam? Could he want her to stay with him, forever? Did he still consider it a weakness to love a white woman?

But, no. He could now never believe that loving her was a weakness. Her love gave him *strength*. He now understood so much about his true father . . . why he had loved who he had loved . . . !

He ached to have Jeanine as his woman, as his *wife*. But he could not ask her this. Not yet. This was not the time. He had much to discover in his life that had nothing to do with her. He had *brothers* to learn about . . . *everything* about them. He had studied Strong Hawk from afar. He must now travel to Duluth, to study Silver Fox, his other brother.

He now understood about his one brother's choice of wives. Lone Wolf had tested Jeanine in many ways, even now the *ultimate* of tests. And now he knew . . . now he knew. . . .

He did want her to be his wife! But he did not want to think that she might be in his way. Yet, wasn't that the way it would be, should he ask her to marry him? Such a commitment would have to come later, even if she would agree to it!

Lone Wolf ceased his strokes for the moment, yet held

himself sensually within her. He did not plan to wait forever to teach her the full pleasures of their bodies. He looked down at her, with love.

"Is this why you held me captive, Lone Wolf?" Jeanine asked, fearing his answer. "You only wanted to seduce me? If so, why did you wait . . . so . . . long . . . ?"

"Now is not the time for questions or answers," Lone Wolf said thickly. "But Lone Wolf will tell you that, no, from the beginning, *none* of the seduction was planned. It is my heart that has guided *me* to wanting you in such a way. Only my heart, my beautiful white woman. Only . . . my . . . heart. . . ."

He crushed his lips hard against hers, twining his fingers through her hair as he lifted her head closer. His hips moved in rhythm with hers. It warmed his heart that she responded to every nuance of his lovemaking.

The fires within Jeanine were spreading into her limbs. And then her body exploded with spasms of desire, sweeping through her such pleasure she felt as though she might faint. She was aware of the shuddering of his body and heard his sensual groans against her parted lips, and knew that he had also reached that same pinnacle of pleasure as she, leaving them both breathless and clinging.

Lone Wolf moved gently from atop her and spread himself out on the grass beside her, breathing heavily. "It was good," he said huskily, seemingly in awe that this could be so. "Never before has it been as good."

Jeanine crept to her knees and knelt over him. She placed her cheek on his heaving chest, not ashamed for her nakedness nor for what she had just shared with him. She looked at the part of him which had just pleasured her, and even that did not send her senses reeling with guilt. Instead, she reached and gently touched him, circling her fingers, moving her hand slowly, causing Lone Wolf to emit a soft gasp of pleasure as he began to harden again against her fingers.

"I shall never forget this day," Jeanine murmured. "Never."

She turned her eyes to him. "Lone Wolf, I love you, so dearly love you," she added.

"Though I hold you captive?" he dared to ask.

"Had you not, I would have never been catapulted into the world of rapture as I have just been to, and returned from," she said softly. She removed her hand from his hardness and scooted to lay fully upon him, not denying his entrance again inside her. She inched her mouth to his and kissed him. Her lips trembled and her body arched as the pleasure again began to mount.

"Tonight we feast alone in my wigwam," Lone Wolf whispered as he drew his lips from hers. "Are you not hungry?"

"Yes," Jeanine sighed. "But I am hungry only for you."

Again they kissed, blending together as one soul, one body, one heartbeat. Jeanine could hardly bear the thought of ever leaving him. . . .

Twelve

Feeling almost shy for what she had just recently shared with Lone Wolf, Jeanine entered his dwelling alone while Lone Wolf went to check on his father. Evening was nigh; the fire was casting dancing shadows on the curved inside walls of the wigwam.

Suddenly in the shadows Jeanine caught sight of Pale Dove hovering close over something placed before her on the floor. Pale Dove's back was to Jeanine so she could not see what the tiny thing was so absorbed in.

The soles of the moccasins she wore were soft and quiet on the bulrush mats beneath her feet, as Jeanine crept across the wigwam and bent to look over Pale Dove's shoulder, then gasped. Pale Dove had gotten into Jeanine's satchel and had taken her journal. She had even removed the pencil and was scribbling all over the pages, softly giggling as she enjoyed this new type of plaything found in the white woman's belongings.

Pale Dove heard Jeanine gasp. She dropped the pencil

and turned around slowly, her shoulders hunched in shame. Guilt and fear were written on her face, showing that she knew she shouldn't have bothered Jeanine's journal and pencil.

Jeanine stepped around Pale Dove and picked up the journal, anxiously thumbing through its pages. Pencil scribblings were on the entries that she had made each day of her journey north. Her insides pained her at the discovery, yet if she looked closely enough she could still see what she had written beneath the terrible, childish markings.

Jeanine again looked down at Pale Dove. She had a strong urge to scold her, yet decided not to. The look etched across Pale Dove's face stopped her. She knew the child was not to blame for her innocent behavior. No doubt she had never even seen paper and pencil before. The opportunity at hand had been too great for her to ignore.

"Pale Dove, do you like my book and pencil?" Jeanine asked softly. She knelt down before Pale Dove. She turned to a clean page, closer to the back of the journal. "Would you like to write something else in my book? Perhaps I could help you write your name. Would you like that?"

Pale Dove breathed shallowly as she looked wide-eyed at Jeanine. She had expected the woman to be angry, for Pale Dove knew that she had done something wrong by the white woman's reaction when she had found the markings all over her book of leaves. Pale Dove hadn't ever seen such a large, nice book. Its leaves were smooth . . . were so white! It had thrilled her so to make markings in it.

And now the white woman was offering to teach Pale Dove how to write her name?

Lone Wolf had been smart to bring this white woman to the village of Chippewa. She was a smart white woman . . . she was a generous white woman! Pale Dove would have expected less. She would have expected the white woman to hate her because Pale Dove was a close friend to the man who had abducted her! But she was offering even more than friendship. This so warmed Pale Dove all over, a shiver of anticipation coursed through her blood and across her flesh!

Nodding her head eagerly, her long, greased pigtails bobbing up and down on her frail shoulders, Pale Dove smiled up at Jeanine. "*Ay-uh*," she said excitedly. "Teach Pale Dove. Please teach?"

Jeanine's heart held a strange ache within it. She saw the eagerness of the child to learn and recalled how most Indians were refused in the schools of the white man. Oh, the ignorance of man! Hopefully by writing her book and by lecturing, she could teach the world of the wrongs done to these beautiful people!

Settling down on the bulrush mats beside Pale Dove, Jeanine looked Indian, herself, if not for the creamy white of her skin. The fringed blouse and skirt, the colorful beads sewn onto them, made her *feel* Indian. Her insides thrilled with remembrances of what she had shared with her Indian in the wilds of the forest. Oh, to do so again made a sensual thrill embrace her, as does a cocoon encase the beginnings of a beautiful butterfly. She dared to think of what the night would bring. Another metamorphosis of herself . . . into becoming more and more woman in Lone Wolf's arms . . . ?

Her face flushed with her wanton thoughts, Jeanine smiled down awkwardly at Pale Dove as she placed the journal on her lap. "It should be easy to teach you how to write your name," she said softly. "Pick up the pencil, Pale Dove."

Her fingers trembling, Pale Dove picked up the pencil and held it out for Jeanine to take. But Jeanine shook her head.

"No. *You* hold the pencil," Jeanine softly urged, then wrapped her fingers around Pale Dove's hand, which held the pencil clumsily. "Now just hold onto the pencil thus and watch as you write the first letter of your name."

Slowly Jeanine guided Pale Dove into shaping the letter *P* on the page. She smiled to herself as Pale Dove quietly gasped when seeing the rewards of her efforts. "See? You did it," Jeanine encouraged, smiling down at Pale Dove as the young girl looked up into her eyes adoringly. "That is the first letter of your name. It is called a *P*. Can you say the letter, Pale Dove?"

Pale Dove formed the letter on the tip of her tongue, then laughed softly, eager to get on with her lesson. "I like this," she murmured. "White woman, is this what it is like to go to white man's school?"

"Partially," Jeanine said, embarrassed when again thinking about this child who seemed full of eagerness to learn, knowing that she would probably never get the opportunity.

Jeanine let her gaze move slowly over Pale Dove, reflecting on the child's frailness, the curve of her back, and recalling her limp when she walked. Even if Pale Dove did get the opportunity one day to enter a school for learning, children would torment her for the way she looked. It would not be easy to be both Indian and crippled.

Jeanine realized that Pale Dove still did not call her by name. She always called her white woman. "Give me the pencil for just a moment," she softly encouraged, smiling a quiet thank-you to Pale Dove when she did as asked.

Jeanine placed the pencil to the page and began slowly printing her name. "My name is Jeanine," she murmured. "I am showing you my name as it is written on the page. J-E-A-N-I-N-E. See how it is done, Pale Dove? Can you call me Jeanine, instead of white woman?"

Pale Dove blushed and nodded. "Pale Dove call you Jeanine," she said, then smiled warmly up at Jeanine as Jeanine again placed the pencil in her hand. "Me now write the rest of my name, Jeanine?"

"Yes. The rest of your name. . . ." Jeanine said, almost choking on the words. She was feeling drawn to this beautiful child as one is drawn to a sister. She guided Pale Dove's hand until her full name was in bold black letters beneath Pale Dove's feasting eyes.

"My name?" Pale Dove said, breathless, running her fingers over the written name on the page. "P-A-L-E D-O-V-E?"

Jeanine beamed. She was compelled to draw Pale Dove into her arms and did so. She hugged the tiny thing to her chest. "Yes. You wrote your name and it is beautiful," she sighed, then pulled away quickly from Pale Dove when a shadow fell over them both.

Jeanine looked up quickly, then smiled with relief when she discovered that it was Lone Wolf who was making the shadow.

Scurrying to her feet, she held the journal open for Lone Wolf to see and placed it beneath his wondering eyes. "Lone Wolf, see what Pale Dove has done," she said, excitement fueling her words. "She has written her name." She urged the journal even more closely to him. "See? Didn't she do it so beautifully?"

Pale Dove rose to her feet and began creeping toward the closed entrance flap. She saw a sudden anger in Lone Wolf's eyes and did not understand why, but she did not want to stay to find out. Limping, she turned and left the wigwam, yet a part of her heart stayed behind. She felt a strange sort of camaraderie with this white woman and knew that she would do anything for her. Anything . . .

Lone Wolf jerked the journal from Jeanine's hands. In one stroke he had the page removed that had Pale Dove's name written on it. He dropped the journal to the floor, then knelt down beside the fire and fed the page into its flames.

Jeanine sucked in her breath, aghast at what he was doing. "What do you . . . think . . . you are doing . . . ?" she said in a shocked whisper.

"You tease the child with such nonsense as this," Lone Wolf said, dropping the last of the burning page into the fire. "It is not good to tease my friend." He looked up at Jeanine, a coldness in his eyes. "Lone Wolf not let you tease her again!"

He picked up the journal and began tearing pages from it, burning them one at a time. Jeanine was so stunned by what he was doing, she stood by mutely, frozen in place, it seemed. But then her full senses and mobility returned to her, realizing that he was destroying her only means to recall moments of her journey north and her means to transcribe her interview with Judith McMahon, should she even ever have the opportunity to go to Chief Strong Hawk's village of Chippewa!

Scrambling to her knees beside Lone Wolf, Jeanine grabbed her journal away from him, fuming. "Stop that immediately!" she shouted. "You have no *right*!"

Lone Wolf grabbed it back away from her and placed the whole journal into the fire. "You forget whose dwelling you are in," he said flatly. "It is *you* who have no rights here, white woman."

Frustrated, Jeanine boldly reached into the fire and jerked her journal from the flames. She emitted a soft cry of pain when its heated binding scorched her fingertips. She dropped the journal to the floor and bent to blow on it, to blow out the remaining flames at its edges.

Then when the fire was out she rose to her full height and glared down at Lone Wolf. "You are despicable," she hissed, placing her hands on her hips. "First you take me captive, then you tell me you will release me soon, you make love to me, *tell* me you love me, then you again tell me I have no *rights*? Lone Wolf, I wish you would make up your mind. Which am I? Am I still a captive in every sense of the word? Does being your captive mean that I must even stifle thoughts that I've written on paper? And why don't you want me to teach Pale Dove such a simple thing as the skills to write her name? I was not teasing her. I was *teaching*. I love children. I spend a lot of my time lecturing to children."

Lone Wolf pushed himself up to tower over Jeanine. He wanted to remain angry with her for introducing Pale Dove to the outside world's intrigues, yet the storm in her eyes, the demand in her voice made him love her even more. She was an individual, not one whose mind could be shaped and molded. It would not be so bad for Pale Dove to *be* like Jeanine. But it was impossible. In every way, it was impossible. . . .

"Do you not know the harm in teaching her?" Lone Wolf said, angrily folding his arms across his chest. "She will hunger for more and more."

"And what is wrong with that?" Jeanine stormed, yet felt herself wavering beneath his steady gaze, a gaze which was always melting.

"She has no way to *learn*," Lone Wolf grumbled. "Do you think she would be welcome in your schools? Or do you see that she would be scorned?"

Jeanine was shaken by his answer, having thought along those same lines only moments ago. Now she understood why he had become angry, even defiant. She could see why he wouldn't want Pale Dove to desire learning, when she could never be given the chance to let her brain feed on these desires.

She glanced down at her scorched journal, then back up into Lone Wolf's commanding eyes. "You didn't have to burn my journal to make your point," she said softly. "All you would have had to do was *tell* me, Lone Wolf. I would have understood. I understand."

"Do you truly?" he grumbled, then turned his back to her as he left the wigwam.

Jeanine looked at the shimmering entrance flap, feeling the void once he left the wigwam. Her heart pounded. She wanted to reach out to him, tell him that she would be happy to teach Pale Dove. Yet to do so would mean that she would have to stay in Lone Wolf's village. She was not ready, yet, to make that sort of commitment to him *or* to Pale Dove! She had to test her feelings for Lone Wolf. Perhaps when away from him, in her own sort of world, she would find that it had just been the intrigue of him and who he was that had made her succumb to such sensual feelings for him . . . to share the ultimate in intimacy with him.

Hopefully he would let her leave soon. She must. For many reasons! She hadn't found the sort of answers she was seeking while in an Indian village. When she had left Duluth to learn the ways of Indians, never had she dreamed her research would uncover the only man who could ever speak with love to her heart.

Then it came to her that she still did not know why he had taken her captive. He had only told her that he had done so to observe her. But why? And he had not been given answers to why *she* had been traveling north.

They were both withholding secrets. They each seemed to have a purpose for the other, but neither speaking of it any longer, seemingly awaiting the right moment. Could it be they were seeking some of the same answers?

Shaking her head, confused, Jeanine settled down on the bulrush mats beside the fire and lifted the scorched journal back onto her lap. Slowly, she opened it and turned to the next blank page after her last entry. Picking up the pencil she began to write of her experiences while with Lone Wolf. She wrote of hating, then loving him. She wrote of her total confusion brought about by knowing him.

Then her eyes were drawn upward when he was again standing over her, watching her, holding a large tray of food.

"What do you write in the book now?" he asked, an edge of caution in his words.

Jeanine slowly closed the journal. She smiled mischievously up at him. "Oh, nothing . . ." she murmured. She eyed the tray of food as she placed the journal on the mats behind her, trying to remove the wonder from Lone Wolf's mind. If he knew that she was writing about him, surely he would be furious. He was a secret sort of man. He wouldn't want the world to know that he knew how to be gentle. In most eyes he would want to look the fierce warrior . . . that surely required of a brave who would one day be chief. . . .

"We eat," Lone Wolf said, yet he looked farther than her eyes, still not trusting the book she seemed to protect so fiercely. He still did not know why she had been writing that night by the campfire, when the heavens were dark. Would he ever? She had her secrets . . . he had his. . . .

"Yes, I am suddenly famished," Jeanine said, forcing a soft laugh when she saw his gaze still on the journal that was not hidden well enough behind her. "And it looks so good, Lone Wolf," she added, seeing an assortment of cooked meats, corn, and squash.

Lone Wolf eased down beside her. Together they enjoyed the evening meal, yet neither saying a word. There seemed to be an awkwardness now between them and Jeanine was beginning to become uneasy over this.

"Lone Wolf," she finally blurted. "Are you still upset with me for what I did with Pale Dove? You have been so quiet, since. I told you I understood why you were angry with me. Need I apologize?"

Lone Wolf glanced again at the journal, then looked deeply into Jeanine's eyes. "Lone Wolf take you back to your home tomorrow," he stated flatly, having learned enough of her for now, and fearing answers he had not yet been given. He had postponed learning of his other brother, Silver Fox, long enough. Waiting to again be with the woman he loved would be a true test of his willpower! If he returned her to her way of life, would *she* even want to be with him again, in any capacity? It would be a test for both of them, possibly a test sorely needed if their future were to be decided.

"You will release me of my captivity . . . so . . . soon . . . ?" Jeanine said shallowly, glad, yet unhappy.

"It is best," Lone Wolf said flatly. He scooted the platter of food aside and eased a piece of roasted venison from Jeanine's hand. "Earlier you said you were not hungry for food. You were hungry for something else."

Jeanine's insides rippled with a sudden desire, realizing exactly what he was referring to. "That is true," she murmured, understanding quite well that he was evading any more mention of her captivity or release. He had told her once. To him, once was always enough when he stated something.

"You were hungry for loving?" Lone Wolf said. He drew her to him and placed his hands beneath her hair, at the nape of her neck. He urged her lips close to his. "You are hungry now for Lone Wolf's lips?"

"I hunger *always* for Lone Wolf's lips," Jeanine whispered. She again did not recognize this new self who behaved so wantonly . . . so mindlessly, when placed under the spell of Lone Wolf's fathomless, dark eyes and his voice of pure magic.

Lone Wolf crushed his lips down upon hers, his tongue finding entrance inside her mouth. Her tongue responded and met his in an almost seductive dance against it. He lowered his hands to her waist and urged her to lay down on the bulrush mats where he spread himself atop her.

With a knee he parted her thighs and reached a hand up beneath her skirt and found the soft juncture of downy hair at the base of her abdomen. He began softly stroking her there, feeling her love mound swelling against his fingers. When she began to moan softly, he stopped and leaned away from her, his fingers now busy disrobing her.

"Tonight will remain uppermost in your thoughts when you are away from me," Lone Wolf said huskily. "You will hunger more and more to be with me. Then when we are together again, our union will be twofold in its passion."

Jeanine's breasts heaved with her erratic breathing as she watched Lone Wolf lower his loincloth, revealing to her his proud readiness for pleasure, beneath the fire's glow. Her heart thundered inside her as he wrapped his fingers about it and guided it downward, until she felt its hardness at the entrance of her womanhood.

Closing her eyes, she reveled in how he now filled her and was so skillfully moving himself in slow thrusts inside her, taunting her into mindlessness.

Then he again embraced her. It was an embrace so torrid she felt as though her body were being set afire. Her arms twined about his neck, she received his lips upon hers almost worshippingly. The blood spun wildly through her veins, dizzying her as his hands now molded her breasts, his thumbs circled her nipples, urging them into an even tighter peak against them.

And then he pulled gently away from her, but only far enough to have access to her eyes, his own darkening with the depths of his emotion. A soft smile touched his lips, one that Jeanine would never forget.

"Surely this is not real," she murmured. "This must be a fantasy . . . one that has lain dormant inside my brain since the day of my birth. This surely isn't real, Lone Wolf. Never had I dreamed that being with a man could be so . . . beautiful."

"This is real," he said thickly, teasing her face now with soft kisses. "You are real. Lone Wolf is real. My only regret is that the outside world is real and that Lone Wolf must deliver you back to that world. So much tells me to keep you captive, forever, white woman. So much . . ."

He again claimed Jeanine's lips with his, kissing her gently . . . kissing her endlessly. The kiss erased the word captive from her vocabulary and imbedded this need of him more deeply inside her consciousness. She could not even fathom how long she could live without being with him again . . . being kissed by him . . . being held in his arms. Even that she must, made a sick ache circle her heart. He had introduced her to a loving so intense, she could easily forsake all else but him. . . .

His hands began a sensual exploration of her body, as though he were readying himself for her absence in his life. It was as though he were memorizing her every curve . . . every dip . . . as his hands ran from her thighs to her hips, to her breasts, and then to the softness of her buttocks, lifting her even more closely into his continuing strokes.

His mouth slipped from her lips and fastened gently on a breast. His teeth nipped at the taut peak, his tongue swirled around it. Jeanine threw her head back in ecstasy; her breath was coming in short rasps.

And then his lips were at the gentle curve of her neck, and then at the hollow of her throat.

He twined his fingers through her lustrously long hair and directed her lips back to his. While he kissed her heatedly, their bodies met in a love-song as each reached that plateau of soaring, gratifying explosion of need . . . of rapturous, exchanged love.

Burying his face into her hair, his breath hot on Jeanine's cheek, Lone Wolf whispered of his undying love. Goosebumps rose on Jeanine's flesh; she was so caught up in feelings for him, realizing just how much he loved her. It still felt as if a fantasy, for surely in life, one did not find one to love so quickly . . . so fiercely. . . .

Lone Wolf turned on his side and molded Jeanine's back to his frontside, holding her like that until he fell into a restful sleep. But Jeanine was wide-eyed, too keyed up with emotion to drift off to sleep so easily.

She lay like that for an eternity, it seemed. And knowing that sleep was going to be elusive for some time this night, she focused her attention on her journal and an idea began to form. While Lone Wolf slept she could continue recording her adventure of this day . . . even include her deepest feelings for him in her writings. He would never know. He was . . . fast . . . asleep. . . .

Feeling how limp his arm and hand hung across her abdomen, Jeanine eased from beneath them. She slipped a blanket around her shoulders and went to where her journal lay on the other side of the fire. Her eyes searched and found her pencil. Eagerly, she sat down before the fire and began writing.

So caught up in what she was writing, Jeanine was not aware of eyes suddenly on her. She did not even hear Lone Wolf when he began stealthily crawling around the fire, toward her. It was only when he grabbed the journal away from her that she understood that she had been discovered.

"Again you write in your book by fire's light," he said, looking from her, to the journal. "Why is this, Jeanine? Why do you leave Lone Wolf's side to spend time with book? I have asked you before. Why did I find you in forest, alone? That is not the common practice of a white woman, is it?"

Jeanine didn't know what to say, yet she had expected

him to ask her all of these things again. But how could she tell him that she was on her way to another Indian village? He surely wouldn't understand any of her reasons for *anything*.

"No. It is not a common thing for a white woman to do," she uttered softly. "But I am not like most other women. I like to . . . to . . . *explore*."

"You write of exploring in your book?" Lone Wolf prodded.

"Well, something like that," Jeanine said awkwardly. "I couldn't sleep. I felt that it wouldn't matter if I wrote in my journal until I . . . I . . . got tired enough to sleep."

"And what were you writing about?" Lone Wolf grumbled.

Becoming irritated . . . annoyed, Jeanine folded her arms across her chest angrily. "I don't feel that I should be questioned so, Lone Wolf," she said heatedly. "And what I write about is not all that important."

She watched, mortified, as Lone Wolf placed the journal into the fire with its pages hanging out loosely for the flames to draw up into them, then held the journal in place and let it burn.

"If the book is not important, then you won't mind if I burn it," Lone Wolf said matter-of-factly. "It will not come between us again."

Jeanine scampered to her feet, ready for a fight. Twice he had attempted this! Well twice he would not get away with it. "No!" she screamed, grabbing for the journal. "You can't do that. It's mine. It has all of my entries of my travels in it. It is the beginning of the book I plan to write!"

A rush of cold spread throughout her, realizing she had mentioned her book. She hadn't intended to tell him that she was planning to write a book about Indians. She didn't believe any Indian would understand. Her only hopes were that she could eventually be able to find Judith McMahon and Judith would be the sort to understand the need for such a book and cooperate enough to tell her all that she needed to know.

But this was now and Lone Wolf was standing at his full height, towering over her, glowering. "Book? You are writing a book? What sort of book?" he demanded, while Jeanine watched the final remains of her journal go up in smoke. She felt suddenly detached from herself, sad for both herself and for Lone Wolf. It seemed that no matter how much they loved each other, there would always be misunderstandings to battle.

"It truly doesn't matter," she murmured, settling down beside the fire, staring blankly into it.

Lone Wolf eased down beside her on the bulrush mats. He drew his knees up before him and hugged them. "You do not tell me all truths about yourself," he said thickly, also staring into the fire. "It *is* best that you leave my village tomorrow. When the sun colors the sky in the morning we shall be already far away from this dwelling in which we have found both peace and warring between us. It is best. *Ay-uh, it is best. . . .*"

Jeanine gave him a quick, sudden glance, oh, so missing him already. . . .

Thirteen

Sweet ferns, trailing arbutus and wintergreen covered the natural openings in the great pine forest Jeanine was traveling through alongside Lone Wolf. The aroma was a mixture of pine and honeysuckle, tantalizingly rich, as though a rare perfume had been sprayed into the air. It felt good to be on her horse, Daisy. It was as though her life had been handed back to her, yet in a sense it hadn't. Lone Wolf was now a part of her and she would soon be saying good-bye to him.

Jeanine was torn with feelings. Still not knowing the true reason Lone Wolf had abducted her, she could not help but feel used. He *had* used her. He had not given her any valid reason for having made love with her except to say that is had been his heart that had guided him.

But Jeanine could not let herself believe that. It was as though he had tested these moments with her while in her arms, comparing her with all of his other lovers.

And hadn't he tested her in so many other ways? Why?

Would she ever know? Soon she wouldn't even have the chance to ask him again. When he rode away from her, back north, it might even be the last time she would see him. . . .

"Why, Lone Wolf?" she suddenly blurted, wheeling her horse around, placing it directly in the path of his stallion. "You must tell me why you abducted me, Lone Wolf, or I shall never have a full night of peaceful sleep again for wondering about it. You told me that you wished to observe me. *Why*?"

Lone Wolf's eyebrows arched with surprise at Jeanine's sudden decision to question him again. His fingers tightened involuntarily on the reins and his horse jerked sideways, then came to a shuddering halt. Since they had left his village it had been a journey of strained silence. After burning her journal, she had seemed drained of all energies *and* questions. It seemed to Lone Wolf that even her spirit . . . her determination . . . had joined and followed the smoke from her burning book, on up through the smokehole of his dwelling.

Then he pondered her question. It would be so easy to tell her about his discovery of his brothers and his need to know all about them. He had the need to confide in her . . . tell her of the battle raging inside him over his decision to challenge Strong Hawk or *not*. He knew that it would be a noble cause to unite the two tribes of Chippewa! But how should it be done? Should Strong Hawk die so that Lone Wolf could do this uniting? Or should blood brothers share in this cause?

But Lone Wolf did not feel free to divulge such torments to *anyone*. And especially to Jeanine. Had not she been writing entries about her journey in her journal? Had not she mentioned writing a book? She had not said what sort of book . . . or what it would be about.

He could not chance telling her anything about his secret findings, fearing that she might somehow choose to write even about this in her planned book. Though he had burned all her entries up to this point, he knew that she would surely have all that she had written stored in her memory storage house inside her brain and would still use it to her advantage, later.

"Lone Wolf cannot say," he stated flatly. He nudged his horse and stubbornly edged it around Jeanine's mare. He then rode away from her, his chin held high, leading his horse into a slow, easy canter.

Frustrated, Jeanine stared openly at Lone Wolf for a few moments, then clucked to her mare and sent it bounding into a gallop after him. Her hair was flying, the tailend of her travel skirt was slipping up, exposing her boots and the calves of her legs. She had left the Indian attire behind, hoping that by doing so she could also leave all remembrances of Lone Wolf and those sensual moments with him in the past, as though they had never existed.

She was glad that even he had chosen a different sort of attire for traveling this day. Only his handsome face was exposed to the naked eye. Instead of the usual loincloth Jeanine had become so accustomed to, he wore fringed leggings and shirt. With him at least dressed more decently, she could keep a level head.

Before, seeing his muscled shoulders and legs and the outline of his manhood pressing against the flimsy loincloth always disturbed her to the point of wanting him. she wanted him now as much. But with his physical attributes hidden beneath a layer of clothes it was easier to put a halt to such feelings when not reminded of just how virile he was.

Again alongside Lone Wolf, Jeanine glared over at him. "I'll never know, will I?" she half shouted. "You take me captive and I will never even know *why*. And that you released me so soon and so easily? Lone Wolf, you so confuse me!"

"No more than you confuse me," Lone Wolf said, frowning over at her, yet seeing so much about her that would forever speak to his heart of loving and wanting her. She was a haunting image of perfect features, with her raven-black hair swirling around her shoulders, and the ripe curve of her breasts so obvious to the keen penetration of his eye, as they strained against the cotton of her blouse.

As the breeze blew softly down the front of the half-buttoned blouse, slightly filling it out away from her body with its air, Lone Wolf's loins ached when he saw the pink of a breast. He was recalling how sweetly her breast had tasted and how soft it had been against the tips of his fingers.

Yet he was having to forfeit her to those other drives troubling his insides. And even she was driven with needs of her own which did not include him. As he had been rebellious in not answering her questions, so had she been, in not answering *his* questions about *her*.

"What do you mean by that?" Jeanine asked hotly, smoothing a lock of hair back from her brow as the breeze continued to whip it around like rivulets of grass blowing wildly on the windblown stretches of the prairie.

"You have never fully explained why you were in the forest alone," Lone Wolf grumbled. "Thus far your answers have not been logical ones. You keep your secrets from Lone Wolf. Lone Wolf keeps secrets from *you*."

Jeanine's eyes widened. "Are you saying that if I tell you why I was traveling alone, you would tell me, in turn, why you abducted me?" she asked cautiously.

Lone Wolf's spine stiffened, feeling as though one being led into a trap. "You wish that I . . . ?"

Lone Wolf's words were cut short when several riders were made out in the distance where the tall pines trailed off into a vast meadow of sunflowers. Instinct drew Lone Wolf's hand to the gunsling at the side of his stallion. He withdrew the rifle in one swift movement and held it snugly onto his lap as he gave Jeanine a troubled glance. He then again looked straight ahead, squinting against the brilliant rays of the sun.

His insides did a strange rolling when he recognized that his brother, Chief Strong Hawk, was one of the lead riders, with several of his Braves following dutifully along behind him.

And then Lone Wolf's eyes drifted to the men flanking Strong Hawk's sides. Two white men were riding as though they belonged with his brother, yet this did not come as a surprise to Lone Wolf. If his brother's wife was white, so must his brother's friends be white! Could this brother, Strong Hawk, even one day join his other brother, Silver Fox, and live his entire life *as* white?

Ah, it would be so easy for Lone Wolf to become the chief over both bands of Chippewa! This brother who mingled too easily with the white man did not deserve to be a Chippewa chief!

Jeanine followed Lone Wolf's studious gaze and gasped when she saw the approaching men. She then just as quickly paled when, after she had studied the men, she had discovered that one was her uncle and one was Cameron Tyner! And they were traveling with Indians . . . ?

"Lord, it can't be. . . ." she said, placing a hand to her throat, feeling the pulsebeat growing stronger there. "Uncle . . . Fred . . ."

Her uncle hated Indians. She could never believe he would ride with them, for any reason. And it was obvious that he and Cameron were not being held captive. They were riding alongside the Indian, as though mutual acquaintances . . . even friends . . . ? "Uncle Fred . . ."

Lone Wolf had caught Jeanine's surprised look and had heard the wonder in her tone of voice. "You speak a name," he grumbled, drawing his stallion closer to Jeanine. "You know these white men who ride with my . . ."

He caught himself. He had almost said the word "brother," which would identify Strong Hawk more to Jeanine than Lone Wolf intended. His thoughts were on brothers so much, even his words were filled with brothers!

"You were saying?" Jeanine said, tilting her head, looking more directly into Lone Wolf's eyes. She was seeing something strange about him . . . a cautionary air she had never seen before. And the approaching horsemen were the cause.

"Do you know the white men who ride alongside Chief

Strong Hawk?'' Lone Wolf said, drawing his eyes away from her full attention. She seemed to be learning the skills of looking into his soul. That was surely because they had a bond forming between them . . . a bond that could either grow stronger, or break apart, as though nonexistent.

For now, Lone Wolf could not even begin to know how it was to be for them. They were far apart in so many ways. Only their love for one another was the same. Such a love could never be duplicated. It was theirs to keep, either separate, to savor only in memories, or together, to blend as one in marriage. Only time would tell how it was truly to be. . . .

Jeanine's head turned with jerks back in the direction of her uncle and his party of Indians. Her gaze settled on the lead Indian. Strong Hawk! Lone Wolf had said this was Strong Hawk . . . Judith McMahon's Strong Hawk!

Now she understood. Her uncle had gone to Chief Strong Hawk's village, searching for her. Strong Hawk must have offered his assistance in continuing the search and had searched for her beyond his village after reassuring her uncle that she had not been in his. And her uncle had agreed. *She* had caused Sheriff Fred Hunter to forget his dislike of Indians for a while at least. He had thought the Indians would possibly be the only means by which to seek her out in the wilds of the forest so far from his more familiar stamping grounds of Duluth!

A slow smile lifted her lips, feeling gratitude toward her uncle for loving her so much, and a warmth for Strong Hawk for showing her uncle that Indians were as civil, sometimes even more human, than the white man! Perhaps, now, she could even eventually interview Strong Hawk personally. It seemed that her uncle had done her two favors in one. By making Strong Hawk's acquaintance in this way, he had opened the road to conversation between his niece and this great chief of the St. Croix Band of the Chippewa! Her travel north had been fruitful in many ways.

Lone Wolf grabbed Jeanine's reins from her hands, startling her into looking over at him quickly. "You know the white man?" he growled. "You mentioned a name. Who is this with Chief Strong Hawk? Is it someone to be trusted?"

Jeanine glanced down at her reins curled around the fingers of Lone Wolf's right hand, mingled with his own, and then at his right hand grasping strongly onto the butt of his rifle. Then she gave him a soft look. When their wondering eyes met, her heart melted into his, understanding his hesitance to trust. She reached and touched his hand.

"You do not need the rifle," she reassured, smiling. "I know the white men with Chief Strong Hawk. One is my uncle. The other is his deputy."

A cornered look surfaced on Lone Wolf's face. He raised the rifle and secured it firmly beneath the elbow of his right arm. "Deputy?" he said shallowly. "I had forgotten. You said your uncle was a sheriff. If he is sheriff . . ."

"Do not fret so," Jeanine said, smoothing a hand over his proud, sculpted cheek. "My uncle will never know how it was that I came to be with you. Do you think that I could tell him that you took me captive? Lone Wolf, we have our differences between us, but none is severe enough for me to want to see you *hang*."

The roar of hoofbeats drew closer. Jeanine turned her head just as Fred began shouting her name. She gave Lone Wolf a lingering look, relaying a silent message of love to him that she did not wish to speak aloud. She then thrust the heels of her boots into the flanks of her horse and rode on away from him, meeting Fred halfway between the larger group of Indians, and the one, lone Indian, cautiously watching from afar.

"Damn it, Jeanine," Fred said, drawing his horse to a halt beside her mare. "Where in the hell have you been? What're you doin' with that damn Injun? In my mind I had you mauled by a bear and left for wolves to feast on."

Jeanine looked almost shyly over at her uncle, in her

mind's eye recalling moments which could never be spoken about to him. And it seemed that being with one generous Indian did not change her uncle's mood about any others. He had used Chief Strong Hawk's generosity to his own benefit, and now was ready to cast aside any sort of respect for him and those whose skins were of the same color.

"As you see I am just fine," Jeanine said haughtily. "I told you that I could take care of myself."

Cameron Tyner rode up to Fred with Chief Strong Hawk by his side. Jeanine felt a coldness touching her all over when Cameron gave her a knowing stare, his lips lifting into a smug smile. She knew that he was going over his threat to her in his mind. She was thankful that Fred hadn't sent Cameron alone to find her!

Then her gaze moved slowly to Chief Strong Hawk. A sudden liking washed through her for this handsome chief. There was such a friendship reflected in his eyes, she didn't see how her uncle could ever again say a dark word against him. And when he smiled at her . . . it was as though the whole world had smiled. And in his handsomeness she saw so much that reminded her of Lone Wolf. Their eyes . . . their noses . . . their sculpted facial features . . .

She reached a hand of friendship out toward him. "My uncle isn't good at thank-you's," she said softly. "But please let me say thank you for him."

Chief Strong Hawk's eyes found pleasure in her loveliness, but he did not find the same sort of beauty that he had found in his wife, Judith. *His* woman was unique, as surely this woman with the name of Jeanine would be as unique in the eyes of the man who would eventually love her.

"*Nee-may-nan-dum-wah-bum-eh-nawn,*" he said, clasping his fingers about her hand, shaking it.

Jeanine's eyes widened; she forked an eyebrow. "Pardon . . . ?" she murmured, easing her hand away from his when Lone Wolf was suddenly there, edging his way in between Jeanine's uncle's horse, and Jeanine's.

"He says in Chippewa that he is glad to see you," Lone Wolf said thickly, now truly puzzled over Jeanine and Strong Hawk's relationship. They did not appear to be old friends. They were being too stiffly cordial as though meeting for the first time. Had Lone Wolf been wrong? Did his woman not know Strong Hawk or his wife at all? Why then *had* she been traveling so close to Strong Hawk's village? Would he ever . . . ever . . . know . . . ?

He looked over at Strong Hawk intensely. His insides quivered when up so close he saw so much of himself in his brother's features. A part of him, the brother in him, wanted to clasp his brother into his arms and hug him fondly. Yet another part of him wanted to hate him, for a part of Strong Hawk was of a white *gee-mah-mah*, mother. And he was bearing the title which, in truth, was Lone Wolf's. The firstborn son of Gray Wolf should now be chief! Not Strong Hawk!

A bitterness gnawed at his insides for so many reasons, but he did not want this to show on his face, for the world to see. Instead he smiled at Chief Strong Hawk and placed a fist to his heart. "I am Lone Wolf of the Cedar Falls Band of Chippewa," he said proudly. "You are Chief Strong Hawk. Lone Wolf has heard much about you."

Chief Strong Hawk nodded, his eyes warm with friendship. "*Ay-uh*, I know of your village . . . of your father, the great Chief White Cloud," he said. "It is good to meet you, Lone Wolf." He glanced over at Jeanine, then back to Lone Wolf. "How is it that you know the white woman?"

Fred edged his horse closer to Lone Wolf's. "Yeah, why *was* she traveling with you?" he said, a daring tone to his voice.

Jeanine squared her shoulders. She knew that she must speak up now or things could get quickly out of hand. "I was lost," she said dryly. "Lone Wolf found me. He was escorting me back to Duluth." She looked over at Lone Wolf, half smiling. "I owe him my life," she said in a white lie. "I again thank him."

"I damn well hope gettin' lost teaches you a lesson or

two,'' Fred snapped. ''I hope you damn well forget wantin' to go to the Injun village to get information from Judith McMahon for the Injun book you plan to write. I'd damn well think you'd have had enough of Injuns to last you a lifetime.'' He nodded toward Lone Wolf. ''You've surely been with him long enough to know what to write about him and his kind.''

Jeanine blanched. She sucked in her breath as Lone Wolf's eyes lit up with fire. She watched, horrified, as he wheeled his horse around and thundered away from her.

And then her gaze moved to Strong Hawk. He was glaring from her to her uncle, and then, too, galloped away from them, leaving them alone, except for the sneering Cameron Tyner, who was half laughing beneath his breath over what had just transpired.

''No . . .'' Jeanine softly cried. ''Oh, Uncle Fred, look what you've done. You've . . . spoiled . . . *everything*. . . .''

''I ain't spoiled nothin' that didn't deserve spoilin',''he said, yanking a half-smoked cigar from his shirt pocket. He lit it and flipped the match into the air. ''Now, young lady. It's time we head for home. I know *I've* had enough of Injuns and this desolate land to last *me* a lifetime.''

Jeanine looked over her shoulder, scanning the horizon for any signs of Lone Wolf. But there were none. It was as though he had disappeared from the face of the earth. Her heart cried out to him. Surely he hated her now. And would she ever get the chance to truly know . . . ? She doubted if he would ever even give her the chance to explain, should she even see him again. . . .

Her shoulders drooping, her face sullen, she nudged her horse with her knees and followed alongside her uncle, wishing he would learn to think before he spoke.

Fourteen

Though she had been art curator for two years now, it seemed strange for Jeanine to be working in that capacity this day. It was as though she were in a world separate from herself—her thoughts elsewhere since having returned the day prior from her time in the forest with Lone Wolf.

The sun dimming through the window as the afternoon waned, Jeanine finally got the energy needed to sit down at her desk, and began thumbing through mail that had accumulated while she had been gone. Only halfheartedly she glanced at the return addresses, trying to decide which was important and which could wait another day for her to read.

After tossing a couple aside she stopped and sighed, still too restless to sit for long. Combing her fingers through her hair, she rose from behind the desk and began to walk away, but a glance back down at the letters caused her to stop in mid-step when she saw a return address on an envelope that caused her blood to pump wildly through her veins. She read the name again.

"Giles Thomas . . ." she whispered. "Danette Thomas's other son. Surely he hasn't changed . . . his . . . mind. . . ."

Grabbing the letter up, her fingers trembled as she tore open the envelope and jerked the letter from inside it and unfolded it. Her face broke into a sudden smile when she read the invitation to come to the Thomas Mansion, to view Danette Thomas's paintings. Giles Thomas had decided to sell most of them to the art museum if the art museum was interested.

"Well I'll be damned," Jeanine said, her eyes shining. "He's not asking me there for the reason I had requested, but it's just as *good*."

Jeanine's mind recaptured the stormy letters she had received back from Giles Thomas the two times Jeanine had written to him to request that she meet with him and his mother, Danette, to interview them for her planned lectures and book on Indians. He had been adamantly against Jeanine going to the Thomas Mansion for such an interview. He had even threatened her, telling her that if she showed up at the mansion after he had told her not to, he would call the sheriff and have her arrested, surely not realizing that Jeanine's uncle *was* the sheriff. The different last names tended to confuse most about this uncle and niece being related.

Jeanine had honored such a strong "request" and hadn't bothered Giles again . . . had even given up on interviewing Danette. She had hoped that Judith McMahon could have given her all the information about Danette and her late husband, Chief Gray Wolf. And hopefully, one day *still* Jeanine could speak with Judith.

"If only Uncle Fred hadn't spoken so openly against Indians in Chief Strong Hawk's presence," she mulled to herself. There had even been a chance for her to speak with *him* if her uncle hadn't spoken so out of turn. He had even caused Lone Wolf to ride away in anger.

But Jeanine knew that it was more than what her uncle had said against the Indians. It had also been what he had said about her writing a book *about* the Indians. That surely had not sat well with either Indian—Strong Hawk *or* Lone Wolf.

Wanting to not get caught up in worries of Lone Wolf and possibly never seeing him again, Jeanine flung the letter down on the desk and grabbed a shawl and slipped it around her shoulders. In her full-skirted paisley-designed dress with its myriad colors of blues, greens, and purples, its neck high, its sleeves long, Jeanine hurried from the museum into the bustling streets of Duluth. She wouldn't give Giles Thomas the chance to change his mind. She would go there, now, yet it seemed unlike the Thomas family to want to sell Danette Thomas's paintings. The paintings had been a part of the family for so long. Jeanine could even remember hearing that they had been on display at the Duluth National Bank a few years back.

Even now, before Jeanine had ever seen the paintings, she had guessed their unique quality. She had been told that many had been of Indian scenes. Jeanine had been told that these must have been painted by Danette while she had been in the Indian village, living with her husband, Chief Gray Wolf; that nothing could have looked so real unless having been painted while there, seeing it, first-hand. . . .

Yet inside Jeanine's mind she was remembering so much about Lone Wolf's village, as though painted onto her memory, forever. There was something surrealistic about the Indian village and the people residing therein. When she began writing about it, it would surely be as real as Danette's paintings. . . .

Going to her waiting horse and buggy, Jeanine was soon among those traveling the streets of Duluth. She edged her horse and buggy around other horses, then heard Daisy's familiar, soft whinny when being introduced now and then to the noise of an automobile making its way along the street.

Jeanine was in awe of these fascinating machines, yet had no desire to own one herself. She had enough trouble maneuvering her horse and buggy up the steep streets of Duluth, much less having to worry about an automobile whose motor might quit at any moment and make a backward plunge down the street, possibly ending up in the waters of Lake Superior.

At least Daisy's footing was sure enough to take Jeanine to any destination she preferred—even now, while traveling up the straight stretch of street which eventually turned off onto a flatter plane which then would lead to Giles Thomas's fancy mansion. Jeanine wasn't sure if Danette resided with Giles at the mansion now, or still lived with the Indians, since her husband, Gray Wolf's, death.

If Jeanine were lucky, Danette would be in Duluth. Perhaps . . . just perhaps, Jeanine might get the opportunity to sit down and talk with her about that which had nothing to do with paintings. For the moment, Jeanine's book and her desire to secure interesting material for her lectures were more important to her than her art curator position. If a book was to be written . . . if lectures of Indians were to be made, she must let her research overtake her every thought . . . her every whim. . . .

The sun was now only spreading its orange splash in the sky along the horizon as it was sinking in the west. Jeanine shuddered when a damp chill touched her face. She drew the shawl more closely about her shoulders, glad to have finally reached the street that would take her to her destination.

As she made her way along this street, she looked from side to side, seeing the houses that made up this most affluent section of Duluth. She looked past green, flat lawns, onto two- and three-story imposing residences that were classified as mansions by the Sunday travelers who came to gawk after their mornings at church . . . the habit of the poor, wanting to get a glimpse of the rich.

And then, immediately impressed, Jeanine saw the Thomas Mansion. She urged Daisy to turn into a long, narrow drive that led up to the house. Her gaze moved, capturing it in its greatness. Its granite steps led to the front door of the austere and beautiful Victorian house. The granite sills of the windows were a soft, pale gray against the warm brick facade. It *was* one of the finest houses in Duluth, two-storied and rectangular, with a wide porch and stained glass windows.

Jeanine felt her first twinge of uneasiness when she saw someone at an upstairs window drawing a drape partially aside, to look down upon this unannounced caller. Giles hadn't said when to come and call . . . had only offered her an invitation to make arrangements.

Jeanine felt that perhaps she should have sent back a proper sort of reply to Giles, yet in her mind, time was of the essence. Her excitement to find answers for her book and lectures prompted her to move less carefully than usual. Hopefully this person watching from an upstairs window welcomed a caller. What would Giles say when she began asking questions about his relationship with the Chippewa Indians instead of the price of Danette Thomas's artwork? Did Jeanine truly even *dare* . . . ?

"I only wish I'd had had the opportunity to meet him before this meeting," she whispered to herself.

All she knew was that Giles was Danette's son, and Jeanine had only met her one other son, and he was *Indian*. When Jeanine had questioned her uncle about Giles—what sort of person *he* was—her uncle had refused to talk about him, saying that Giles Thomas was a helluva person to deal with. He had a hot temperament, one not to tamper with.

Her uncle had also told Jeanine that Giles Thomas spent most of his time inside his office or at home. He had become some sort of recluse. And her uncle would not explain *why*. . . .

The fact that darkness was closing in on Jeanine, making her now only a vague outline for anyone to see from the house, made Jeanine even more uncomfortable. She slapped her horse's reins and was glad to finally be at the house where, within moments, she would hopefully be invited in, where there was light and warmth from a fire.

Securing her reins around a hitching rail, Jeanine quietly climbed the marble steps and took a deep breath before raising the knocker which hung on the heavy, oak door.

Lone Wolf left his stallion hidden within some deep brush behind the stable that sat back behind the Thomas Mansion, on the far side of the property. He had only had to question one man on the streets of Duluth to find out where he could find Giles Thomas's dwelling. Lone Wolf had followed the directions well and had welcomed the cloak of night, for it had given him the best cover for which to enter his brother's property undetected.

Having heard a horse and buggy arriving ahead of him, Lone Wolf had slipped behind bushes close beside the porch of the house and had waited until this caller had secured her buggy and was now on the porch, waiting to be invited inside. Through the darkness Lone Wolf had not been able to make out the driver of the buggy. But the horse had been easy enough to identify! Even now he was looking at Daisy, wondering why Jeanine was at the Thomas dwelling. Did she know Giles Thomas? If so, in what capacity?

He was recalling when Jeanine and Strong Hawk had met, when Strong Hawk had directed Jeanine's uncle through the forest, in search of her. She hadn't acted as though she had known him at that time. Perhaps she didn't even know Giles all that well and was now seeking him out, to find more answers for this book of Indians her uncle had spoken about.

Lone Wolf's lips set into a straight line of anger when he thought of how she had used him. All the time they had been making love she was surely thinking of ways to write these feelings into a book! He was Indian. Perhaps that was *all* he was to her! An Indian from whom she could gather information for a book!

Then he let himself remember just why he had captured *her*. At first it was to only learn of her . . . of her *ways*. . . .

He had meant to use her. Only use her. But his feelings had run deeper. He now loved her . . . would always love her. And to believe that she was so close *now*, that he could only speak her name for her to know that he was there? It was his self-restraint taught to him as a child that kept him silent.

Stealthily, he crept to a window and peered through the sheer curtains, breathless as he waited for Jeanine to be invited into the house, for him to totally see her again. And to see his brother Giles at the same moment! He had never planned that his journey to Duluth would be so fruitful!

The front door finally opened. Jeanine was met by a stiff-collared butler. She quickly explained that she was there to meet with Giles Thomas . . . at Giles Thomas's request. She was then ushered into a wide entrance hall that opened into three spacious parlors and a dining room.

The portraits of the Thomas family stared back at Jeanine from where they hung at the staircase, and then she looked further, against a far wall which lined the one side of the hallway, seeing many magnificent paintings. Their grandness sent a shimmer of anticipation through Jeanine, almost forgetting her *true* purpose for being here, for her own personal, selfish reasons. It would be easy to get lost in the talk of these beautiful paintings. But she could not chance losing this opportunity to speak with Giles Thomas about his relationship with the St. Croix Band of the Chippewa.

Jeanine was led on into a parlor. When the butler left her alone, she went and stood close to the warmth of the fire on the hearth. Letting her shawl drape loosely about her arms, she began looking slowly about her, marveling at the wealth of the Thomas family.

In this parlor, dramatic, red-glazed walls set off a massive mahogany Chippendale mantel and overmantel, refinished in antique Chinese red and carved with pagodas and figures of Chinese men.

A bronze French Dore crystal chandelier sent a warm glow from its gaslights, settling on elegant wall and ceiling frescoes, quartersawn oak woodwork and European carpeting. The Chippendale chairs and sofas were covered in the finest imported silk. Dropleaf and lamp tables were arranged generously around the room.

Upon closer observation, Jeanine could see that someone in the Thomas family had purchased rare items abroad, and from leading American dealers. There was the English Regency oak center table richly carved with animal, floral, and military motifs; a Chinese porcelain punch bowl with its original stand; and two magnificent twelve-foot by ten-foot Flemish tapestries, dated 1661. . . .

Footsteps drawing close drew Jeanine around. When she saw an Indian stepping into full view, yet one dressed in an expensive suit and with his hair cut to lay just above his shirt collar, she was stunned into speechlessness. Now she understood why her uncle had refused to talk to her much about Giles Thomas. Now she even understood why Giles Thomas just might choose not to mingle among the white community. Though he was a rich Duluth businessman, he was also Indian. And he was not only Indian, he was the exact replica of Chief Strong Hawk. He must be Strong Hawk's twin. It had been a secret closely guarded. . . .

''Do you always arrive unannounced when you decide to go calling?'' Giles grumbled, his dark eyes fierce as he gave Jeanine an angry stare.

Jeanine recoiled somewhat, now fully realizing what she was up against. It was certain he was not going to be a pushover. If she was able to get him to open up to her, to talk about the Chippewa Indians, *she* would be surprised. He was Indian *himself*. . . .

Jeanine firmed her shoulders and let her shawl flutter away from her, into a chair. She would meet him dead on. She would show him that she was not one to be frightened away by a few harsh words.

Fifteen

Lone Wolf crept from window to window, then stopped when he found the room in which Jeanine and Silver Fox stood. Rage and wonder fused inside him when he saw Silver Fox, his brother, for the first time. Though Lone Wolf had expected it, he was finding it hard to cope with this Chippewa brother who was dressed fully in white man's clothes. Lone Wolf had never seen a Chippewa who was ashamed of *being* Chippewa. Well, it seemed that his brother was an exception.

Then his gaze moved to Jeanine. He wanted to so desperately know how she and Silver Fox knew one another.

But then a slow smile lifted his lips. He could tell by closely observing their attitudes toward one another that they were meeting for the first time, and that neither was comfortable with the other.

At least Lone Wolf knew that this meeting wasn't between two lovers. . . .

* * *

"You are Giles Thomas?" Jeanine asked guardedly, not wanting to show her complete surprise at discovering that he was Indian. To him, the fact that she had not known this would probably be described as "ignorance." He did seem the sort to label women in such a way. His demeanor was that of cool arrogance, as though he never allowed anyone beyond that barrier he seemed to have placed around himself.

"And the butler tells me that you are Jeanine Thaxton," Giles said coolly, walking farther into the room.

"You have come to check out my mother's paintings?" he then said with an air of caution, suspecting her true selfish reason for being there. He was just now placing the name. This was the same lady who had asked earlier to meet with him and his mother, to discuss their relationships with the Chippewa Indians. She was not only an author, but also the Duluth Art Museum curator. His spine stiffened, wishing that he had recognized the name earlier.

"That is why you summoned me here, is it not?" Jeanine said almost as coolly, not able to relax in his presence. He did not radiate Lone Wolf and Strong Hawk's same sort of friendliness. There seemed to be some sort of pain in the depths of his eyes, as though he were tormented for some reason or other. It took away from his handsomeness . . . defined as such since he was the exact replica of Chief Strong Hawk. He even closely resembled Lone Wolf!

Jeanine studied him more closely, trying to understand the man, this Indian. Perhaps his torment was because of how he had chosen to live his life. He had left the Indian way of life and was living as a white man, dressed in white man's clothes, and living in a luxurious mansion. He even spoke in succinct English.

Perhaps now, for some reason, he was regretting having selected this sort of life over that which his brother had chosen.

Then Jeanine's blood turned cold. If this was Chief Strong Hawk's twin, how had a choice been made between brothers for the title of Chief . . . ?

"I would have rather made a choice as to *when* you were to arrive," Giles said, then gestured with a hand toward Jeanine. "But since you *are* here, let us go to my study and discuss the arrangements for the sale of my mother's paintings."

Jeanine's eyes widened, struck dumb by his abruptness. She hadn't even had a chance to view the paintings fully, and he was ready to discuss selling them. He seemed much too eager. Jeanine had to wonder why.

"But, Sir, I have yet to view them. . . ." she said in a soft, almost whisper, yet began walking behind him when he turned and headed briskly toward the door that led out into the spacious hallway.

Giles turned on his heel and glowered toward Jeanine. "We will first discuss what it is that I wish to do with the paintings and *then* you shall be allowed to fully view them."

Giles did not wish to waste his time if Jeanine Thaxton was meeting with him for reasons other than those she represented for the art museum. She did seem too anxious to be interested only in the sale of the paintings.

But he hoped that it was his suspicious nature that was urging him to be cautious. He sorely hoped to get this all over with once and for all. The fact that he had even put himself in the position of selling his mother's precious paintings cut away at his insides, paining him more than he would ever admit to.

He ignored Jeanine's puzzled look and turned and walked on away from her, again lost deep in thought. Perhaps it would be simpler and less humiliating for him, even easier, to go ahead and do as he had silently planned.

But placing the revolver to his temple those many other times had proven to him that he was not only a failure in business and life, but also . . . a coward. He now wished that he had not urged his partner, Judith's brother Rory McMahon, to sell out to him. Rory had had a good head for business. Perhaps he could have saved the Thomas Lumber Company.

But no one, not even Rory, could second-guess the fear of locusts that most said would arrive with a vengeance this year. The newest sprouts of trees that could guarantee some sort of future, should they be given the chance to reach full maturity, would be destroyed by the damnable pests. The tender sprouts of trees would not stand up against the devouring scourge of locusts. The fear of this happening was just one too many burdens to worry about on his already overtaxed mind!

Jeanine grabbed her shawl from the chair and hurried along behind Giles, trying to understand his attitude. She was beginning to doubt her sanity for even having come for *any* reason. If she got any answers out of him for *anything* she would be surprised. He was not approaching this sale in any normal way. How could she talk seriously about it if she hadn't first viewed the paintings objectively?

But then again . . . hadn't she come with hopes of speaking more of her planned book and lectures, than of the paintings? She *had* to give it one more try. So far, all other means by which to get research material about the Chippewa had failed.

Draping her shawl across an arm, Jeanine followed Giles into a paneled room where a fire burned bright on the hearth on the outside wall. Bound books lined the opposite wall, and a spacious oak desk sat in the center of the room, a kerosene lamp aglow on one corner of the desk, its flames drawing shadowy designs on a clutter of papers and opened, yellowed ledgers.

Lone Wolf strained his neck, watching Jeanine and Silver Fox leave the room. Then he again crept stealthily from window to window until he found them once more. Hiding behind forsythia bushes richly heavy with blossoms, he again watched the activity inside the house between the woman he loved and this brother who did not seem appropriately fitting to be called brother.

Lone Wolf forced himself to envision Silver Fox in Indian attire, proud, instead of ashamed. . . .

* * *

"Please sit down," Giles said flatly, motioning toward a thickly-cushioned chair on the opposite side of the desk, while he eased into a high-backed leather chair. He eyed a drawer at his right side that was partially open. The shine of the snub-nosed revolver that lay at the bottom of the drawer teased his eyes. It had become a seductress, luring him into using it. As though willed to, he again picked up the revolver and began moving it idly from one hand to the other, his eyes now focused on Jeanine.

Jeanine paled of color. Her eyes moved with the revolver, from hand to hand . . . from hand to hand. Then she looked up slowly into Giles's eyes, almost afraid to speak. But she must, to at least try to ease the strain that lay thickly in the air between them.

"I must apologize for coming without first making proper arrangements," she felt the need to say. "But, you see, I have been on . . . on . . . an extended vacation. I only returned today and discovered your letter. I thought maybe it was best that I come ahead and meet with you personally."

"You have wanted to meet with me at other times," Giles said, his hands still busy with the revolver. "I had failed to notice the familiarity of your name until only moments ago. My . . . uh . . . mind has been occupied by too many other things of late other than *names*."

His gaze shifted to the revolver as he placed it gingerly on the desktop. "You see," he added weakly, "my lumber company has fallen on hard times." His shoulders slumped. "Bankruptcy," he mumbled, placing his fingertips together before him. "Isn't that a nasty word, Miss Thaxton?"

Jeanine leaned forward in the chair. She rested her hands on the desk, intertwining her fingers. "Bankrupt? Your company has gone bankrupt?" she murmured, her eyes wide.

"It will if I don't sell my mother's paintings," Giles nodded. His eyes rose upward and held Jeanine's. "That is why I asked you to come. I would like to get a substantial sum from the sale of the paintings. Perhaps then my company—my family's company—can be saved."

He rose so quickly from the chair, Jeanine jumped with a start. She placed a hand to her throat as she watched him begin to pace frantically.

"I don't even want to talk about it, though," Giles said thickly, kneading his brow. "Those paintings mean so much to my mother." He gestured with a hand as he looked toward the ceiling. "She's up there now in her room, trusting my judgment. God, how could I have let her down?"

Jeanine rose slowly from the chair and stood numbly watching him, seeing a man in total defeat. Her heart went out to him, but she knew that she could do nothing to help him. It seemed that he would not win either way he turned. If he sold the paintings, he would forever feel guilty. If he did not, his company would fail, filling him with the same sort of guilt, for the company, as well as the paintings, was a part or his family.

Jeanine could not impose herself on him, by asking him about him or his family. This was not the time. He was not the person to interview, ever. He had separated himself from his family of Indians. He had already let Jeanine know that he did not wish to talk about this to anyone. She had been wrong to think that he might change his mind.

"Giles . . ." Jeanine said, reaching a hand out to him, realizing that he needed a friend, not an interfering author to complicate his life.

Giles turned around and glared down at her. "I can't do it," he said, his voice breaking. "I just can't sell my mother's paintings."

He took Jeanine by an elbow and began guiding her from the room. "I was wrong to ask you to come here," he said thickly. "I'm sorry if I have inconvenienced you in any way."

Jeanine half stumbled over the tail of her skirt as Giles led her on toward the front door. Though she didn't know the man, she was hurting for him. She even feared for his life. In her mind's eye she was still seeing how he had so absently been toying with the revolver. She hadn't felt threatened by it herself. It was his preoccupation with it that had made her become concerned for *his* welfare. Was he planning something foolish? Was he going to seek the easier way out? Surely he wasn't planning to shoot himself!

Jeanine stopped and eased away from him, her mind circling with confused worry. She glanced up at the staircase. "Your mother," she murmured. "You said she was upstairs?"

"Yes. But we mustn't disturb her," Giles said, again claiming Jeanine's elbow, half forcing her on to the door. He opened the door with his free hand. "Now please just go on your way. I cannot talk of selling my mother's paintings now, or *ever*."

"But, Sir . . ." Jeanine stammered. "Are you alright? I feel that perhaps you shouldn't . . . uh . . . be left alone." She looked across his shoulder and glanced up the staircase. "Perhaps your mother wouldn't mind being disturbed. If she knew you needed—"

"I need nothing nor nobody," Giles said from between clenched teeth, urging Jeanine out onto the porch. "Please just leave. Neither my welfare nor my mother's is any concern of yours."

Jeanine drew her shawl up around her shoulders, quietly studying Giles, then knew that she had been close to crossing that threshold which spoke of being a busybody if she interfered any further in Giles Thomas's decisions of the moment. She had no right to suggest anything to this man she didn't even know. She only hoped that he was more rational than she had just witnessed him to be. It seemed to her that he was at his wit's end and *was* capable of violence against himself. But she was helpless in any endeavor she might pursue to help him. She had no choice *but* to leave.

As she reached the steps, Giles released her elbow. "Thank you for coming," he said thickly, then swung around and hurried back inside the house.

A chill seemed to touch Jeanine all over as the door slammed in her face. She listened to the silence all around her for a moment, then rushed to her buggy and grabbed her reins from around the hitching rail. Feeling all out of sorts, she climbed into the buggy and rode away, joining Giles in his feelings of defeat, though hers were for very different reasons. Danette had been there, so close, for the interview! Yet, Jeanine had been forced by circumstances not to ask to see Danette at this time.

Again she had failed to gain much needed information for her book. Would she ever . . . ?

She slapped the reins against Daisy's rump and rode away briskly beneath the silver shine of the moon.

Lone Wolf moved from the bushes and stepped far enough away from the house to watch Jeanine. His heart ached to go to her, to draw her into his arms and kiss her. But when he recalled her uncle's words, as to why she had been in the forest, a bitterness stung his tongue with the thought of how she had used him when she had shared in their lovemaking.

Though he knew that he had been the first with her sexually, would she have gone that far to get the answers she most surely needed to write her book about Indians? Was she the sort to use, then discard? When they had kissed, she had seemed to have put herself into the kiss. It *hadn't* been a kiss of pretense. It hadn't!

Wrestling these feelings around inside him, Lone Wolf felt torn between needs. He wanted to go to Jeanine, yet he wanted to observe his brother further. His brother had showed many weaknesses this night. And the revolver had been a dangerous weakness! One did not play with a revolver as though it were a toy. One only dealt with a firearm if one meant to *use* it!

But watching Jeanine moving farther and farther away from him on the drive, only a turn away from the street, not knowing when an opportunity would arise when they would once again meet, Lone Wolf turned and began running to where he had left his stallion reined. He must go after Jeanine. He must!

Giles moped back to the study and quietly shut the door that separated the study from the hallway. With his shoulders slumped in defeat, he went back to the desk and looked down at the revolver for a while, again feeling its seduction, as though it were a lady. His heart began thundering wildly against his chest, his fingers grew numbly cold. This was the moment of decision. Could he? Or was he still the coward he had been the other times he had attempted to fire that bullet into his tired, useless brain?

Forcing his fingers not to tremble, he reached for the revolver and moved as though sleepwalking toward the window. Drawing the sheer curtain only slightly aside, he looked down the long stretch of drive to make sure Jeanine Thaxton was not within hearing range of the gunfire. When he saw no signs of her, he let the curtain ripple from between his fingers and turned his back to the window.

Slowly, but deliberately, he lifted the revolver to his head and placed the barrel to his temple. He closed his eyes and then the trembling began. He tried to will himself to pull the trigger, wanting to end his life . . . his suffering. His courage had always failed him when it came right down to the moment of decision. But this time he must do it! He had already placed a note to his mother in the family Bible out on a hallway table, explaining why. Hopefully she would understand. . . .

Closing his eyes, he pulled the trigger.

Lone Wolf heard the explosion of the gunfire, causing him to stop in midstep. He had just come within footsteps of his horse. Though he had never known his brother, personally, knowing what had most surely just happened made a total emptiness sweep through him.

"*Neen gee-gee-kee-wayn-zee*!" he cried, then turned and ran toward the house. He didn't stop when he reached the door. He swung it open wildly and found his way to the study. He was the first to reach his dead brother.

Tears crept to the corners of Lone Wolf's eyes as he knelt over Giles and eased the revolver from his hand. A loud gasp behind him drew Lone Wolf quickly to his feet. He turned and found crystal-clear blue eyes accusing him. Then he stepped aside as the lady rushed to Giles and knelt down beside him, weeping.

"My son," Danette Thomas cried as she eased Giles's head onto her lap. "Oh, Lord, Giles, Silver Fox, my son . . . my son." Her eyes closed as she pressed her cheek against Giles's cheek. "Oh, Gray Wolf, our son. Our . . . son. . . ."

Lone Wolf's stomach churned strangely; his breathing became shallow. This woman with her dark hair coiled into a tight bun atop her head and dressed in a full-skirted dress of lilac velvet, with a face as pale as snow, was the woman who had married Gray Wolf. She was the woman who had stolen Gray Wolf away from Lone Wolf's beautiful *gee-mah-mah*, mother!

Danette looked up at Lone Wolf sourly, glancing from the revolver in his hand, back up into Lone Wolf's eyes. "Why would you do this?" she sobbed. "Lord, why would you do this?"

His heart skipped a beat, now realizing how it must look with him holding the revolver. Knowing what this woman was accusing him of, Lone Wolf dropped the revolver as though it were a hot coal. But it was too late to convince anyone that he was not the responsible party, for the butler was already blocking the door, holding a very lethal rifle on Lone Wolf.

"Don't you even think of moving," the butler threatened. "I've already sent a stablehand for the sheriff. . . ."

Sixteen

With handcuffs anchoring his hands behind him, Lone Wolf followed alongside Sheriff Fred Hunter into the jail. His eyes were lit with fire. He was sweltering with hate as Fred took him by an arm and shoved him inside a jail cell and slammed the door shut with a loud clank.

"Didn't expect to meet up with you again so soon," Fred chuckled, draping the keys to the cells over a nail on the far wall. "Wonder what my niece'd think of you *now*, Injun?" he added, placing his doubled fists on his hips. "You ain't nothin' but trouble, are you? Well, you ain't gonna cause nobody no trouble anymore. Sunup tomorrow you'll be decoratin' my hangin' noose right purty." His face darkened with a frown. "Sunup ain't soon enough. I didn't like you bein' with my niece no matter that she said you rescued her from the forest when she got lost. The way you were lookin' at her weren't healthy, Injun. Weren't healthy at all."

The jangling of spurs approaching down the long hall of

cells made Fred turn and smile at Cameron Tyner. "You missed all the fun," he chuckled. He gestured with a hand toward Lone Wolf. "We got us a live one here, Cameron. Seems he's killed one of his own kind. He killed Giles Thomas." He kneaded his chin. "Cameron, did ja know that Giles Thomas was a redskin Injun? His Injun name is Silver Fox. Damn. I wonder how many more redskins are hid around Duluth. Guess I'd best get to know my town and its folks *better*."

"Yeah. I heard about Silver Fox," Cameron jeered, his blue eyes silver beneath the dim lighting of the room. "Seems I neglected tellin' you about him, Fred. Sorry 'bout that."

Cameron stepped up to the cell and glowered at Lone Wolf, then his eyes wavered when Lone Wolf stared back at him coldly. The look Lone Wolf was giving Cameron made him feel as though someone had sprayed ice water all over him. He had had enough run-ins with Indians to know when one wasn't to be messed with. And all of his inclinations warned him that this was one of those kind.

Cameron smiled slowly. But *this* Injun was behind bars! Soon he would be blowing in the breeze at the end of a hangman's noose. So Cameron felt that teasing was a safe enough thing to do.

"Hey, there, Injun," he said, kicking the toe of a boot hard against a bar of Lone Wolf's cell. "Where's your fancy stallion? You don't look so smug now without your fancy stallion."

Lone Wolf stood tall proudly, too stubborn to let his feelings show. He felt like a trapped animal without any hopes of escape. The bars were not enough for these white men! The sheriff had manacled his wrists together! Was he going to be left that way?

Then his thoughts returned to the death scene. His insides ached. A brother that he had never gotten to know now lay dead and *Lone Wolf* was accused of the death!

His thoughts went to Danette, the woman who had wrongly accused him. She had not only stolen Gray Wolf from Lone Wolf's mother, but now also Lone Wolf's life! Had she known that Lone Wolf's father was Gray Wolf, would she have been so quick to accuse . . . ?

But, yes. Her son was now dead. She saw Lone Wolf as the one responsible. And Lone Wolf had not told her that her son had taken his own life. She would never have believed this of a son of the powerful Indian Chief Gray Wolf! And even if she had discovered that it was true, she surely would never admit such a truth to anyone.

"Got nothin' to say for yerself, Injun?" Cameron continued to taunt. "Or will you beg for mercy when I place the noose about your neck?"

Laughing raucously, Cameron turned away from Lone Wolf and placed a muscled arm about Fred's shoulders. "Come on, Fred," he said, giving Lone Wolf another quick glance. "Let's go and celebrate. Ain't every day we get us an Injun to hang."

Discouraged, Jeanine paced her living room. She was still seeing the shine of the revolver in Giles Thomas's hand. She was still hearing the defeat in his voice. And the fact that he had changed his mind so quickly about selling the paintings disturbed Jeanine so, she couldn't get it off her mind. Was he capable of shooting himself? Would he . . . ? Was he capable of even more violence with the revolver? . . . ? Would he go on a shooting spree on the downtown streets of Duluth . . . ? This had been known to happen when one's mind becomes too strained, snapping . . .

Combing her fingers nervously through her hair, Jeanine leaned her head back and sighed, her thoughts going beyond just worry about what Giles Thomas might do. He was Indian. Why hadn't she thought earlier that he might be? When she had heard that he was Danette's son, why hadn't it connected inside her mind that surely this son was a brother to Strong Hawk? Jeanine hadn't heard about any earlier marriages of Danette. She should have known that there had been only one. . . .

"Oh, what should I do?" she worried aloud, shaking her hair so that it tumbled fully down her back.

She went to a window and drew back a sheer curtain, seeing the midnight black of the night. Then she went to her double French doors and stepped out onto her balcony. Hugging herself, trying to ward off the chill of the breeze, she looked down toward the lights of Duluth. They were as though golden specks of fireflies in the darkness.

Then she began thinking of her Uncle Fred. Perhaps she should go and warn him of Giles Thomas and the revolver of which he seemed too fond. Though her uncle hated Indians, he hated violence in his town even more. And violence even wrought upon one's self!

"Yes," she whispered. She whirled around and went back inside. "I'll go and talk with Uncle Fred. He *should* know. Giles Thomas *might* go berserk and kill more than himself!"

Drawing on a black velveteen cape with a hood to protect her hair from the damp chill that continuously blew in from Lake Superior, she snapped it together at her neck. She rushed from the house and instead of bothering with harnessing her buggy to her horse, she jumped on Daisy bareback and rode toward town.

The cape flying, the air cold against her face, Jeanine entered the town. In her black cape she blended in well enough with the darkness of night, not drawing undue attention to herself and the fact that she was a lady, alone, at this late hour.

Galloping on down the main thoroughfare, she rode past boisterous noises emanating from saloons on both sides of the street. Shrill laughter rose into the air from women frolicking about in dance halls. Men were loitering along the planked walks, some drinking, some smoking. The street was busy with mingling men on horseback and horsedrawn carriages and an occasional putt-putt of an automobile.

And then she spied the jailhouse at the far end of the street. Jeanine nudged the flanks of her horse with the heels of her boots and hurried along, the gaslights aglow through the barred windows of the jail meeting her approach. She reined in Daisy beside a hitching rail, dismounted, then in a half run slung the reins about the rail and hurried inside the jail.

Tossing the hood from her head, she was disappointed when she found the outer room of the jail empty. Smoke from a half-smoked cigar resting in an ashtray on the desk made her aware that her uncle was not all that far away, possibly only next door for a quick drink.

Deciding to wait for him, Jeanine loosened her cape from around her shoulders and let it flutter downward onto a chair. Nervously fidgeting with objects on her uncle's desk, she looked slowly about the room. It smelled of stale cigars and cold stove ashes. The gaslight on the wall flickered in golden slants across the ceiling, settling on a spider web, where a spider had spun its silken string about a captured moth.

A shiver raced across Jeanine's flesh. She briskly rubbed her arms through her long-sleeved blouse. Her eyes again began moving about the room, then stopped on the gaping door that led into the room where many cells for the most part usually stood empty.

She squinted, trying to see more clearly. Faint flickerings of light from a gas wall sconce revealed that one cell door was closed.

''Hmm,'' Jeanine said, raising an eyebrow inquisitively. ''Seems Uncle Fred's been busy. He's got himself a *prisoner*.''

Curious, Jeanine inched her way toward the door and raised a hand and pushed it open slowly. Her heart fluttered and her knees grew bizarrely weak when eyes darker than any nights she could remember met her gaping stare. She stood momentarily immobile, stunned by her discovery, then her gaze swept fully over Lone Wolf, aghast to find that he was not only incarcerated but also had his hands handcuffed behind him.

In a sweep, not even feeling her feet moving against the

wooden floor, Jeanine went to the closed cell door and curled her fingers about the cold steel bars. Looking into Lone Wolf's eyes she saw a raw, cold hate.

"Lone Wolf, what . . . ? How . . . ?" she gasped, the knuckles of her hands growing white from her steadfast grip on the bars.

Lone Wolf squared his shoulders and clamped his lips tightly together, refusing to speak to her. But his heart was bleeding, painfully bleeding, with her so near, yet so far. His feelings for her were mixed. He was trying to understand the sort of person she was . . . someone who would exploit the Chippewa, yet make love to one all the same? He did not want to believe that she had used him.

Yet, with her being blood kin to such a man as Fred Hunter, was she not capable of such deceit? What more could Lone Wolf even expect of her?

Lone Wolf would have to learn not to love her. But that would not be hard, for tomorrow he would be hanging at the end of a rope, with all desires and hopes drained from him, as though he had never even existed!

Circling his fingers into tight fists, Lone Wolf thought of death. He did not welcome it, but he would die a proud Chippewa! Though he was accused wrongly, he would not beg to be released as do cowards! When word was received at his village that he was dead, he only hoped that someone would come for his body and treat it respectfully. His spirit would not rest anywhere but with his people!

Jeanine's insides grew cold, her spine stiff, slowly realizing that Lone Wolf had decided not to answer her. "Lord, Lone Wolf, speak to me!" she cried. "Tell me what happened? Why are you here?"

"He killed one of his own kind. *That's* why," Fred said, stepping suddenly to her side. "Didn't this savage tell you? Duluth'll witness a hangin' tomorrow at sunup."

Jeanine had been so totally wrapped up in her feelings for Lone Wolf she hadn't heard her uncle enter the room. Turning with a start, she looked up at him and saw a look of greed etched across his ruddy face. He puffed eagerly on a cigar that hung from the corner of his mouth. His hands rested on each of his holstered pistols. His green eyes were dancing with humor as he glanced from Lone Wolf, back to Jeanine.

In a state of semi-shock, Jeanine found it hard to speak. Her mind raced, trying to capture her uncle's true meanings. Lone Wolf had killed another Indian? Who? Why?

Then she finally composed herself and her thoughts. She spun around and totally faced Fred. "What do you mean . . . Lone Wolf killed one of his kind? Who? When?" she blurted. "Uncle Fred, surely you are wrong."

"You'll be surprised to find out just who this Injun *did* kill," Fred chuckled, taking the cigar from between his lips. He dropped it to the floor and ground it out with the toe of his boot.

Jeanine glanced over at Lone Wolf. His expression hadn't changed, nor had that same look of cold hate in his eyes. She so wanted to reach out and touch him, whisper in his ear that she loved him no matter what he was being accused of. She knew him well enough to know that he would not go around killing, unless he were doing so to defend himself. He was gentle in ways no man like Fred Hunter would understand. It was this gentleness that made a sensuous warmth spread throughout her when just recalling how Lone Wolf's hands and lips could send her mind soaring to heights of pleasure never known to her before. She loved him. She would always love him. No . . . matter . . . what. . . .

Fred lifted a shoulder into a shrug. "Giles Thomas," he said casually. He tilted his head to the side and smiled mockingly at Jeanine. "Didn't know Giles Thomas was part Injun, did you? He's also known as Silver Fox. He's Chief Strong Hawk's twin *brother*. You'd have been there faster than spit to interview *him* for your damn Injun book had you known, wouldn't you?"

Paling, Jeanine's hands went to her throat. "Giles is dead?" she gasped. "And you think Lone Wolf . . . ?"

Again her mind became cluttered with thoughts. Giles

was dead? And . . . Lone Wolf . . .? How could Lone Wolf be accused unless Lone Wolf had *been* there?

She turned a slow eye to Lone Wolf, silently questioning him, yet still he kept his lips tightly sealed, only burning her now with the dark command of his eyes.

"Lone Wolf, tell him. . . ." she said in a rush of words, grabbing tightly, desperately, to the bars of his cell. "You *know* how Giles died. *I* know. He shot *himself*. Tell Uncle Fred. Tell him."

"What's that you say?" Fred said, idly scratching his brow. "What are you jabbering about, Jeanine? What's this you say about Giles shootin' himself? Why would you say such a dumbass thing as that?"

Jeanine turned and grabbed onto Fred's arm. "Because it is true!" she half cried. "Uncle Fred, I was with Giles Thomas a short while ago. He was toying with a revolver as we talked. He was a tormented man! He shot himself! You must believe me! Don't you even wonder what brought me here, to your jail, at this late hour of the night? Uncle Fred, it was to warn you about Giles and how he was behaving while in my presence. I feared that he might do something reckless. And, Lord, Uncle Fred, he did!"

Fred grasped onto Jeanine's shoulders and slightly shook her. "Hey there, Jeanine!" he growled. "You're plumb talkin' outta your head. What is this nonsense about you being with Giles Thomas?"

Jeanine squirmed free of his grasp. She smoothed the skirt of her dress down and stubbornly dared her uncle with a tilted chin. "Giles Thomas summoned me to his house to discuss the sale of his mother's paintings," she said stiffly. "I also went there to discuss the book I plan to write. I had hoped to seek information from him *for* the book."

Then Jeanine cringed when hearing a soft intake of breath from the direction of Lone Wolf. Her confession had finally drawn some sort of response from him. She understood this response. He did not like the mention of her book in his presence. Hopefully one day he would understand her reason for writing it. But first she must make sure he was set free from this jail cell or there would be no tomorrows for either of them to share!

"But what was it you said about Giles Thomas shooting himself?" Fred demanded, his face growing red from frustration.

Jeanine thought quickly, knowing Lone Wolf's only chance was *her*. Her uncle would never believe that Lone Wolf wouldn't have killed Giles . . . and that Giles had behaved as one who would most surely kill himself. There it was again, this strange hatred of her uncle's toward the Indians. He wanted this hanging. He wanted to hang an Indian no matter if this Indian was innocent of the accused crime. She must help Lone Wolf escape. She would ask him questions later! She just knew that he was innocent. That was all that she needed to know for now.

But how could she help him escape if she continued ranting and raving to her uncle about how Giles had most surely died? She had to pretend to believe that Lone Wolf had done it after all. To pull attention from herself and what she must do, this was the only way!

"Oh, just forget that I said that," Jeanine said, shrugging. "It's just that he seemed so strange while I was with him. That's all." She forced a haughty, hateful look on her face when she looked toward Lone Wolf. "I guess I was wrong about Lone Wolf. If you say he killed Giles Thomas, he *killed* him."

"Damn right he did," Fred said, nodding. "Danette Thomas found this here Injun standin' over Giles Thomas's body with a revolver in his hand. Don't need no more proof than that, do you?"

Jeanine's gaze wavered, she flinched with her uncle's words, now truly puzzled. Lone Wolf had been found standing over Giles with a revolver? Why . . .?

She looked up at Lone Wolf intensely. Her face splashed crimson when she read the look in his eyes as he returned her steady gaze. There was a wounded hurt in their depths. When she had said that she believed Lone Wolf had killed

Giles after all, Lone Wolf had believed that she had meant it. He couldn't know that this was said only to divert attention away from herself so that her uncle would feel free to leave the keys to the cells hanging on the nail, for her to claim later then, when she was with Lone Wolf, who would then be free of those damnable handcuffs and bars, she would explain. He could, in turn, explain how he could have been put in the position of being accused of Giles Thomas's death. . . .

Fred placed a hand about Jeanine's waist and began ushering her from the room. "Come on," he said thickly. "This ain't no place for a lady. Anyways, you need to get your beauty rest. You'll have to rise bright and early tomorrow mornin' if you want to witness a hangin'. This one will be a colorful one, don't you think?"

He doubled over with laughter. "Don't you catch the joke?" he said, straightening his back, wiping laughter tears from the corners of his eyes. "Colored. An Injun's skin is colored. Get it, Jeanine? We're havin' us a colorful hangin' in the morning."

Jeanine's insides quivered. She now knew that she must find a way to release Lone Wolf *tonight*. Tomorrow or tomorrow night would be too late. Her uncle was not going to waste any time in setting an example for the rest of the stray Indians wandering the streets of Duluth, penniless.

She forced an awkward laugh. "Yes. You have a way of telling jokes, Uncle Fred," she murmured. "Yes, that was very funny."

As she stepped into the office with her uncle, Jeanine cringed when she almost ran full-bodied into Cameron Tyner. He was so close she could smell his tangy aftershave and the warmth of his breath blowing down into her face. She could even sense his animal heat as a slow smile lifted his lips, baring to her his straight, white line of teeth.

"Cameron, you stay put for the night," Fred said firmly, yanking his Stetson hat from a peg on the wall. "Don't let anythin' happen to our prize prisoner, do you hear? Come mornin', after the hangin' you can catch up on your rest."

Jeanine stepped hotly around Cameron, yet felt meekly afraid of what she had to do the next few hours. She would have Cameron to come up against when she returned to the jail to help Lone Wolf escape.

"Sure as hell can depend on me," Cameron said, plopping down on the chair behind the desk.

Fred placed Jeanine's cape around her shoulders. With a firm grip on her elbow he led her from the room. But before she left, she took a backward glance at Cameron and smiled to herself when she saw him slip a bottle of whiskey from a desk drawer. When he tipped it to his lips and took a long swallow, she knew that before long he would surely fall into a drunken sleep.

Seventeen

Creeping through the dark, around the side of the jailhouse, Jeanine scarcely breathed. Her eyes peered through the darkness, alert for any sudden movement ahead, hopefully having waited long enough to return to the jail to release Lone Wolf. She had separated from her uncle several hours ago and most of the activity on the street had lessened. It was the time of the night when most were asleep. Even Jeanine was finding it hard to stay awake. Her eyes felt as though there was sand scratching them.

With luck, Cameron Tyner had become as sleepy as she after drinking his whiskey. If not, Jeanine would have no way to explain her presence back at the jail in the middle of the night. If worse came to worst, she might even have to hold Cameron at gunpoint while she unlocked Lone Wolf's cell.

But Jeanine prayed that wouldn't be necessary. She would become hunted along with Lone Wolf if it were to become known that she had released him. Though she didn't approve of what her uncle had done, she didn't want to lose his love *or* respect. If she could release Lone Wolf unnoticed, her uncle might suspect that one of Lone Wolf's friends had done the sneaky deed. Her uncle would have no cause to suspect Jeanine. While with her uncle in the jail, after she had discovered Lone Wolf there, she had acted disinterested enough in Lone Wolf's welfare to deter any suspicion.

At first though, she had almost revealed feelings for Long Wolf that she would never want her uncle to know about; he wouldn't understand. She wasn't even sure that she did, or ever would. Lone Wolf's mystique continued to draw her to him as though it were just meant to be. Each time she saw him, the feelings he had created inside her strengthened. There seemed to have been a missing link in her life, until him. . . .

The velveteen cape whipped about Jeanine's ankles as the breeze blew in briskly from Lake Superior. Her hair fluttered about her face as it was drawn from beneath the hood of the cape by the wind. With nervous fingers she brushed her hair back from her eyes, then stepped out into the open and moved surefootedly to the door of the jailhouse.

Jeanine didn't stop to look around. Instead she inched the door open, her heart pounding from cautious fear in the hollow of her throat. Eyes wide she looked toward the desk where she had last seen Cameron Tyner. Something grabbed at her insides. He was gone! He wasn't at the desk. Had he deserted the post assigned to him by her uncle? If so, her uncle would most surely horsewhip him! Her uncle had left strict orders for Tyner to stay with Lone Wolf, to make sure he was given no opportunity to escape!

Smiling softly to herself, Jeanine crept across the room, glad that Cameron had proven to be hardheaded at a time that would benefit her. Of late, his neglect in following orders would be enough to force her uncle to take his deputy's badge and send him on his way.

This couldn't be too soon as far as Jeanine was concerned. She knew that her days could be numbered with

Cameron, when he would finally try his hand at approaching her in ways warned by him. Hopefully her uncle's next deputy would be a more respectable sort!

The gaslight on the wall, burning dimly in the inner, spacious, cell room, emitted only enough light for Jeanine to see her way inside, to move stealthily along the lined cells.

Her eyes searched and found Lone Wolf's cell. It was too dark for her to tell if he was asleep on his bunk, or awake.

Whichever, he would be surprised to discover why she had returned. And would he even be glad? When she had last seen him he had been anything but responsive to her.

Would he trust her? He had seen how she had left with her uncle. At that time she had only pretended that she could care less about Lone Wolf, but had Lone Wolf truly believed her?

Oh, surely he had seen it as only the ploy she had meant it to be! How could he not know the depth of her feelings for him? They had shared so much, and in so little time!

Moving as does a thief in the night, Jeanine hurried to the nail on which hung the keys to the cells. She flinched when they jangled as she took them from the nail. She quieted them by holding them to her chest, then swirled around and moved determinedly toward Lone Wolf's cell. When she got there, she again made out his figure on the bunk. His back was to her and his breathing was quiet and even, surely proof that he was fast asleep.

Jeanine's gaze settled on the handcuffed wrists at his back. A strange sort of hatred for her uncle was aroused inside her, feelings never before felt by her toward him.

But never before had she loved a man . . . a man wronged *by* her uncle.

If Jeanine were forced to choose between these two men, she dared to think which would be the winner in her eyes. It would be her heart that would guide her decision, as it was her heart that had led her to do this dangerous deed this night!

It was all because of Lone Wolf. Oh, how she did love him. This sort of love was dangerous. She knew that. Yes, she knew that. . . .

Her fingers trembling, Jeanine sorted through the keys. She tested first one and then another in the keyhole, growing frustrated at being unable to find the right one.

Then a slow smile touched her lips when finally a key totally fit. In a matter of moments she would awaken Lone Wolf and find another key . . . one that would unlock the handcuffs. They would flee into the night together. She would first see to his safety, then return home, as though nothing had happened.

When her uncle came to her with the news of Lone Wolf's escape, she would gasp and shake her head, tsk-tsking, saying what a shame!

She could already feel the triumph when watching her uncle's anger at Cameron Tyner for letting Lone Wolf escape!

But then she would have to worry about a posse being formed. Lone Wolf must find a safe place to hide . . . at least until the truth about Giles's death was proven!

A loud, sudden snore erupting from somewhere behind Jeanine startled her so, she almost dropped the ring of keys. Instead she held them safely within the palm of her hand and slowly turned, to trace the root of the sound.

She finally discovered Cameron Tyner's whereabouts. He was stretched out on a bunk in a cell at the far end of the room, snoozing. Jeanine jumped when he flopped over and placed his back to her drifting into a deeper sleep.

Jeanine emitted a heavy sigh of relief, feeling a cold bead of nervous perspiration lacing her brow. Her heart thundering, she turned back around and inched the cell door open. She watched Lone Wolf for any signs of awakening. But he was still breathing easily, his back to her.

Not wanting to startle Lone Wolf and cause him to cry out at suddenly being awakened, Jeanine didn't know how to approach him. But then her eyes widened and her heart seemed to stop dead when Lone Wolf turned around swiftly and rose to stand giantly over her, his eyes dark pools in the night as he gazed down at her with wonder.

"You weren't asleep at all," she whispered. "You knew I was here. Lone Wolf, why didn't you let me know? You almost frightened me to death."

But it was the same as earlier in the evening. Lone Wolf refused to speak to her. Instead his gaze moved and settled on the keys in her hand. He turned around and gave her full access to the handcuffs, a silent request for her to unlock them.

Again Jeanine searched through the keys until she found the right one, casting Cameron occasional worried glances. Should he awaken, he might shoot first and ask questions later, not even stopping to see that *she* was there, stealing Lone Wolf away in the night.

Sighing, she was finally able to remove the handcuffs. She watched, wide-eyed, as Lone Wolf turned around and again faced her. His fingers were rubbing his raw wrists. His jaw was set firmly in his continued silence.

And then Lone Wolf grabbed Jeanine by an elbow and began to guide her from the cell. His eyes found Cameron and looked at him with fire. This white man's scalp should be taken for insulting Lone Wolf!

But this was not the time. It was necessary to leave the dreaded white man's animal trap with iron bars. It was necessary to get Jeanine far away from this place and the accusations of her uncle should he discover her there, freeing a Chippewa!

Lone Wolf was torn with wonder about this woman, who seemed to speak with two tongues. But he was slowly beginning to grasp the truth of her. She had cared that he had been wrongly accused!

But was this only because she again planned to use him? Was her need to write a book about the Chippewa so great that she would endanger herself to free the Chippewa she wished to interview?

Lone Wolf would not let himself think about this now.

His safety . . . *her* safety . . . were the most important things at this moment. The forest. Lone Wolf must find his way back to the safety of the forest. Jeanine could return to her dwelling.

Side by side, Jeanine and Lone Wolf made their way toward the door that led out to the outer office. They both tensed when Cameron emitted another loud snore, then again became quiet behind them.

Giving Lone Wolf a troubled glance, Jeanine stole alongside him through her uncle's office, and then to the door that led to the outside. "Let me check things outside first," Jeanine whispered, edging away from Lone Wolf.

Her pulse raced as she opened the outside door and leaned her head out, to peer cautiously from side to side. When she saw that no one was in sight, she motioned for Lone Wolf to follow as she stepped outside onto the plank walks, with Lone Wolf moving gingerly along behind her.

Jeanine nearly panicked when Lone Wolf began to walk away from her in the opposite direction. Was he just going to leave her like that? Without a word of thank-you? Or *what* . . . ?

She suddenly discovered the answer to her questions. He had spied his black stallion reined close by, beside Cameron Tyner's horse. Cameron had found and had brought the horse with him, more than likely planning to keep it for his own private use once Lone Wolf was dead.

Jeanine didn't stop to watch Lone Wolf mount his horse. Instead she ran to the back of the jail and swung herself onto her own mare. She was worrying again that Lone Wolf was not going to thank her, but instead, ride away and ignore the dangers she had placed herself in to steal him away from the jail. Hopefully she would get back around to the front before he had a chance to fully disappear from her view!

But she didn't have to worry about that. Lone Wolf was suddenly there on his steed, beside her, his eyes telling her so much that he had said aloud those times when they had shared heaven while in one another's arms. She only wished that he would say something now instead of just exchanging looks with her. She was quickly becoming unnerved, wondering why he was choosing silence over words!

"*Mah-bee-szhon,*" Lone Wolf finally said, gesturing with a nod of his head toward the edge of town.

Jeanine's eyes widened, wondering what he had said. But she did not labor over such wonder. Lone Wolf had wheeled his stallion around and was galloping away from her in the direction that he had just shown her.

Feeling as though he had summoned her to follow him, she thrust her knees into the sides of her horse and slapped her reins and went galloping after him, her cape and her skirt flying up around her legs, as though wings. The hood of her cape loosened and fell about her shoulders, freeing her hair, to lift, then billow back down to her shoulders as the breeze fluttered through and about it.

Lone Wolf's shadow trailed along the ground beside him as the moon cast its silver rays along his tall, handsome outline. The fringes of his shirt and leggings quivered in the wind, his long, coarse black hair shone as though blue, the bear grease in it so distinctly evidenced.

Jeanine urged her horse into a faster gallop, then fell into stride beside Lone Wolf. When she looked over at him, she almost melted from the knowing smile he gave her. He *had* intended for her to follow him. He had accepted her help and, hopefully, he would accept her reasons for doing it. It was only because of her love for him. Only because of her love . . .

With her head held high, Jeanine rode beside Lone Wolf on past the last of the buildings of Duluth and into the outer edges of the forest. Then it became dark as a threatening black storm cloud when they moved farther into the towering oaks and elms whose leaves were so thick the moon could not penetrate with its guiding light.

Feeling the cold dampness of the night piercing the flesh of her face, Jeanine trembled. Yet she continued to follow

Lone Wolf until they were far from Duluth, now totally alone . . . now totally safe. . . .

Lone Wolf cast Jeanine a frowning stare. "You were *gee-wah-nah-dis*, foolish, to come and steal keys and help Lone Wolf escape!" he grumbled. "If your uncle would have discovered you there . . ."

Jeanine interrupted him. "But he didn't," she said, smiling mischievously back at him. "And he will never know it was I who helped you, Lone Wolf. In the morning I shall arrive at the jail for the hanging as though I didn't know a thing about your escape."

Lone Wolf wheeled his horse around and stopped. He grabbed Jeanine's reins and stopped her horse. "Then you must return to town *now*," he said thickly. "You do not have long. The sun will soon replace the moon in the sky."

"But I don't want to return home until I know where you plan to be," Jeanine argued softly, pleading with her eyes. "Surely you don't plan to return to your village. That will be the first place my uncle will look for you."

"No. He will not look for me there," Lone Wolf said flatly. "He would know I would not return there, to endanger my people with troubles of the white man. He will look for me elsewhere."

"Then you do plan to return to your village?" Jeanine said, smiling a thank-you to Lone Wolf as he returned her reins.

"*Gah-ween*, no," he said, shaking his head. "It is not best that I return at this time."

"Then where will you go?"

He motioned with a hand in the direction they had just been traveling. "A day's ride away there is a cavern," he said quietly. "That is where Lone Wolf will spend the next sunrises. When I know your uncle is weary of the hunt *then* I will return to my people. My father is not well. I cannot stay away for too long. Should he die . . ."

His voice trailed off as his hand lowered and his head bowed. "Only recently did Lone Wolf lose a mother," he said thickly. "Father follows along behind mother much too soon, I fear."

Jeanine edged her horse closer to Lone Wolf's. She touched his arm gently. "I am so sorry," she murmured.

Lone Wolf's head jerked up. "Later you will come to me so we can be together and talk," he said, taking her hand, squeezing it. "Lone Wolf has many questions. And you?"

"All I want to know is how you happened to be at Giles Thomas's house," Jeanine dared to say. "Why did you go there, Lone Wolf? Did you follow me there? Was that the reason . . . ?"

Lone Wolf's hand jerked away. He grasped onto his horse's reins, again silent. He still was not free to tell anyone of his discovery of brothers and that he now only had one brother left! Some day! But not yet. . . .

"Oh, Lone Wolf," Jeanine said, frustration setting in. "First you talk and then you *don't*. Why do you do this to me?"

"It is best you return to your dwelling now before you are missed," Lone Wolf said flatly.

"But you said . . ."

"You return. It is best. . . ."

"But . . ."

Lone Wolf quickly dismounted his horse and went and placed his hands to Jeanine's waist and lifted her from Daisy, to the ground. Twining his fingers through her hair he drew her face close to his.

"In two sunrises come to this exact spot at this exact time," he gruffly ordered. "Lone Wolf will meet you and take you to hideout. We will then share much talk . . . much love. . . ."

He grazed her lips with his. "But do not tell a soul where you are going," he whispered. "Even if you must lie to your uncle. Tell him you are again taking a journey alone through the forest. If he let you go once, he will not stand in your way a second time."

Jeanine didn't get a chance to tell him that her uncle had

not let her leave willingly that first time to travel north in the forest. Lone Wolf had her lips pinned beneath his, and was kissing her ardently.

And then in a wink of an eye he was again separated from her and on his horse, riding away from her.

Jeanine tasted his kiss on her lips, watching him become as one with the shadows of the forest.

Then she began looking around, trying to memorize some of the trees and bushes of this exact spot, for she *would* return, whether or not her uncle approved! She would find a way. She hadn't risked her life tonight to free Lone Wolf, not to be with him again. Solely with him . . . again. . . .

Eighteen

Jeanine's head bobbed at her desk, having taken a quick wink of sleep. Then her eyes jerked opened and she glanced toward the clock on her office wall, then toward the window, seeing the ripples of orange in the sky as morning erased night from the sky.

Rising shakily to her feet, she yawned, having spent the rest of the night at the art museum after she had left Lone Wolf in the forest. Straightening the lines of her skirt, trying to smooth away wrinkles, she felt her pulse begin to race. It was time for her to make her appearance at the jail. Her uncle had planned the hanging for about this time of morning. It could be just about now that he was discovering Lone Wolf's absence. Jeanine must look the picture of innocence when her Uncle Fred saw her there, asking what had happened to Lone Wolf. It would sorely please her to ask if Cameron Tyner had been lax on the job.

Smiling half wickedly, Jeanine opened a desk drawer and took from within it a hairbrush. In eager strokes she made her hair presentable enough, then rushed from the art museum out to her horse and swung herself up into the saddle. The streets were empty as she rode toward the jail. . . .

Stretching his arms lazily above his head, yawning, Fred left his horse reined at the hitching post and went into the jail, feeling smug. It wasn't every day he had the chance to hang himself a damn Injun. He would enjoy watching the Injun's eyes bug from his head when his neck snapped. In Fred's mind he would be hanging a Sioux, not a Chippewa. He would pretend he was getting at least a little bit of revenge for his wife's death all those years ago. One Injun was the same as another as he saw it. That Chief Strong Hawk could pretend to be civil all he wanted, but Fred knew that nothing could make a savage turn civil. Nothing!

The fact that this incarcerated Injun who called himself Lone Wolf hadn't harmed Jeanine after he had found her in the forest didn't mean that he didn't eventually plan to. Surely he had happened to be in Duluth for her, then had come across this Injun, Silver Fox, and killed him because of some past dispute. Perhaps Lone Wolf had killed Silver Fox because Silver Fox had betrayed his people by living the life of a white man, having even taken a white man's name.

But it mattered not why Lone Wolf did anything. Lone Wolf was now taking his last breaths of life. In only a matter of moments he would be dangling from the end of a rope!

Stepping into the jail, Fred glanced at the desk and smiled a lopsided smile. He chuckled low and moved on past the desk and to the gaping door that led into the long row of cells. Cameron was already in the back, probably taunting the Injun about the hanging. It seemed that Cameron was enjoying this almost as much as Fred. They might even end up arguing over who would place the noose about the damn savage's neck!

Still chuckling, Fred shoved the door wide open and stepped into the back room. But when he looked toward the cell in which he should have found Lone Wolf, his insides grew numbly cold. The cell was empty, the door open. The ring of keys was on the floor.

A loud snore erupting from the far end of the room drew Fred around quickly. His face and eyes grew hot with anger when he discovered Cameron in another cell, fast asleep on a bunk. And it was obvious that he hadn't been forced there by whomever had helped the damn Injun escape, for the door to that cell was also open. Cameron had gone there on his own to get a wink of sleep and had even slept through Lone Wolf's escape!

A low growl rumbled through Fred as he stormed to the back of the room. When he reached the cell in which Cameron still slept, he stepped inside and stood over him, glaring down at him. Bending, he swept his hand back and slapped Cameron on the face, awakening him with a jolt, so much so that he fell from the bunk before scrambling clumsily to his feet.

Surprise in his eyes, Cameron rubbed his burning cheek and stared at Fred, then let his gaze move slowly to the cell that no longer imprisoned Lone Wolf.

"You damn, blundering idiot," Fred growled, slapping Cameron again, on his other cheek. "The Injun escaped while you just lay there and *let* him. You ain't worth nothin' to me no more, Cameron. Nothin'."

Fred turned on his heel and stomped away and went immediately to his desk. Opening a drawer he rifled through a stack of wanted posters and grabbed one out and slammed it on the top of his desk.

When Cameron ambled into the outer office, red finger imprints on each of his cheeks, Fred met him with handcuffs ready.

"Like I said, Cameron," he said flatly. "You ain't no good to me anymore. Seems you're goin' to take the Injun's place in the cell." He nodded toward Cameron's hands. "Hold 'em up, Cameron. I've a pair of handcuffs that'll fit your wrists this mornin'."

Cameron's blue eyes were awash with puzzlement. "What . . . ?" he gasped, then saw the poster on the desk on which was a likeness of himself.

"Yeah. Seems your runnin' days are over," Fred chuckled. "I was going to spare you had you continued to be worth somethin' to me. But as it is, you ain't, so take your medicine, Cameron. Get these handcuffs on without a fight. A few days behind bars and then I'll ship you down south, where you're wanted for more than bein' a deputy."

Cameron laughed awkwardly and combed his long, lean fingers through his blonde hair. "Now, Fred, you ain't serious," he said. "You know you ain't serious. You've always liked me as your sidekick. Don't you remember how fast my draw is? Who'll ride alongside you who can shoot as fast as me? Huh? Who? Who saved your *life*? Who'll be there the next time?"

"Sleepin' on the job, Cameron? Lettin' a prisoner escape?" Fred said in a low growl. "Your shootin' fast ain't worth that much to me no more, so that I would forget your failings. And don't think I ain't seen the way you've looked at my niece. There ain't no way I can allow the likes of you to get ideas of marryin' her. She'd want a man of breeding . . . not a scalawag like you."

Fred's tone of voice softened and his eyes wavered. "And you don't know what losin' that Injun means to me, Cameron," he said thickly. "The hangin' was going to represent more to me than just a mere hangin'."

"So I slipped up," Cameron said, his hand easing toward his holstered pistol. "Let me make it up to you, Fred. Let me go and find that Injun. I'll see to it that he hangs alright. We'll make an example of 'im. Okay, Fred? Let me go after him for you? And I'll forget my notions about Jeanine. You got my word on it, Fred."

Fred's gaze lowered. He fingered the handcuffs contemplatively, then began shaking his head. "No. Nothin' you'd say—" he began, but before he could finish his sentence or raise his eyes again he felt a sharp blow on his head. He dropped the handcuffs and grabbed at his temples, only seeing a blur before his eyes as Cameron raced past him and out the door.

His knees buckling, Fred sank to the floor and slipped into a void of black unconsciousness. . . .

Jeanine dismounted before the jail and slung her reins about the hitching rail and walked determinedly toward the door. Her eyebrows lifted when she saw the door ajar. Stepping gingerly up to the door, she pushed it open slowly. Her breath was stolen momentarily away when she discovered her uncle sprawled out on the floor, groaning as he was rubbing a lump on his head.

"Lord!" Jeanine said, hurrying inside. She knelt beside her uncle and helped him into a sitting position. "What happened, Uncle Fred?"

Fred squinted as he looked up at Jeanine, still seeing everything as only a blur. "Damn him," he grumbled. "Wait'll I get my hands on him. I'll tear him limb from limb."

"Who, Uncle Fred?" Jeanine asked, now helping him to his feet.

"Cameron, *that's* who," Fred said, bending to pick up the handcuffs from the floor. "He ain't worth nothin,' Jeanine. Absolutely nothin'. How'd I ever get suckered into believin' he *was*? I should've locked him up the minute I saw that wanted poster on him."

"Wanted poster?" Jeanine gasped, then her gaze moved to the desk and saw the poster. She went to it and picked it up and read it. "He's wanted in Texas? Lord, Uncle Fred. Did you know this and just let him continue being your deputy?"

"Seems that a-way, don't it?" he said, lumbering to the door that led back to the cells. He nodded toward Jeanine. "Come here. Take a look, Jeanine. Cameron ain't the only one doin' a disappearin' act. The damn Injun escaped.

While Cameron slept his damn fool head off, Lone Wolf *escaped*."

"Lone Wolf escaped?" Jeanine said, forcing a surprised tone to her voice. She walked alongside Fred into the back room. "And you said it's Cameron's fault?"

"Yeah. Like I said," Fred grumbled, slamming the cell door shut with a bang. "He slept while someone walked right in here and opened the cell and let the Injun out. Don't that beat all?"

"Who would do that?" Jeanine asked, wide-eyed.

Fred shrugged. "Another *Injun*. Who else?" he said matter-of-factly.

He thundered from the room, to his office. Jeanine followed behind him. He grabbed a rifle from a rack on the wall. He took bullets from a drawer and thrust them into his pants pocket.

"Well, I'm going after them *both*—Cameron *and* the Injun," he snarled. "I plan to see them share a hangin' rope!"

"You're going to form a posse?" Jeanine dared to ask.

"Hell no!" Fred half shouted. "I intend to take care of both those savages all by myself."

Jeanine went to Fred and separated his hair, where the lump protruded. "Are you sure you're able to, Uncle Fred?" she asked softly. "You've got quite a lump on your head. Cameron ought to be horsewhipped."

Fred turned with a start. He forked an eyebrow. "How'd you know which of the two critters gave me this bump on my head?" he snapped. "I never told you, Jeanine."

Jeanine blanched. She lowered her eyes, afraid that he would read the lie that she was about to tell. If she wasn't careful, he would know that it hadn't been another Indian who had helped Lone Wolf escape. Then it wouldn't take much for him to figure out the truth, especially if he *caught* her in lies.

"Why, Uncle Fred, you *did so* tell me," she murmured. "The very moment I walked into the room and found you.

You just don't remember. The blow to the head half robbed you of your senses, I guess."

Fred kneaded his brow. "I could've swore I only mentioned Cameron runnin' out on me," he mumbled. "I sure as hell don't remember tellin' you that he hit me over the head. Guess I'm in worse shape than I thought."

Then he frowned as he looked Jeanine up and down. "Now ain't those the same clothes you had on last night when you came to the jail fussin' over somethin' or other?" he said, taking a quick step around her. "Hell. It looks as though you slept in those clothes. It *is* the same outfit. Why, Jeanine? You usually take better care of your appearance than that."

For a moment Jeanine was at a loss for words, feeling cornered. If he looked close enough he would also see dark circles under her eyes and would know that she hadn't had much sleep. If he should pin her down, to exactness, what *could* she tell him?

She had to think fast to cover her tracks. She must protect Lone Wolf at all costs. Her uncle was now out for blood. If he suspected she had anything to do with Lone Wolf's escape, he might even add *her* to the list of those to be hanged.

"I didn't get much sleep last night, Uncle Fred," she said smoothly. She forced a light laugh, lifting the tail of her skirt, as though inspecting it. "And, no, I didn't change my clothes from last evening. I spent most of the night at the art musuem, preparing for an art showing. Since I was gone so many days, I had to work at least this one full night to get caught up."

"An art showing? Where?"

"In St. Paul."

"Oh? You haven't mentioned anything about that to me before. When *is* this art showing?"

Jeanine dropped the tail of her skirt and found the rest easy to say. In her mind she had practiced her deceitful plan throughout the night. It must look as though she was needed elsewhere for many days, or how could she ride into the forest, to be with Lone Wolf, and farther still, to go on and try to have that interview with Judith McMahon?

Her life was becoming one of lies and deceit. But her uncle was forcing her into this. If he were more understanding, less overbearing, then perhaps they could work together on this project of hers.

But it was his hatred of the Indians that stood in the way this time more than his desire to control *her* life. Some day she hoped to know the reason behind this drive of her uncle's to never give up on his hatred of Indians. . . .

"The art show in St. Paul?" she said, smiling sweetly up at her uncle, who still seemed to be studying her much too closely, as though he wasn't believing one word that she was saying. "Soon. I must leave tomorrow. I'll be gone for over a week. Is there a problem with that? You seem to have enough to do to keep you occupied while I plan to be gone. You won't even be in Duluth, yourself. Your search for Cameron and Lone Wolf should take you away from the city for several days, don't you think?"

She was finding it strange that she was not concerned about her uncle's plan to look for Lone Wolf. It was as though she knew that Lone Wolf knew well enough how to keep himself hidden.

As for Cameron, Jeanine hoped her uncle would find him and lock him up and throw away the key. It was Cameron who was now more a threat to Jeanine than anyone or anything else. If he was out there, loose, hating Fred Hunter for what he had done to him, he could just be awaiting the opportunity to accost Jeanine. It would be done out of spite now, for it was she who had forced her uncle's hand to discover Cameron's worthlessness!

The thought of running into Cameron while alone in the forest was chilling. Did she even dare set out on her own again . . . ? She would be with Lone Wolf only a short while. The rest of the time she would be traveling to Chief Strong Hawk's village alone, very vulnerable . . .

"The fact that you'll be away from here for a spell sets my mind at ease," Fred said, again moving around the room, gathering things together for his trip into the forest. "And by damn, you're much safer on a train goin' to St. Paul than stickin' around here. Until I get Lone Wolf and Cameron Tyner behind bars again you ain't safe, Jeanine. You bein' my niece makes it dangerous for you. I guess I don't have to paint a picture to explain why, do I?"

"No. Not really," Jeanine said, her eyes innocently wide.

"So you're leavin' when?"

"Probably early in the morning."

"Well, hon, take care of yourself."

"I will, Uncle Fred. I will."

Jeanine gave her uncle a quick kiss on the cheek then walked toward the door. She stopped and turned to face him. "Uncle Fred, *you* be careful," she murmured. "Please? Be careful."

Fred chuckled and waved her away with the brisk movement of a wrist. Jeanine went out into the early morning sun, the breeze soft on her face, like a caress. She looked in the direction of the forest, her heart anxious. Lone Wolf had said to meet him after two sunrises. One sunrise was now behind her. Only one to go. . . .

Nineteen

The night air was flavored with the musky odor of fallen leaves and dew-dampened grass. A sense of loneliness and isolation pressing in on her, Jeanine sat stiff and silent on her horse within a dark circle of bushes. Her eyes had grown accustomed to the blackness of night long ago, yet the wilderness of the thicket and trees of the forest were so black, she still could hardly see a foot ahead of her. The night was ghostly with sounds from an owl hooting in the distance and an occasional howl of a wolf tearing through the thick cover of trees.

Jeanine squirmed on her saddle. She had been waiting for Lone Wolf now for what seemed an eternity. She was beginning to worry that perhaps she had come to the wrong spot for the rendezvous with him. But she had been so careful to watch for familiar trees and bushes, she didn't see how she could be wrong. Perhaps Lone Wolf had decided against coming.

The fact was that he *was* free now. He could go on with

his life without her interference, that is if he *saw* her as an interference. The way he had kissed her good-bye, though, had spoken to her of very different feelings than that. Jeanine's insides warmed even now with the remembrance of his lips pressed hard into hers. It had been a kiss of possession . . . a kiss of fire. . . .

Afraid to let herself think of Lone Wolf in such a way, now thinking he might have played her for a fool since he had not arrived at the designated place and time, Jeanine forced herself to think of other things. She was glad that she was refreshed, ready for the journey ahead. After meeting with her uncle she had gone home and had slept the full day away. She had expected not to have the opportunity to rest so fully again for the next several days if everything that she planned came about.

Every nerve inside her was alive, anxious. Her eyes were rested, her stomach was filled with a hearty breakfast. Now if she could only get her mind relieved. If only Lone Wolf would arrive.

But if he didn't, she would travel onward, alone. She would go on to Chief Strong Hawk's village. She *would* meet with Judith McMahon! Yet she would have the constant worry of running across her uncle *and* Cameron Tyner. Her uncle thought that she was safely on her way to St. Paul. Cameron Tyner . . . ? Who could even venture to guess what was on his mind . . . ? He could be only a few feet away from her even now, watching her!

The thought of Cameron and what he might have planned for her sent a nervous tremor through Jeanine. She clutched her cape more securely about her neck and tucked loose strands of her hair back inside the hood, as though doing this could hide her from the world.

She had chosen to wear a plaid shirt, jeans, and boots on this journey north. She needed all possible defenses against the cold of the night and the briars along the trail that constantly seemed to be reaching out for her legs.

A horse snorting from somewhere close by drew Jeanine's attention from her wandering thoughts. She stiffened in the saddle; her eyes became two points of searching as she peered in all directions around her. She wanted to speak out, say Lone Wolf's name, to test and see if it was he who was approaching.

Yet she knew the dangers in doing that. If it was Lone Wolf, he would know where to find her without her saying anything to guide him to her.

If it was someone else, the person might pass on by her, the fact that she was there, hiding, remaining unnoticed.

Her heart thumping hard against her chest, she watched and listened. And then her shoulders slumped with relief when she saw the familiar outline of Lone Wolf approaching her on his beautiful stallion. They both blended so beautifully in the night . . . proud man atop as proud a steed!

It stirred Jeanine's insides into a familiar loving of this man who had stolen her heart . . . her sense of caution.

And then he was there beside her, his eyes telling her that which words were not required to say. He reached a hand and touched her cheek, then wheeled his horse around and began moving back in the direction from whence he had come without saying even that first word to her, knowing that she would follow.

Jeanine's horse's hooves squished in the sodden ground of the forest; her saddle creaked as she did follow him. She edged Daisy up next to Lone Wolf and glanced over at him, seeing how beautifully he was dressed for this occasion of being with her. His shirt was of buckskin, beautifully embroidered. His leggings were made of deerskin that fit tight to the leg, extending from the feet to the hips, and fastened to a belt that passed around the waist. A band worked with porcupine quills of richest dyes passed down the seam on the outer part of the leg and was fringed also along its whole length. His moccasins were buckskin, beautifully embroidered with porcupine quills.

And now that they had traveled away from the thick cover of trees and the full moon was beaming its silver rays, Jeanine could see the full detail of Lone Wolf's bow, slung across his one shoulder. It was of bone and as white and beautiful as ivory. Over its back was laid and firmly attached, a coating of deer's sinews which gave it elasticity and surely death to all that stood inimically before it. Its strings were three stranded and twisted of sinews. The quiver for the arrows that hung upon his back was made of panther's skin and charged with deadly arrows, feathered with hawk's and eagle's quills.

Though she was glad to have this opportunity to be with him again, and this time not as captive, Jeanine was becoming annoyed by his silence. He had yet to say one word to her. Being of a stubborn nature, she had not chosen to be the first to break this bond of silence between them. He seemed to be satisfied that she was there, agreeing to go with him. It was as if for now, that was all he needed to feed his desire of her.

And if she confessed the full truth of her feelings to herself, she would know that being with him in this same way was all that was needed even for herself at this time. She knew what would transpire later. The moments of silence would be followed by moments of sharing, and not only words, but touches and kisses as well.

They both had accepted, it seemed, this destiny that had brought them together, and would let it grow, as it would grow. . .

Even trust seemed to be a part of their sharing. She hoped to never give him reason to lose this trust.

Glancing down at her satchel secured at the side of her horse, Jeanine knew not to let Lone Wolf see its contents. She understood quite well his dislike of journals. She would not give him cause to burn *this* one. She would make sure this time that she was totally alone when she made her entries each day. Either while he slept, or while he hunted. . . .

The darkness of night had faded away and had been replaced by a bright day of sunshine and blue sky. But even this was changing back into night as the sun became only a small, orange disc on the horizon. A half night and full day of travel was behind them. They had stopped only long enough to take occasional drinks from streams, and to eat fruit and cheese that Jeanine had packed for the trip. And still they traveled onward.

This land through which they now ventured was different than Jeanine remembered the last time she had been this far north from Duluth. Time, wind, and water had created a rugged, beautiful landform of steep limestone bluffs, caves, streams and sinkholes. Some limestone cliffs towered over Jeanine and Lone Wolf, as high as eighty feet. Majestic red cedars, gnarled and bent by the passage of time, adorned the cliffs.

On the hillsides and fertile valleys could be seen Dutchman's breeches, trout lily, phlox and trillium. In the oak-hickory forest various flowering shrubs dotted the land.

A sudden gobble of a wild turkey made Jeanine turn her eyes toward Lone Wolf, to see if he would make chase. But she smiled to herself when she saw that he was too determined to get to his destination, to waste time on the hunt of a turkey.

And then he wheeled his horse around and faced Jeanine. "We have arrived," he said, gesturing with his hand toward space that did not show anything to Jeanine, other than just more covering of brush.

"Where?" she said, forking an eyebrow.

"Follow Lone Wolf," he said, his eyes twinkling. "It is a place formed through many, many years of rainwater filtering through leaves, rotting ground vegetation. The acidic groundwater slowly dissolved limestone, forming the cave in which I am about to take you."

Relieved to be there, Jeanine did not care where, only that they were there and she would be able to get off her horse. Her thighs felt glued to Daisy, her buttocks were numb.

Again she found herself following Lone Wolf without questioning him. She bent low, clinging about Daisy's neck, beneath low, jagged rocks clustered green with vines.

They rode deeper and deeper into vegetation where the ground now slanted lower and lower. A rush of cold air warned Jeanine just before entering a great mouth of a cave. At the far end she could see another vast tunnel of light turning orange from the lower creeping sunset.

Lone Wolf rode through the darkness of the cave, toward the light. Jeanine followed behind him, wincing when droplets of water splashed down onto her bare head from the cave roof, her cape and its protective hood having been shed early in the morning, when the sun had become almost unbearable in its heat.

A flutter overhead caused Jeanine to emit a low shriek when a bird suddenly dipped low, then flew away again into the darkness.

With a heavy sigh of relief, Jeanine led Daisy out into the light where Lone Wolf was already dismounting his stallion beside a luscious, wide stream shaded by immense, towering elms. Their limbs hung low over the water on either side, as though they were giant umbrellas.

"We are safe from all who search for us now," Lone Wolf said. He went to Jeanine and eased her reins from her tired, aching fingers. "*Mah-bee-szhon*. Come. Dismount. You build a fire while I draw net from water which should now be filled with fish. We will eat and enjoy each other's company at leisure."

His dark eyes grew moody. "Are you happy or sad you have come?" he added. "The day was long in the saddle, was it not?"

Jeanine smiled down at him warmly. "I am glad I came," she murmured. She laughed lightly, rubbing her aching rear end. "But I must admit, I *will* be glad to get out of this saddle. The day *was* long. I didn't think we'd ever get here."

Her insides trembled as he placed his hands to her waist and helped her from the horse, to the ground. His eyes drew an amused glint into them as he raked them over her. "You are dressed strangely," he said chuckling low. "You wear man's breeches? It is the first time Lone Wolf sees a woman dressed as a man."

His fingers wove through her hair as his gaze moved upward. "But even so, you are still *mee-kah-wah-diz-ee*," he said huskily. "My woman, you are always beautiful."

Slowly he drew her into his arms. His lips were sweetly warm as he tested her with teasing kisses along the planes of her face, driving Jeanine wild with desire. Twining her arms about his neck she encouraged his lips to hers and fit herself into the hardness of his body, having known all along that the long ride would be worth it. She would ride to the ends of the earth, it seemed, now, for just a single kiss from his beautifully shaped lips.

Oh, that he would have never found and taken her captive! She would have never known such heaven as this. To think of parting from him again was almost too much to bear.

Yet as soon as he knew where she must go next, he would perhaps even hate her. But she *must* travel onward, to talk with Judith McMahon. Jeanine never started something unless she finished it. Hopefully Lone Wolf would one day understand.

But there was just now. She would relish this time with him. She would absorb each and every touch, each and every kiss, as though they were the last. . . .

And then he drew away from her, his fingers tracing the outline of her breasts that strained against the cotton of her shirt. "You have not questioned me again about how it was that I was at Silver Fox's house," he said thickly, his eyes touching her breasts, as though they were his bare fingers. "You trust me so much, Jeanine? You came with me, yet not knowing for sure it was not I who killed Silver Fox? You even helped me escape from your uncle's jail?"

His hands framed her face, then tilted it so that their eyes could meet and lock. "Do you love me so much that you let trust grow stronger between us?" he said softly.

"I love you. I *trust* you," Jeanine said hoarsely. "You know that I couldn't have gone against my uncle's wishes unless I felt both things strongly for you, Lone Wolf. Do you trust me . . . love me . . . as *much*?" Her gaze shifted momentarily to the satchel, then back to Lone Wolf.

"Trust is earned, is it not?" Lone Wolf said, lowering a soft kiss to her nose.

"Yes . . ." Jeanine said in an almost whisper.

"Then we will not talk about Silver Fox or why I was there?"

"Not if you don't want to."

Lone Wolf swung away from her, smiling widely. "You prepare fire while I pull net from water," he again said to her in more a request than an order. "We will have feast. Then we will enjoy the peacefulness of the campfire as though we were one."

Jeanine stretched her weary arms then looked about her and found where he had earlier formed a firepit with rocks placed in a wide circle where in the center were gray, cold ash. Close by he had already piled firewood. All that was required of her was to place it in the center of the rocks and get the fire started.

She strolled to the firepit, feeling contentedly happy, this time free of the dreaded word captive while in Lone Wolf's presence. He still had not told her valid reasons for her earlier captivity. They were two who trusted, yet who held secrets from the other. Perhaps one day they would not have reason to hide full truths from the other. But until then, she had something to accomplish as, it seemed, did *he*.

Bending to her knees, Jeanine began placing wood in the firepit, yet absorbed now in watching Lone Wolf and what he was doing. Before he had left to meet her he had set out a net of nettlestalk twine with stone sinkers and cedar floats. Now he was pulling in the net and, as he had hoped, it was filled with fish.

The fire was now in full flame. A skillet with fish cooking inside it simmered over the fire. Jeanine and Lone Wolf sat arm-in-arm, waiting for the delicacy to be cooked through and through. The sky was now dark overhead; frogs croaked from the stream.

"It's so peaceful here," Jeanine sighed. "How did you know of such a place?"

"Lone Wolf knows many secret places," he said huskily. Then he grew silent.

"What's wrong, Lone Wolf?" Jeanine asked softly. "You seem troubled."

"I cannot stay here with you past this one night," he said, staring into the flames of the fire. Then he moved his gaze slowly to her. "But you will wait for my return, will you not? I would be gone for only one day and night. Then Lone Wolf will return and make you happy for many days and nights while your uncle is making a fool of himself searching through the forest not finding me."

Jeanine fidgeted nervously. She had her *own* destination. She so badly wanted to go to Judith McMahon and get the information she needed for the book, then get on with the rest of her life which, hopefully, would include Lone Wolf!

"But where must you go?" she blurted.

"If I told you, you would not understand," Lone Wolf said, plucking a blade of grass, thrusting it between his lips.

"Tell me. I will try to understand."

Lone Wolf gazed down at her. He studied her deeply with his fathomless, dark eyes. "It is something you cannot understand," he said softly. "It is something I do not understand even *myself*."

Jeanine shook her head. "Lone Wolf, you are speaking in circles," she sighed. "If this is something you don't understand, why do it?"

"It is required of me," he said, taking the blade of grass from his lips, tossing it away from him. "As it is, I may even now be too late. Silver Fox's spirit is already fast traveling to the shades of his father, toward the setting sun."

Jeanine paled. She leaned away from Lone Wolf. "Silver . . . Fox . . . ?" she said in a bare whisper.

Lone Wolf turned to her and clasped his fingers to her shoulders. "I will tell you this but nothing more," he said flatly. "I must go and be witness to burial rites of Silver Fox if I am not even now too late. Then I will return and be with you."

Jeanine's thoughts were spinning, full of wonder. Why would Lone Wolf want to go to Giles Thomas's—Silver Fox's—funeral? Was it guilt? Yet, it had to be something more. She was always forgetting that Lone Wolf had been outside Giles's house when Giles had shot himself. There had to be a reason for that. Would she ever know what?

But for now, her thoughts were turned to a sweet spinning as Lone Wolf stretched her out on the ground and kissed her ardently. The smell of food cooking and the mystery of Lone Wolf's connection with Silver Fox took second place in this night of aroused senses. . . .

Twenty

Lone Wolf eased away from Jeanine and began to loosen the buttons of her blouse. His smoke black eyes were charged with growing passion. Jeanine looked up at him, the glow from the fire illuminating his finely chiseled features.

With trembling fingers she reached and began untying the leather strings that held his fringed shirt in place. As his powerful chest was revealed to her in its total smoothness, all the hair having been carefully plucked as was the custom of the Indians, she scooted the shirt back and over his wide shoulders, then let it drop to the ground behind him.

Running her hands over his chest, Jeanine reveled in the touch of him, quite aware that her blouse was removed and that her breasts were free. She quivered sensually when Lone Wolf reached and cupped both her breasts within the palms of his hands. She closed her eyes and sighed when his thumbs circled her nipples, causing them to harden against them.

Lone Wolf gazed down at Jeanine with the same haunting desire that had plagued him since that first time he had seen her. He was seeing her long, drifting hair spread out on the ground like a black, silken halo, and her slim, sinuous body almost begging for him to again fully possess her. He could not believe that she had come so willingly with him. But he would not worry about the whys of it, just that she was there.

Smoothing his hands downward, he removed the rest of her clothes and her boots until she lay perfectly nude beneath him.

His eyes savored her invitingly rounded breasts, her narrow and supple waist and slim thighs, her long and silken calves. If ever there was a perfect specimen of a woman, Lone Wolf knew that he had found her. Even if her . . . skin . . . was white. . . .

Forgetting what was required of him in only a matter of hours, that he hoped to at least witness from afar the burial of his brother because they *did* have the same blood running through their veins, Lone Wolf lost himself in the moment.

Rising to his feet, he stood over Jeanine and slowly began removing his fringed leggings. He watched her as she lay there looking up at him, proud to see passion in her eyes. And when she smiled up at him as he stepped fully from his clothes, revealing his ready hardness to her, he knew that she welcomed this time of building pleasure with him.

It was the look in her eyes and her smile as sweet as a child's that made Lone Wolf truly believe that she was with him only because she desired to be. They loved as surely no other man and woman did! It was their destiny *to* love.

Lone Wolf would not let remembrances of a white woman stealing his father away from his lovely mother stand in his way of what his body and heart ached for. That was another time . . . another place. This was now. There was no Chippewa maiden being slighted by Lone Wolf loving a white woman. There had been no special woman *until* Jeanine. Nor would there ever be, *again*. He would not let guilt stand in the way of what he desired. He would not let the color of her skin stand in the way of what he would *have*!

Bending to his knees over Jeanine, supporting himself on each side of her with the palms of his hands pressed against the ground, Lone Wolf welcomed her fingers that were again searching his body. His flesh quivered beneath her gentleness. Their eyes were locked, their smiles were true.

Lone Wolf could wait no longer. He knelt lower and spread himself gently atop her. Twining his fingers through her hair, he brought her lips against his and kissed her with intensity as he slowly nudged her thighs apart with the persuasion of a knee.

Jeanine shuddered as she felt his hardness softly probe, then enter her. Surely her heart had been momentarily misplaced, for where he was now taking gentle strokes inside her, she could feel a pulsing. It was a feeling of heat rushing, sending delicious shivers of desire throughout her.

And then he cupped her swelling breasts. His mouth searing hers, his tongue was a warm probe as it entered between her lips, searching hers out, until they met, exploring the other. Jeanine clung to his sinewed shoulders. She locked her ankles together behind him and rode with him, again taken down the road to stormy rapture.

"My *ee-quay*," Lone Wolf whispered as he drew his lips from hers, breathing the sweet scent of her breasts as he placed his face there. "My *mee-kah-wah-diz-ee ee-quay*."

Jeanine knew not what he had just said but the husky tone of his voice spoke of his intense passion for her and that was enough. She bent her neck and gently kissed his brow. "I so love you," she whispered. "Lone Wolf . . . Lone Wolf . . ."

Lone Wolf slowed his thrusts and leaned up away from Jeanine. He smiled down at her. "The night speaks to you in a loveliness," he said softly, seeing how the moon's beams had found entrance between the thick canopy of leaves overhead, setting Jeanine's face aglow with its silver light. He caressed her face with the tips of his forefingers. "You are wedded to the moon and stars this night, my woman. One day you will be wedded to *Lone Wolf.*"

His words thrilled, yet frightened Jeanine. She could not ever envision life without him, now that she knew the feelings they shared. Yet could she give up her career, the life of freedom that she had built for herself?

She had never expected to meet a man who could take precedence over these important aspects of her life. But she had never thought she'd meet a man like *Lone Wolf. He* had made all the difference in her life, in her decisions.

To be his wife! Oh, to be his forever! To wake up each morning with him at her side. Could there ever be anything as beautifully perfect? His hands always there to caress her. His lips always there, to send her into a tailspin of pleasure . . . ?

Yes, she would give up everything for him. But when . . . ? She wasn't quite ready. She had things to accomplish. A book to write . . . lectures to carry to children who hungered to learn! Even Lone Wolf didn't seem all that ready. He had things yet to conquer. Oh, in time . . . in time . . .

Placing an arm about her, Lone Wolf drew Jeanine briskly against his hard frame and kissed her with a wildness, almost even that which could be defined as savage. Jeanine's lips ached beneath the pressure. His teeth even seemed to be cutting into her.

Yet this made her desire him more. She arched her hips upward and met his deep thrusts. Almost frantic with the need of him, she dug her fingernails into the flesh of his shoulders. She moaned against his lips as the fingers of his free hand circled her breast and squeezed, making it swell into his palm.

Jeanine had never felt so alive. Her breath quickened as she felt the pleasure build more intensely and spread through her in fiery splashes. Lone Wolf's lips left her mouth. He lay his cheek against hers as he groaned in his found release.

Lone Wolf's body quivering into hers, Jeanine felt the momentary loss of sense of time and place, as the wonders of pleasure also engulfed her in their wondrous splashes of warmth. She seemed to glow from the rapture.

And then it was over, that moment which sometimes could be measured as surely only a fantasy when over and done with, for it was always much too short a time of pleasure. But that seemed to make the next time even more looked forward to. Jeanine even now, as she lay limply in Lone Wolf's arms, dreamed of a next time, wondering *when*. Would they even be given a chance to be together again? There could be so many obstacles getting in the way. Her uncle . . . ? Cameron Tyner . . . ? This strange connection of Lone Wolf with Giles Thomas . . . Silver Fox . . . ?

As Lone Wolf eased away from Jeanine to spread out on his bare back on the thick cushion of grass beside the fire, Jeanine turned to face him. She leaned up on an elbow. "Lone Wolf, why *would* you want to go to Giles Thomas's funeral?" she blurted, without thinking further about it. "By going back to Duluth you will be placing yourself in mortal danger. Should you be seen . . ."

Lone Wolf frowned at her. He then pushed himself up from the ground and quickly dressed, ignoring her question. Once fully dressed he stooped onto his haunches and removed the frying pan with its sizzling fish from the fire and set it down on the ground beside two wooden platters.

Frustrated by his choice not to talk with her again, his times of silence always so annoying to her, Jeanine followed his lead and quickly dressed. She then plopped down on the ground beside the fire and nodded a thank-you to him when he offered her a platter of fish, then sat down beside her and began eating heartily.

Jeanine took several bites, enjoying the savory juices of the fish as it blended onto her tongue, then gave Lone Wolf a silent, questioning stare.

And then she couldn't keep quiet any longer. She set the platter down on the ground and turned to face Lone Wolf, positioning herself onto her knees. Gently touching his cheek, she pleaded with her eyes. "Lone Wolf, you *can't* return to Duluth," she softly encouraged. "I was able to release you from jail *once*. But I wouldn't be given the opportunity again. In fact, if you were caught, they wouldn't hesitate to hang you *then*. You wouldn't be given that second chance to escape, Lone Wolf. Surely you know that."

Lone Wolf placed his empty platter on the ground and gently took Jeanine's wrists and drew her to him. "You think Lone Wolf a foolish Chippewa?" he said, amusement in his eyes. "Duluth is not my destination. Lone Wolf understands the dangers there."

"But you said you were going to Silver Fox's funeral," Jeanine softly argued. She was again feeling the passion weaving between them, her breasts crushed against his chest, his breath so enticingly warm on her face, his lips so close. . . .

"Lone Wolf said nothing about funeral."

"But I'm certain you *did*."

"Lone Wolf speaks of burial *rites*."

"But isn't that the same as a *funeral*?"

"White man's funeral?"

"Yes."

"*Gah-ween*," Lone Wolf said, shaking his head. "No. No white man's funeral. It will be Chippewa burial *rites*. No Chippewa, no matter if Chippewa lived as white, would be buried in white man's ceremony. Silver Fox will return to his people in death. He will be buried as *Chippewa*, in Chippewa *fashion*, in Chippewa *village*."

Jeanine's heart skipped a beat. "Are you saying that you are going to go to Chief Strong Hawk's village of Chippewa?" she dared to ask, knowing the possibilities for her if this were true. She still didn't know the exact location of the village. Now might she? If Lone Wolf could direct her . . . ?

"*Ay-uh,* that is so," Lone Wolf said thickly. "But only to observe from afar. No one will even know that I am there."

Jeanine frowned in wonder up at him. "Will I ever understand why you must do this?" she murmured. "Why or how you even know Giles Thomas? Lone Wolf, surely his people think you are responsible for his death. Should they find you close by, what would *they* even do?"

Lone Wolf's thoughts returned to that night, when he had foolishly entered the white man's dwelling and picked up the revolver. He was remembering, in his minds's eye, that look on Danette Thomas's face, a look of total accusation. Even when she spoke to him it had been in an accusing tone. If she had been a part of the Chippewa way of life so long, how could she think one Chippewa could take the life of another so easily? Without reason?

What did Strong Hawk think now? Was Lone Wolf a condemned man inside Strong Hawk's mind and heart, without even questioning him to find out the truth? Would his remorse over the loss of a brother blind Strong Hawk to his sense of logic where Lone Wolf was concerned?

What *if* Strong Hawk discovered Lone Wolf close by, observing the burial rites? What would he do? And what, even, would Lone Wolf say as to why he was there, a mourner . . . himself . . . ?

Jeanine jerked free of Lone Wolf and doubled her fists onto her lap. "Lone Wolf, you almost drive me insane with your moments of silence," she said hotly. "Sometimes it goes way further than moments. It goes on forever. Why do you do this to me? Why are you so quiet now?"

Then her tone softened. She splayed her fingers onto her thighs and leaned closer to Lone Wolf. "Or is it because I cause awkward moments for you by questioning you so much about things you do not wish to speak about?" she said softly, her eyes searching his face for answers. Her insides melted when his dark eyes met hers in a gentle warmth. "Lone Wolf, I never want to make you feel awkward. I love you. I *love* you. But please don't shut me out. Love me as much. Talk to me. Whatever you tell me won't go any further. Honest, Lone Wolf. Honest."

Lone Wolf's eyes grew instantly cold. His gaze shifted as he looked toward her satchel, then back into her eyes. "You bring journal again on your journey north?" he said thickly.

Jeanine paled. She eased away from him and sat down beside him. Nervously she raised her knees before her and clasped her arms about them and hugged them to her chest. She stared into the fire, afraid to answer him, but she knew that she must.

"And if I did?" she said, still avoiding his eyes.

"It is because of this that Lone Wolf cannot tell you all truths *about* Lone Wolf," he said, rising angrily to his feet. "If you must write of Chippewa, you write of other Chippewa. Not Lone Wolf!"

He turned on his heel and glared down at her. "It is now time to sleep," he said flatly. "Sunrises come quickly. Lone Wolf will be gone by sunrise."

In a near state of numbness Jeanine watched Lone Wolf spread blankets and furs on the ground beside the fire, ignoring her as though she weren't even there. And when he spread himself comfortably atop these, ignoring her as though she didn't even exist, she quickly decided what tomorrow would also bring for her at sunrise. As soon as Lone Wolf left, she would also. She would follow him. She would *also* silently observe the Chippewa burial rites! She would finally know the location of Strong Hawk's village!

Smiling mischievously, feeling smug, Jeanine got her bedroll from Daisy and soon had herself also comfortably bedded for the night. Sleep came easy for her. It had been a long, arduous day. Tomorrow . . . ?

Twenty-One

Jeanine coaxed Daisy through the thick underbrush, only far enough behind Lone Wolf so that he did not know that she was following him. The sponge of leaves beneath her horse's hooves silenced its approach; an occasional reassuring caress of Daisy's thick mane kept her horse from nervously whinnying.

But Jeanine's lips, parched from thirst, made her realize that Daisy was surely almost as thirsty and knew that time must be spent in stopping to quench both their thirsts. Yet there was more than one risk in doing this. Jeanine could lose sight of Lone Wolf and become quickly lost, *and* the sudden appearance of her Uncle Fred *or* Cameron Tyner was always a constant threat. Though the forest was widespread in all directions, her Uncle Fred and Cameron could be anywhere . . . anytime. . . .

Softly moaning, Jeanine squirmed on her saddle. Her bones ached, her head throbbed. She *must* stop, not only to get a drink of water, but to stretch out the tightness of her body. The stream that snaked through the forest not that far from where Jeanine traveled teased her with its fresh, clear water.

"I *must* . . ." Jeanine whispered, urging Daisy in that direction. "It will only take a moment."

Reining her horse in beside the shine of the water, Jeanine quickly dismounted. Daisy dipped her head down and eagerly refreshed herself with deep gulps. Jeanine fell to her knees and sank her cupped hands into the water and brought them to her mouth and enjoyed the coolness as the wetness crept down her dry throat. She then bent her head down closer to the water and splashed several handfuls onto her face.

But fearing losing Lone Wolf altogether, Jeanine rose back to her feet quickly. She cringed when Daisy snorted a greeting to her, then whinnied.

"Be quiet, Daisy," Jeanine whispered, running her hand down her mare's thick, brown mane. Placing a foot in a stirrup she got herself halfway up to the saddle when she heard the approach of a horse and the familiarity of a voice that suddenly spoke from close behind her.

"Jeanine, what the hell . . . ?" Fred Hunter grumbled, his thick eyebrows arching. "What the hell are you doin' here? I thought you were in St. Paul."

Jeanine was so startled she lost her footing. She fell backward and landed on the ground with a loud thump. The pain in her backside quickly reached her brain and caused her to emit a loud cry of pain.

Then she looked up at her uncle guiltily as he rode up next to her, glowering down at her with his cold, green eyes.

"Hello, Uncle Fred," she said, smiling up at him sheepishly. "Fancy meeting *you* here."

"Jokes? You think my findin' you here calls for jokin' around with me?" Fred half shouted, flailing a hand in the air. "God-damn, Jeanine, what the hell *are* you doin' here?"

* * *

Lone Wolf's ears caught the sound of voices. He tensed, suddenly recognizing them both. One was Jeanine's uncle's . . . the other was *Jeanine's*! Why had she followed him? He had ordered her to stay behind, to wait for his return!

Confused, Lone Wolf drew his stallion to a quick halt and dismounted. After he secured his horse's reins on a low limb of a tree, he moved stealthily toward the sound of the voices. His right hand went instinctively to the knife sheathed at his waist. He knew the dangers of being seen by Fred Hunter. It was apparent that this sheriff would only be this far from Duluth because of Lone Wolf!

Lone Wolf's life was being threatened by Fred Hunter's presence. And was not Lone Wolf's woman being threatened also? Fred Hunter was using white man's curse words on her now. His voice held an ugly threat within it as he shouted at her. Her uncle would never understand why Jeanine had accompanied Lone Wolf into the forest, to be with him.

Did Lone Wolf even understand? Had she done it to only use him again? Didn't the fact that she was following him to Strong Hawk's village prove that?

His heart ached with the thought that his woman was someone he would possibly never know, definitely would never *understand*.

Fred quickly dismounted and stood over Jeanine threateningly. "You lied to me," he growled. He grabbed her by a wrist and yanked her to her feet.

Paling, Jeanine felt the scald of her uncle's eyes as he continued to glare at her. "Uncle Fred, had I told you what I had planned, you would have only thrown a fit and tried to stop me," she said in a tone of apology. She cast a troubled look in the direction of the forest, where she knew that Lone Wolf was traveling. Thank God her uncle had seen *her* first instead of Lone Wolf. But Lone Wolf was still not all that safe! Her uncle's loud voice carried wide and far! What if Lone Wolf heard . . . ?

"You know of my determination to gather research material for my new book," she blurted, looking frantically into her uncle's rage-filled eyes. "If you don't give your approval, then I must continue to do what I must *without* it."

"But to downright lie?" Fred said, tightening his hold on her wrist.

Anger was rising quickly inside Jeanine for both the rough treatment from her uncle *and* his continuing to treat her as something less than a woman. She was no longer a child. Would he ever see that?

Yanking herself free, Jeanine stormed away from him and stubbornly placed her back to him. "Uncle Fred, I don't have to ask why *you're* here, do I?" she said shallowly. "You're still searching for Lone Wolf, aren't you?"

"Hell, yes!" Fred stormed. "He's a murderin' bastard. I plan to hunt him down and kill him. I'm not going to bother with hangin' the sonofabitch."

Jeanine turned with a start. Her eyes wavered. "You . . . plan . . . to shoot him if you find him?" she gasped. "Just like that? You won't give him a chance to prove his innocence?"

"Innocent?" Fred said, kneading his chin. "Since when do you think he's innocent?"

Then he recalled how she had at first defended Lone Wolf that night at the jail. Hadn't she changed her opinion strangely fast that night? Something seemed amiss here. Why hadn't he wondered about it earlier?

"Jeanine . . ." Fred began, but the sound of a twig breaking close by behind him caused the hair to rise fearfully at the nape of his neck. And when he saw Jeanine's eyes widen in recognition as she looked on past him, Fred wondered *why*?

Words stuck in Jeanine's throat when she saw Lone Wolf suddenly there behind her uncle. She saw the initial threat here! Her uncle had said that he planned to shoot and kill Lone Wolf!

Oh, Lord, she had to warn Lone Wolf!

She placed her hands to her throat, still unable to speak. She glanced from Lone Wolf, to her Uncle Fred. She watched almost painfully as her uncle swung around and drew his pistol from its holster. . . .

"No!" Jeanine then managed to scream. She flung herself at her uncle and grabbed for the pistol. As its cold steel made contact with her hand and she was able to knock it from her uncle's grip, she recoiled and screamed again when the blast of gunfire exploded in the air.

Jeanine's insides grew numb when she heard the gurgle of surprised pain erupt from deeply inside her uncle and saw that the stray bullet had ripped through her uncle's clothes at his right shoulder.

In mute horror, she watched her uncle slowly crumple to the ground, clutching at his shoulder, where blood poured profusely from the fresh wound.

Jeanine trembled as she dropped to her knees beside him. "Uncle Fred!" she cried, desperate now that her uncle's eyes were closed. Was . . . he . . . dying . . . ? "Oh, Lord, I didn't *mean* to . . . !"

Lone Wolf stared in disbelief from Jeanine to her uncle. He was filled with many emotions—rage, hate, surprise . . . *love*. . . .

Jeanine had saved Lone Wolf's life, yet while doing so, could now lose her *uncle*. Though Lone Wolf had many questions to ask Jeanine, he knew they would have to be asked later. He must tend to her uncle for *her*, because he knew that she would want him to. She would find it hard to live with the fact that if her uncle died, she would have caused his death.

Lone Wolf went to Jeanine. With gentle hands he eased her away from Fred Hunter.

"Tear some of your shirt away and give it to me," Lone Wolf said thickly, dropping to his haunches beside Fred. He glared down at the white man who was in this area only because he wanted Lone Wolf dead. Would he still, once he knew that Lone Wolf was helping to save his life?

Could Lone Wolf's kindness prove to the white man once and for all that Lone Wolf was innocent of the accused crime?

Seeing the blood still seeping from the wound and how Fred was paling, Lone Wolf gave Jeanine a stern glance. "*Wee-weeb*! Hurry! We must get the bleeding stopped!"

Jeanine looked disbelievingly at Lone Wolf. He was helping her uncle even though he had to know what her uncle had planned for *him*. This Indian whom she loved continued to reveal to her in many ways that he was, oh, so very, very special.

"*Wee-weeb*!" Lone Wolf persisted, making pressure on the wound with the palm of his hand.

Jeanine seemed to awaken from the shock of the moment. She nodded to Lone Wolf. Ripping the tailend of her shirt away, she handed it to Lone Wolf. She watched him remove her uncle's shirt, then wad up the piece of her shirt that she had given him, to hold over the seeping wound.

"*Gee-ah-bi*!" Lone Wolf ordered, watching Fred's eyes begin to flutter open and draw a look of dread into their depths when he discovered Lone Wolf there, tending to his wound.

Lone Wolf's shoulders squared, understanding the white man's look of terror . . . a man who saw all Indians as savages. It was only right that this white man should be afraid! If not for Jeanine, Lone Wolf would be tempted to let the heartless man die! Fred Hunter was a white man who was looking at Lone Wolf even at this moment as though Lone Wolf were a . . . savage!

"*Gee-ah-bi*," Lone Wolf again said to Jeanine.

Jeanine squinted and shook her head. "Please speak to me in English," she murmured. "I don't know what you are asking of me."

Lone Wolf nodded toward Fred's shirt. "More. I need more bandages," he said dryly. "Rip shreds away. Tie some together so they will be long enough to wrap around your uncle's body, to secure them in place."

"Yes . . . I see . . ." Jeanine said, nervously ripping her uncle's shirt into strips. Her fingers trembled as she began tying these pieces together. She sighed with relief after handing the strips to Lone Wolf and seeing that her uncle was awake, looking up at her.

"He will be alright," Lone Wolf reassured, securing the last strip of cloth about Fred's thick chest. "The gunshot did no mortal damage. The bullet is no threat. It passed through the other side and is now gone."

"Thank God," Jeanine sighed, smiling down at her uncle. But her smile quickly faded when Fred's eyes closed again and his breathing became shallow.

"Lone Wolf!" she softly cried. "Uncle Fred. He's lapsed into some sort of unconsciousness. He . . . he is not breathing normally."

Lone Wolf checked Fred's wound again. Then he looked deeply into Jeanine's eyes. "We will take him to my village. Pale Dove knows magical ways of treating all kinds of wounds," he reassured, knowing that he must cast all anger at Jeanine aside for following him. She had been put through enough this day without adding to her burden of anguish. He would scold her later . . . when they were alone in his wigwam!

Tears silvered Jeanine's eyes. She placed a hand to Lone Wolf's cheek. "You would do this for my uncle?" she said, choking on a sob.

"I do this for *you*," Lone Wolf said. "Only for *you*."

"But, Lone Wolf, you were on your way to Strong Hawk's village. . . ." she dared to say.

"As were you. . . ." he said dryly.

Jeanine felt a cold splash of apprehension touch her all over. For a few moments there she had forgotten that Lone Wolf had reason to be angry at her . . . to even love her less, for he knew that she had tricked him. She knew to expect to have to answer to him very soon. . . .

Lone Wolf saw the wavering of her eyes and understood. "Let us not talk of Strong Hawk or why you or I were traveling there," he said, knowing that fate was surely leading him away from Silver Fox's burial rites. He would not question or argue with fate. "Let us take your uncle to my village so that Pale Dove can use her special skills with medicines."

Jeanine wiped a stream of tears away from her face, then eased into Lone Wolf's arms. "Thank you," she murmured. "Thank you. . . ."

Twenty-Two

The village was hushed with a strained, puzzled silence when Lone Wolf entered, dragging the makeshift travois that he had made behind his stallion, upon which lay Fred Hunter in a deep, troubled sleep. Jeanine rode beside Lone Wolf. She glanced down at her uncle, cringing when she saw how the blood had seeped through his bandages. Though Lone Wolf had tried to reassure her that her uncle wasn't all that badly wounded, Jeanine was beginning to doubt that. Her uncle lay much too quietly, breathing much too shallowly. He needed a doctor, *not* the herbs that Lone Wolf said would be used on his wound.

But Duluth *and* its doctors were much too far away. Her uncle surely couldn't survive such a journey. Jeanine had no choice but to let Pale Dove try her Indian magic on her uncle. Then perhaps in a few days she could take her uncle on to Duluth.

The farther the silent procession of two traveled into the village with the travois, Indians stepped aside and made space for them. Lone Wolf looked straight ahead, uneasy for having to bring the white man into his village for any reason. This white man had shown his hatred for Indians! He had even hunted Lone Wolf as though he were a mad dog . . . *ay-uh*, a *savage*.

But the white man was special to Lone Wolf's woman. Lone Wolf must see that he survived the wound she had inflicted. If not, his woman could very easily carry blame inside her heart forever. To be free to love, Lone Wolf's woman must not be filled with remorseful torments and regrets!

Lone Wolf's spine stiffened, now again wondering if even she did truly love him. If he could only cast all doubts aside! But he could not help but wonder over and over again if she knew the art of deceit too well. Did she only . . . pretend to love him to get information *from* him?

Yet, he could not recall one instant when she had tried to prod him for answers that she would seek for a book. From the very beginning she had not seemed to be using him, unless she had made love with him only to know what it was like to be with a Chippewa!

But could she not accuse him of the same? From the beginning, when he had taken her captive, he had done so to learn *of* her, hadn't he? Perhaps he was being unfair to accuse her of that which he was guilty of himself!

Her main interest for her book seemed to lie with another band of Chippewa. Strange how fate had brought Lone Wolf and Jeanine together! Besides sharing love, Lone Wolf and Jeanine shared more than one mutual interest . . . they shared not only their love for one another, but also the wonder of the St. Croix Band of Chippewa!

Pale Dove's wigwam came into view where she stood with wonder in her eyes as Lone Wolf continued to move toward her with the trailing, dragging travois, then reined in his stallion close beside her. Dismounting, he went and stood over Pale Dove, his face solemn.

"Lone Wolf must ask favor of Pale Dove," he said

thickly, gently lifting a hand to touch the frailness of her cheek.

Pale Dove looked up into Lone Wolf's fathomless, dark eyes, then looked down at Fred. "*Way-nen-dush-win-ah-ow*?" she asked softly. Then she glanced up at Jeanine, tensing. "White woman with the pretty name Jeanine returns as captive, Lone Wolf?" She again looked up at Lone Wolf, imploring him with her eyes. "You bring *two* captives this time?"

Lone Wolf smiled down at Pale Dove warmly. He understood how she might think Jeanine and her uncle might be captives. Was that not even what the rest of the village of Chippewa was thinking? Is that not why everyone had become so still, even dropped their daily chores to look upon these two who entered with Lone Wolf, one injured, the other familiar from the other time she had been there?

"*Gah-ween*, no," he chuckled. He gave Jeanine an amused glance. He turned and went to her and helped her down from her horse then strolled with her back to Pale Dove, his arm possessively about her waist. "White woman not captive, Pale Dove. Nor is her uncle. They are here willingly."

He then broke away from Jeanine and went to Fred and knelt down on a knee beside him. "The favor Lone Wolf asks of you, Pale Dove, is that you look after this white man and medicate him with your special herbs until he is well enough to travel back to his people." He untied the leather bindings that had been placed around Fred to secure him on the travois for the long journey back to Lone Wolf's village.

"Lone Wolf even asks that you let the white man stay in your wigwam while you are treating him. No Shaman will be called. Only you, Pale Dove, will perform your magic. White man will accept gentle young girl with her magic more than a Shaman that he would not understand, might even *fear*." He glanced up at her. "Is that understood, Pale Dove? Do you agree to help white man?"

Pale Dove looked from Lone Wolf to Jeanine. "He is white woman's blood relative?" she murmured.

"*Ay-uh.*"

"Then Pale Dove will gladly treat white man."

Jeanine's insides warmed with love for Pale Dove. She went to her and embraced her. "Thank you," she sighed. "Thank you so much."

Pale Dove beamed in the embrace of Jeanine. She had begun to idolize this white woman who knew the skills of books, paper, and writing tools. The white woman had even been generous enough to take the time to teach Pale Dove how to write her name! *Ay-uh*, Pale Dove idolized her. She would do anything for her. Anything!

Lone Wolf tested the bandages around Fred's chest. "Pale Dove, go inside and prepare a place for white man," he ordered quietly. "Place the bed close beside your fire. He must be kept warm at all times."

"*Ay-uh*," Pale Dove said, nodding. She eased away from Jeanine and hurried toward the entrance flap and lifted it, then turned and tilted her head, questioning Lone Wolf with her doeful eyes. "How did white man become injured?"

Lone Wolf's eyes drew within them a coldness. His jaw became tight. He gave Pale Dove a look that caused a chill to ripple up her spine, making her understand that she should not ask him any more questions. She was only to do as instructed. Perhaps she would find out the answers later.

Scurrying on inside, Pale Dove began to place cedar boughs close beside her firespace and covered them with mats, then blankets. Jeanine followed along behind her into the wigwam. The roof sloped both ways from the peak and there were two posts set into the ground to hold the roof solid. Cords of string were strung between these posts and weighed down by all manner of skins and baskets of woven grass.

The fire was in the center of the lodge, set in a little depression, outlined with cobblestones shaped in a perfect circle. Back from the center and about a third of the distance from the rear was an altar upon which was burning incense believed to be pleasing to the dream totems, the sun and the Great Spirit, Wenebojo. It was said that the smoke from the altar rises when these mysteries are spoken to.

On the north side of the lodge was Pale Dove's personal bed, padded beneath with grass and pelts. Upon these rested a thick pad of old blankets. Over these, better blankets had been placed, and also many pillows stuffed with hair and feathers. Clothes and personal articles were tucked behind the bed. Cooking dishes and similar utensils were stowed on the south side of the doorway. Along the walls were more piles of various skins and Pale Dove's paraphernalia which was used for basketry and beading.

The wigwam smelled not only of the incense, but also of Pale Dove—sweet and pleasant.

Lone Wolf entered the wigwam, carrying Fred. Bending to a knee he placed Fred onto the prepared bed. He then stood with folded arms, staring down at him. "It will be for only a few sunrises, Pale Dove, that this man will inconvenience you," he said thickly. "Work your magic well."

Jeanine fell to her knees beside her uncle and touched his brow. She winced and drew her hand away quickly when she discovered that he was feverish. She watched Pale Dove gather together some different sorts of small bags sewn from the skin of animals, birds, and reptiles and place them beside Fred on the opposite side from where Jeanine so worriedly watched.

"Pale Dove, do you think you can really help him?" Jeanine asked, her voice quivering. Guilt plagued her for having been the one to inflict such a hardship on her uncle. Would he ever . . . ever . . . truly forgive her? "He seems to have a fever now."

Pale Dove's twisted back hunched as she settled down on the woven mats beside Jeanine, and began removing the soiled bandages from around Fred's shoulder and chest. "Pale Dove watch and learn mysteries from Shamans," she murmured. "My feeble body stands in way of being like other women, so I chose to learn mysteries of *medicin*. *Medicin* means mystery. That intrigues Pale Dove. So I watched and learned well. Even our village Shaman sometimes angry for what I know.''

She looked over at Jeanine and giggled. ''But he is only *gah-way*,'' she said.

Jeanine lifted an eyebrow. ''*Gah-way?*'' she questioned.

''Jealous,'' Pale Dove again giggled. ''Shaman *jealous*. He sometimes even calls me a *witch*.''

Jeanine laughed nervously, wondering if that was even all that amusing. From the beginning of time the word witch evoked something less than desirable inside one's mind! But Pale Dove was anything but a witch. . . .

A soft moan caused Jeanine to look down quickly at her uncle. Her pulse raced with happiness when she saw him slowly open his eyes. ''Thank God,'' she murmured, again touching her uncle's heated brow. ''Uncle Fred? How are you? Are you . . . in . . . much pain? How can I ever make you understand just how sorry I am about what happened?''

Fred licked his parched lips and looked about the dwelling with his hazed-over eyes. He winced when a sharp pain shot through his shoulder, where it so unmercifully throbbed at the core of his wound. Then he again began looking slowly about, seeing more clearly now. Struggling to lean up on an elbow, he again groaned with pain and crumpled back down, to lie more comfortably on his back. But he was quite aware of his surroundings. He was in an Indian wigwam! Even the damn Indian that should even now be hanging from a noose was there, gazing down at him sharply!

''Why the hell am I here in a damn Injun's dwelling?'' Fred finally grumbled. He nodded toward Lone Wolf. ''Get me away from that damn savage. Jeanine, take me *home*.''

Jeanine paled. Lone Wolf was most surely hating her uncle even more since her uncle was again verbally abusing him so. Yet a part of *her* was glad to hear her uncle being his usual word-stinging self. It had to mean that he was going to be alright!

Turning her head to look at Lone Wolf, to see his reaction, she wasn't surprised to find him gone. He *had* heard and had surely left in heated anger. And Jeanine understood.

Again she looked down at her uncle, only wishing she could understand why her uncle hated Indians so much. Even after two Indians had done him favors, he *still* couldn't find it in his heart to be kind to *and* about them.

"Uncle Fred, why must you always say such terrible things in front of Lone Wolf?" she asked, sighing.

"Damn it, Jeanine, that Injun'll kill me the first chance he gets."

"How can you say that? He treated your wound. He even brought you here for Pale Dove to treat your wound. Please be kinder to *her*, Uncle Fred. She deserves kindness, more than you have ever given an Indian."

Fred slowly turned his gaze to Pale Dove. His eyes slowly roved over her. He saw how tiny and frail she was and also that she had a sort of twisted back. When she smiled down at him, it was so sweet, it almost melted his insides. Perhaps this was one Indian he could learn to tolerate. It was obvious this tiny thing had not one ounce of meanness in her body!

"I'll behave myself," he said, then winced and cried out when another pain shot through his wound.

"Uncle Fred," Jeanine said, smoothing a hand over his feverish brow. "I am, oh, so sorry about what happened . . . about the pain you are in."

"Don't fret so much over it, Jeanine," Fred said thickly, taking her free hand in his. "Accidents happen. But, damn it, you . . . you should've been in St. Paul, *not* in the forest so vulnerable! You could've been shot . . . not me!"

Jeanine could tell by the haze in her uncle's eyes that he was in severe pain. She glanced over at Pale Dove, wishing she would hurry. If her uncle could be made more comfortable then Jeanine could relax a bit more with the situation. She could even leave, to go to Lone Wolf. His state of mind troubled Jeanine more than anything.

She again looked down at her uncle. She caressed his brow with her hand. "Shh," she murmured. "Don't talk anymore. We can talk later."

Pale Dove began opening her bundles, peering down into them. "I must leave for the forest soon, to search for more *mush-kee-kee*, medicine," she murmured. She placed the bundles aside and went to the fire, over which a kettle of water had been heating. Pouring it into a wooden cup she then added several sprigs of a mixture of herbs.

Taking the cup to Fred she held it down, close to his mouth. Placing a hand beneath his head she eased his mouth to the cup and urged him to drink.

"*Min-ee-qway*," she said softly. "You will sleep. I will doctor your wound while you sleep then I will leave you for awhile, to go and search for more herbs."

Jeanine marveled over Pale Dove's power over her uncle. Her uncle was already looking more at peace with himself as he let Pale Dove help him drink the liquid she was offering him. Jeanine truly felt that her uncle was in good hands. She even felt confident that he was going to be alright. She glanced toward the entrance flap, still worrying about Lone Wolf. How wounded were his feelings from her uncle's loose, spiteful tongue? She must go to him, to help him forget.

"Uncle Fred . . ." she said, turning back around to tell him that she was going to leave him for awhile, but found that he was already in a strange sort of sleep. Jeanine suddenly recalled the time that she had been drugged by Lone Wolf when he had taken her captive. More than likely her uncle had just been given the same sort of drug, to make him rest.

Then she tensed when he began talking in his sleep. She and Pale Dove exchanged quick glances when he began talking about his wife, and then about Indians. And before her uncle had quit jabbering in his sleep, Jeanine finally knew *and* understood why her uncle hated Indians. She finally knew why he had never said much about his wife, *or* how she had *died*.

Tears sparkling at the corners of her eyes, Jeanine leaned over her uncle and kissed him softly on a cheek. "Uncle Fred, now I understand so *much*," she whispered.

Wiping the tears from her eyes, she rose to her feet and walked from the wigwam, with Pale Dove following quietly behind her.

"It was *bad Sioux* who did that to his woman," Pale Dove said, as though apologizing for the terrible deed of those many years ago, even though she had had no part in it, and although she was *Chippewa*, not *Sioux*. "He has reason to hate all people with copper skin. Pale Dove would hate as much had it happened to someone *I* loved!"

Jeanine swept Pale Dove into her arms and hugged her. "It is not for you to apologize for what others did," she murmured. "But now that you know what he has gone through, it will make it easier for you to understand his abusive tone should he decide to use it on you."

"*Ay-uh*, I will understand."

Pale Dove eased herself from Jeanine's arms. She cast her eyes downward, almost bashfully. "Pale Dove glad you back in village," she said softly. Then she looked up quickly into Jeanine's eyes. "But I am happy that you are no longer here as *captive*. I am glad to be able to thank you again for taking time to teach me how to write my name on white man's paper, with white man's writing tool."

Jeanine smiled down at Pale Dove, then turned and rushed to her horse where she had secured her satchel at its one side. Opening the satchel she searched through her belongings and found a pencil and small tablet.

Taking these, she went to Pale Dove and offered them to her. "Please take these as a gift for your kindness to me and my uncle," she said softly. "While you are alone at night you can practice writing your name, and you might even learn how to draw pictures of things. You can draw flowers, the sun, and the moon, as you have learned to do on the skins you make your clothes from." She handed them closer. "Please take them, Pale Dove. I want you to have them."

Pale Dove's heart raced, so anxious, so stunned by the white woman's generous nature. Yet she could not find the courage to accept them. She was recalling Lone Wolf's angered words when he had discovered her using the white woman's paper and writing tool the one other time.

"*Gah-ween*, no," she said, her voice breaking. "Pale Dove cannot. Lone Wolf would not be happy with me."

Setting her jaw firmly, Jeanine looked in silence at Pale Dove for a moment. She then went back inside the wigwam and placed the pencil and tablet on the mats beside the fire, where Pale Dove could find them.

Then she went back outside, winked at Pale Dove, and went to her horse and began guiding it toward Lone Wolf's wigwam. She knew not what to expect from him. He had yet to scold her for following him as he had made his way to Chief Strong Hawk's village. But what could he say? He already knew why she had followed him. He knew of her desire to write the book.

"The book . . ." she whispered. She knew that was a dreaded subject inside Lone Wolf's heart. Perhaps if she explained in length about her *lectures* . . . the good they would do for his people after she taught the school children the Chippewa customs . . . just perhaps he would understand more about the lectures than he ever would a book!

Yes, surely that was the answer.

Twenty-Three

Jeanine removed the satchel from her horse and hesitated before going inside Lone Wolf's wigwam. Then, taking a deep breath of courage, she lifted the entrance flap and stepped inside. Lone Wolf was now attired only in a loincloth. He was squatting down before the fire and staring into it, balancing himself on his heels.

Tiptoeing, Jeanine crept farther into the dwelling, then her heart skipped a beat when Lone Wolf turned his eyes toward her, revealing a burning stare without a trace of friendship. Stopping, exchanging looks with him, she thought that maybe she should retreat and go back outside, not feeling at all welcome. She had expected him to be moody, but not totally unfriendly.

Was he so angered by her uncle's words? Or was it now that he chose to scold her for disobeying him? Did he truly believe that she should obey him, as though she were one of his squaws, ready to jump at his beck and call? He still did not know her if he thought she would do that!

Deciding that she was not going to let his cold stare intimidate her, yet not ready to sleep outdoors with the sniffing, yapping dogs that crowded the Indian village, Jeanine casually moved away from Lone Wolf to the other side of the fire, setting her satchel down on the mats beside her.

"You bring travel bag inside Lone Wolf's dwelling?" Lone Wolf said, startling the air with his decision to finally say something.

Jeanine was taken aback by what he said. "Why shouldn't I?" she said shallowly, her eyes wide.

"If your writing tool and book are inside the travel bag, it is *not* welcome inside my dwelling," Lone Wolf said, stubbornly lifting his chin.

"That is not the only thing inside my satchel," Jeanine said dryly, stooping to open it. She withdrew a fresh blouse and skirt. "I wish to change into something clean. Do you mind?"

Lone Wolf rose quickly to his feet, grabbed the satchel and leaned from the entrance flap to place it outside. He came back inside and positioned himself by the fire again. "It must stay outside," he said, again stubbornly.

Jeanine didn't argue with him. She did not wish to begin the argument anew about the book that she was planning to write. It was a subject that would forever be awkward with them.

"Alright. It stays outside," she said softly, going to pour water into a wooden washbowl. She gave Lone Wolf a swift glance, glad that he was still not looking her way. She was surprised that he had not placed *her* outside, as well, if he was so angry.

But she was glad that he hadn't. She had nowhere else to go. Not until her uncle was well enough to travel again. And she *did* wish to remove some of the dust that had collected on her skin from the long journey.

A bath in the lake would be much preferred, but Jeanine did not wish to do that alone. Cameron Tyner was still a threat to her. While she had been following Lone Wolf in the forest, at least she had been close enough to him to scream had Cameron suddenly appeared.

But to go to the lake alone? No. She would be far too vulnerable.

Unbuttoning her blouse, she sank her hands down into the water and began splashing it along her flesh. She even wet the loose tendrils of her hair, then swept them back across her shoulders.

Quite aware of how her breasts were partially exposed where her blouse hung open, she drew the fabric closer and began buttoning it. Her insides turned into a quivering mass when Lone Wolf quietly came to her and gently unbuttoned it, his thumbs softly grazing the swelling tips of her breasts.

Jeanine closed her eyes and sucked in her breath as he removed the blouse and then began to lower her jeans until they and her boots were also stripped from her.

"We argue no more today," Lone Wolf said huskily. "Time is too short. I must go to my father and be with him. I will spend the night at his bedside. I have neglected my duties of son to ailing chief too long now."

Jeanine's eyes opened. She gazed wondrously up into his eyes. "You are not going to question me as to why I followed you?" she dared to ask. "You can change your mood so quickly? You can forget so easily that I did something that you did not approve of?"

"I understand why you defy your uncle, but never Lone Wolf," he said thickly. "But it is no use talking about it. You are a strong-willed white woman. You have your reasons for what you do, though Lone Wolf does not agree with them. Lone Wolf has *his* reasons for what *he* does."

"I have not questioned you at length about so much that puzzles me about your attitude toward the St. Croix Band of the Chippewa," Jeanine said softly. "It is good that you do not question me further about why I must do what I do. It seems we have our own personal reasons to be interested in Chief Strong Hawk and his people. Perhaps one day we can confide in each other, telling each other *why*."

"There is more between us than secrets," Lone Wolf said. His lips searched Jeanine's lovely, pink face. "My woman, tell me that it is so. Tell me that your love is true."

Jeanine's lips quivered as he kissed her. Her fingers splayed against his chest, reveling in the golden touch of him.

"Tell me . . ." Lone Wolf whispered, speaking softly against her lips.

"I do love you," Jeanine whispered. "I do . . ."

"My woman . . ." Lone Wolf said, lowering her to the cushioned mats. He spread her out while his eyes feasted and his hands savored the touch of her softness, resembling the softest of deer skins. "We argue no more. We forget everything ugly. Even your uncle who wished to see me dead."

It was at times like this that Jeanine could so easily forget *all* barriers that threatened their possible future together. She trembled in ecstasy as his tongue swept between her lips and flicked against her own. His fingers sought and found her breasts and began sensually caressing them. Her own fingers moved wickedly to the waist of his loincloth and began to lower it.

Lone Wolf eased away from her and while looking down at her with eyes of fire . . . eyes of heated passion . . . he disrobed. He then placed himself fully over her. Their breasts touched, their hair tangled where their thighs pressed against the other.

Sighing, Jeanine closed her eyes when she felt Lone Wolf's manhood growing against the flesh of her thigh. She lifted her lips as he then masterfully filled her with his hardness and began his gentle probing, stroking . . . stroking . . .

So desiring her, so wanting to totally trust her, Lone Wolf drew Jeanine into the hard frame of his body. Locking her to him, his lips now met hers in a series of teasing kisses. He held her tightly. Her passion became his. Their bodies fused as though one. At this moment she was his

. . . totally his. She knew so well the art of responding to a man. He was proud to have been the one who had taught her the skills. He must see that she only demonstrate them to him, only him, forever.

Lone Wolf's lean, sinewy buttocks moved rhythmically. Jeanine was breathless, intoxicated by his kiss . . . his body. And then she felt the overwhelming pleasure that always came from reaching that pinnacle of joyous bliss shared with him.

Afterward she still clung to him, reveling in his own moment of wondrous pleasure. She felt how his body stiffened, then trembled. She leaned her cheek into his hair and sighed as he whispered her name into her ear as he, too, found the release he had been patient to receive.

Low shadows crept over Lone Wolf as he rose away from Jeanine to lean over her, to feast upon her serene loveliness. He cupped her cheek in his hand and smiled down at her softly. "With you I always find paradise," he murmured. "I love you, Jeanine. *Gee-zah-gi-ee-nay?*"

Jeanine placed her hand in his. "I recognize what you ask me in Chippewa," Jeanine whispered. "You have asked me before. Many times. My answer is the same. Yes. I love you. Haven't I proven it in so many ways?"

Lone Wolf rose away from her, his eyes troubled. He reached for his loincloth and drew it on. "Ay-uh, you have," he said thickly. He looked down at her. A frown creased his brow. "But is all that you do . . . all that you share with me . . . sincere? My woman, is it? You have much on your mind besides Lone Wolf. You have a desire to write book. Is not Lone Wolf enough for you now? Can you not forget such foolish notions about writing *book*?"

Jeanine reached for her blouse and slipped into it. And then her skirt. She went to Lone Wolf and leaned into his embrace, glad that he welcomed her there. "Lone Wolf, such a book could only help your people," she murmured, looking up at him. "I will write of how beautiful your people are. Everyone will finally understand *about* your people. Please see that my book could not hurt you in any way. And, Lone Wolf, I will not only use my findings to write a *book*. I will lecture to school children. I will teach them everything good about your people, the Chippewa."

"Book *mah-nah-dud*!" Lone Wolf said, jerking away from her. "Book *bad*. Lectures bad! No matter what you say . . . what you *do* will be exploiting my beautiful people!"

Jeanine watched with her mouth agape as he stormed from the wigwam. A small tremor coursed through her. She hugged herself, trying to ward off the sudden chill that his words had caused inside her. He would never understand her. She would never understand *him*. She truly feared the impossibility of them ever being able to be together, as man and wife.

Sad, she crept to the entrance flap and searched her hand outside for the satchel, not expecting it to be there. He most surely had taken it and pitched it into the large outdoor fire!

But she smiled when she found it where she had placed it. Perhaps he was beginning to understand her *after* all. . . .

Pale Dove slipped fringed leggings beneath her skirt, watching Fred's even breathing. She glanced down at his wound with its creamy mixture of herbs and water sealing it. Blood no longer seeped from it.

Smiling, proud of her skills to treat wounds, Pale Dove picked up a basket, and also beads which would be used to sacrifice to the spirits of the plants, and left the wigwam. She went into the deep woods which lay close behind her dwelling, confident that she would find all that was necessary to rebuild her supply of *medicin*. She could collect boneset, spikenard, apple roots, hickory bark, sassafras, prickly ash, wintergreen, witch hazel, spruce, and pine gum. She would carefully choose the finest of these plants, perhaps having to pass four plants before one was chosen.

A noise, sounding somewhat like someone walking on dried leaves, made Pale Dove stop to look about her.

Instinct told her that she was not alone. She could feel eyes upon her, following her every movement.

Scanning the dense forest, she looked in all directions. She saw nothing and heard no other sounds, so again began to prowl the forest, limping, her back stooped, her eyes forever searching for herbs. Pale Dove scoffed at having momentarily become afraid. She even paid no heed to how far away from the village she was traveling. She had done this many times before. She felt no threat in leaving the safety of the village behind. She was only a cripple. Who, animal *or* beast, would bother with anyone with a crooked back and a limp? When in the forest, she became a part of it. She felt free . . . mystically free. . . .

Moving along quietly beneath the trees, the sun slanting through their thick branches overhead, Pale Dove caught sight of bright yellow flowers ahead. Her insides grew warm, hoping that she had found a sassafras tree, also known to be called *ague tree*. Its aromatic root was what she sought. It was one of the most valuable of all that she had found in the forest. It was not only medicinal, it smelled quite pleasant.

Limping faster, she smiled to herself when she stepped up to the small tree and saw its furrowed bark. Its three distinctive forms of leaves all on the same bright green twig were now covered with small clusters of yellow flowers.

Ay-uh. She had found a sassafras tree. It would be easy enough to dig for some of its roots. Only a few were required and then she would continue her search for other valuable herbs, most of which were in this same vicinity. She had been here many times before. She was recognizing many familiar trees and plants from which she had taken her *medicin* before. She would gather as many as her basket would hold and then she would return home, to spend the rest of the evening sorting through and separating the herbs.

These would be dried within her lodge then cut in small pieces and placed in fabric or leather bags. They would be rolled in a piece of blanket or a buckskin and kept in a dry place. Bunches of herbs like boneset would be kept hanging near the fireplace.

Taking a set of special beads from inside her basket, Pale Dove knelt down and placed the beads on the ground beneath the tree. It was now necessary to tell the tree in gentle words what she desired of it before taking some of its roots. It was said in the upper world that it was not right to take a plant for medicine without first talking to it.

Pale Dove looked up at the colorful branches of the tree and began gently chanting a song, using these words:

"You have promised that you would heal the earth,
That you were ready with your healing.
With that promise I now claim you, take you,
Take you for your healing virtues only.

"Oh, give me your power to purge, to cleanse,
Your power to heal our people with your virtue.
I will not destroy you, but plant your seeds,
Plant them in the hole from which I take you.

"You will grow again and more than fourfold,
Oh, spirit of the herb, I'll not destroy.
Nor without purpose take you from the earth.
Accept my thanks for all your benefits."

Again standing, Pale Dove searched the limbs of the tree for some dark blue berries that had already pushed the tree's blossoms from the limbs. She plucked some berries then proceeded to dig up roots, replacing them with the berries and some of the beads from her strand of many, her offering to the tree for being so kind to her.

Then she proceeded on her way, again searching. She wasn't searching for herbs only to heal the wound. She was going to replenish her whole supply of herbs this day. For colds and fevers, boneset tea mixed with prickly ash bark might be used. For stomach ills sassafras and golden seal were effective. Mandrake was a good purge, while blackberry roots were an astringent.

Balms were made of bear grease and pitch, but mud was often used for stings and bruises. In the autumn the juice of the snapdragon was used for insect bites or for bruises. For mosquitoes, sassafras root was chewed up and smeared over the spots.

Pale Dove knew, though, that the best of all medicines were the prescriptions of pure water, plenty of air, exercise and bathing. But when there was an open wound to be healed, all of her knowledge of these herbs was most definitely required.

"*Ay-uh*, I will make Jeanine proud of me," Pale Dove whispered. "I will make her uncle well!"

She pushed her way further into the forest, watching the slant of the sun in the sky. When it came midway to the center of the sky and the earth, she would then turn and return home. The thing that she feared most, even more than man *or* animal, was the darkness of night. . . .

Blonde whiskers hiding his face, Cameron Tyner moved stealthily back toward the Indian village. He had trailed along behind the crippled squaw for a while, finding amusement in the way her twisted back swayed, and the way she limped when she walked.

But even though she was an amusing sight, there was an innocent loveliness about her delicate, copper face. She had caused a twinge in his loins, that which could only be quelled when his needs were fed by taking a woman sexually. Even that little filly who was half crippled could quench his desires. For the moment, at least.

But as Cameron had been watching the village of Indians from afar and had seen Lone Wolf leave his wigwam, leaving Jeanine alone, he knew that she took precedence over all else. He had watched her and Lone Wolf traveling through the forest, dragging Fred Hunter on a travois. He had followed close by until they had reached the village.

Cameron had then positioned himself on a slope that

overlooked the village and had waited and watched for Jeanine to be left alone. He had only toyed with the idea of the small squaw, having the time to waste, giving Lone Wolf enough time to get settled in the greater lodge that Cameron surmised was the chief's. Since Lone Wolf had just arrived back at the village not too long before, surely he would now be meeting with the chief for a while, to report back to him.

This could give Cameron time to steal Jeanine away. He would wait no longer! The wigwam in which she had been left bordered the forest. He could move quickly, get her, then leave without anyone seeing. He had a debt to pay, not only to her, but also to her uncle. It seemed that someone else had done the honors where Fred Hunter was concerned! Fred had appeared close to death on that travois!

A crooked smile lifted Cameron's lips. He placed his hand on the pistol belted at his waist, went down on all fours and began to crawl toward Lone Wolf's wigwam. . . .

Twenty-Four

Having written in her journal about what had transpired these past few days, Jeanine yawned and closed the book. Though it was still only midday, the ordeals she had recently struggled through were finally taking their toll on her. She was bone weary and felt as though she could sleep forever! A nap sounded most delicious to her. And since Lone Wolf was seeing to his father, Jeanine was alone to do just that.

Looking down at the journal, she thought of how much Lone Wolf hated it. If she was to expect a civil tongue from him when he returned, she knew that she should not let him see the journal inside his dwelling again. Not even the satchel.

Sighing, she replaced the journal inside her satchel, then crept to the entrance flap, raised it and gently replaced it where Lone Wolf had left it. He would never know that she had once again defied him. And she would over and over again, for she would not let him dominate her, except where loving him was concerned. He had full possession of her heart, now . . . and forever.

Barefoot, she went back to the gentle burning of the fire in the firespace. Spreading blankets, she stretched out beside the fire and lay on her side facing the warmth. Her eyes golden with the reflection of the flames, she let the fire hypnotize her into an even deeper drowsiness.

Slowly her eyes closed as she snuggled more comfortably into the softness of the blankets, raising her knees halfway to her chest. Surely it had never felt so good to let sleep claim her. Every bone in her body was relaxed: she had everything for which to be thankful. Though Lone Wolf was stubborn, she knew that he dearly loved her. Her uncle was going to be alright. Pale Dove had become a special friend. And portions of Jeanine's research were already compiled in her journal. What more could she ask for? She was happy . . . she was content. . . .

Drifting, now dreaming of Lone Wolf and how he had taught her the sensual side of life, Jeanine smiled in her sleep.

The entrance flap lifted. Cameron Tyner shuffled inside the wigwam quickly. So far undetected. The Chippewa were busy with their personal, daily chores. No one had even noticed the strange white man creeping around Lone Wolf's dwelling. But Cameron Tyner was known for his quick movements, not only with a gun, but also on his feet.

Cameron smiled smugly when he spied Jeanine asleep beside the fire. His feelings for her were mixed. A part of him hated her for being who she was—the spoiled niece of the bastard sheriff, Fred Hunter—yet a part of him had always wanted her. Even now his loins burned as though on fire.

His lusty gaze swept over her, seeing her loveliness . . . her gentle jawline, her midnight black, long lashes hiding green eyes beneath them, and, oh, God, her heaving breasts. Even covered by a cotton blouse he could make out their outline as they strained against the fabric. How often had he dreamed of touching her . . . kissing her . . . *ravaging* her!

But now another ingredient had been added to his list of what he would do when he was with Jeanine. After using her, he planned to *kill* her. He would make her uncle pay for threatening Cameron Tyner! Cameron would rob Fred Hunter of the most precious of his belongings . . . his *niece*!

Composing himself, knowing that time was of the essence should he ever get the chance to do all this, Cameron crept closer to Jeanine. The fire's glow reflected in his cobalt blue eyes afire with passion and hate, and on his shoulder-length strings of golden hair and his face of golden stubble. His plaid, cotton shirt was wrinkled and dust-covered; the cuffs of his jeans were heavy with caked mud.

He had removed his spurs and had left them behind. His cowboy boots scarcely made a sound as he leaned over Jeanine, yet it was his breathing that filled the spaces of the small dwelling. It was loud and raspy, coming in quick snatches, matching the rhythm of his heartbeat.

Removing a handkerchief from his rear pocket, he began inching it toward Jeanine's mouth. He made the lunge and locked it onto her lips, hurriedly tying it behind her head as she awakened with a start and turned searching eyes upward, growing wide and wild as she saw him kneeling over her.

Jeanine tried to cry out but the handkerchief stifled all sound. She began to struggle with Cameron as he grabbed her wrists and drew them roughly behind her. He held them there with one hand while with the other he slipped a thin rope from another rear pocket.

"It's known by many how skilled I am at rustlin'," Cameron chuckled, tying her hands behind her. "But this time it ain't nasty smelling cattle I'm workin'. It's a pretty *lady* smelling like flowers, all sweet and jasminy."

Jeanine cast him a fearful, angry look and scrambled to

her feet. Stumbling over the twisted tail of her skirt, she tried to get to the entrance flap but Cameron was too quick for her. He grabbed her roughly about the waist and drew her into his hard frame.

"Now that ain't wise," he snarled. "We've a score to settle and, by damn, it's goin' to be settled. *Tonight*."

Jeanine's nose curled up and she cringed when the vile smell of his sweaty clothes and flesh entered her flaring nostrils. She looked away from him and closed her eyes, then was forced to look up at him again as he coiled his fingers through her hair and jerked her face around.

"It's time you got to know me better, don't you think?" Cameron said, chuckling low. "But first I've got to get you away from here. For what I want to do with you I need *privacy*."

His eyes twinkled, his voice was filled with husky amusement as he shoved her ahead of him toward the entrance flap. Then he held her at arm's length as he peered cautiously outside. When he saw that no one was near he jerked her to his side and forced her outside with him, then quickly to the dense cover of the forest.

Still barefoot, Jeanine winced as briars and sharp ends of broken twigs pierced the tender flesh of her feet. Her pulse raced as she tried to look back toward the village, wanting to cry out Lone Wolf's name. He wouldn't discover her gone until morning! He had said that he was going to spend the night with his ailing father. By morning she could already be ravaged . . . possibly even *dead*!

Cameron forced her through the forest for what seemed an eternity. She knew that her feet must be bleeding. Her legs ached, her breath was short, her lungs felt as though torn with pain.

And then she spied his horse, a lovely white mustang, awaiting him in the distance. If he reached the horse he could carry her far, far away from Lone Wolf's village. She must get away now, or she was surely doomed!

Using the last bit of her strength, Jeanine yanked herself free and began to run away from Cameron, but her hands anchored behind her made her clumsy. She fell, then cringed when again his hands were on her at her waist, jerking her back to her feet. When he placed his face into hers, she stubbornly glared back at him.

Then surprising her, he removed the gag from her mouth. "We're too far away from the Indian village for anyone to hear so I might as well let you say your piece now and get it over with," Cameron said, laughing. He tossed the handkerchief aside, spread his legs and placed his hands on his hips, smiling amusedly down at her.

"Well? Ain't you got somethin' to say?" he chuckled. "Or are you wordless for the first time in your life?"

"I won't waste words with you," Jeanine said, lifting her chin haughtily. "All I will say is that you won't get away with this. When Lone Wolf finds out . . ."

Cameron took a quick step toward her. He twined his fingers through her hair and twisted hard, making Jeanine cry out with pain. Then her outcry was silenced when Cameron crushed his mouth down upon her lips, kissing her hard . . . kissing her demandingly. His free hand sought and found a breast. He cruelly pinched the nipple through her blouse, firing his insides even more when her newest cry of pain was muffled against his hard pressed lips.

But he knew better than to toy with her this close to the village. Stepping away from her he smiled crookedly. "That was just a sample of the fun I'm going to have with you once I get you where full privacy is assured," he snickered. "I'll just bet you'll find you like my way of lovin' better than that *savage Injun's*."

Jeanine puckered her lips and spat at his feet. "Never!" she hissed. Her head jerked with a snap when he doubled up a fist and viciously hit her on the jaw. Her cry of pain this time was not a soft, quiet one. This time it reverberated throughout the forest. . . .

The shrill scream coming from somewhere close by startled Pale Dove so, she dropped her basket of herbs to the ground. She scarcely breathed as she looked in the direction of the scream. She bent and reached into her basket until she found her knife, then stealthily began to move through the forest. Her limp did not discourage her, for she knew that some woman was in trouble and she must at least try to go to her rescue.

Keeping her eyes alert, Pale Dove ran softly, the forest having become strangely quiet. The birds were not singing; the deer were hiding behind thick brush. It was as though the animals sensed disaster and this made Pale Dove suddenly afraid. If she did not move quickly enough with the knife when she found the one accosting the woman, even *Pale Dove* would be in mortal danger. She must move as quietly and as swiftly as does the panther. The knife must be even *faster*.

Coming to a clearing, Pale Dove was able to see far ahead of her. What she saw made her heart jump with alarm. The white woman! Jeanine! She lay on the ground unconscious while an evil white man towered over her, glaring down at her. And now he was stooping over Jeanine, unbuttoning her blouse . . . ! He was touching Jeanine's . . . breasts . . . !

Pale Dove's insides recoiled with the thought of what the white man had on his mind. He had already rendered Jeanine unconscious. Soon he would be raping her! Pale Dove could not allow this to happen! She owed so much to Jeanine for her kindness. And Jeanine was *Lone Wolf's* woman! No other man could be allowed to defile her lovely body! No one!

Gaining all the strength and courage she could muster for her planned assault on the evil white man, Pale Dove heavily inhaled and exhaled, her fingers tightening onto the handle of the knife.

Then she began to run as fast as her crippled legs would carry her, her moccasined feet making no sound as they fell upon the leaf-covered floor of the forest.

She panted hard and kept her eyes focused on the man

whose lips were now tasting the flesh of one of Jeanine's breasts!

It made a sickness spin through Pale Dove's veins to see the man enjoy his sick, twisted moment of pleasure with a woman who was not awake to defend her virtue. It would be easy to plunge the knife into the back of such a man! Pale Dove would stand over him and laugh as he drew his last breath of life! She would leave his body for the wolves to defile just as he was defiling the beautiful, sweet white woman!

So near now that she could even smell his vile aroma of dried perspiration, Pale Dove lifted the knife and stopped to stand over him, then plunged the knife downward. But she only grazed the flesh of his neck, for he had chosen that very moment to move away from Jeanine.

"Oh, no!" Pale Dove cried as Cameron emitted a loud gasp of pain, then swung around with fire in his eyes, finding Pale Dove there with the blade of her knife red with his blood.

"You?" he said, taken aback by the boldness of this little, crippled creature. "What the hell do you think you're doin'?"

Pale Dove rushed him and again tried to plunge the knife into him but he was too quick for her. His hand moved as quickly as lightning streaks through the sky, grabbing her wrist. He twisted it, causing her to scream and drop the knife to the ground.

"So you want to play?" Cameron growled. "Well, little lady, I'll play."

His eyebrows raised as he looked from Jeanine, who was still in a quiet, unconscious state, to Pale Dove, and then to his horse. He couldn't take both of these playthings with him. There was only room for two on his horse. And he knew who he must take with him. Jeanine.

A slow smile lifted his lips. "Well, I plan to play alright," Cameron snarled. "But since I can't take both of you with me I might as well have my fun with you right here. Fun with Jeanine'll come later."

In a flash, Cameron yanked a pistol from his left holster. He aimed at Pale Dove. "Now, little squaw, you do what I tell you or I'll shoot, *then* have fun with you. Do you understand?"

Pale Dove was numb with fear. She trembled as she nodded that she understood, now knowing that she could no longer help Jeanine *or* herself. But she had tried. Oh, how she had tried. She only wished that Jeanine had been awake to know! Now she never would, for Pale Dove did not expect to live to tell of it.

Cameron inched toward his horse and grabbed a rope from the side of the saddle. He tossed it to Pale Dove's feet. "See the tree over yonder?" he said, nodding toward the thin trunk of a sycamore tree.

Pale Dove gulped hard. "*Ay-uh*, Pale Dove sees," she murmured.

"Pull Jeanine over to that tree, take the rope, then tie her *to* the tree," Cameron flatly ordered. He motioned with the barrel of his pistol. "Now! Too much time has been wasted already. Do it now, you savage squaw!"

Pale Dove recoiled beneath his ugly words, but understood the threat of a gun too well not to do as she was told. Grunting, she dragged Jeanine to the tree. With tears flooding her eyes, she wrapped the rope around Jeanine and the tree several times, then tied a knot, yet made sure the knot was loose, just in case. . . .

Before she could swing around to question with her eyes what the white man's intentions were for her now, he was there. He grabbed her by the arms and wrestled her to the ground. His lips were wet and cold as they searched along the tiny planes of her face. His hands were eager. He ripped the buckskin blouse in half and exposed her tiny buds of breasts to his callused fingers.

But Pale Dove would not give in to this attack so easily. She squirmed from beneath him and limped quickly away, her eyes locked on the shine of the blade of her knife, which lay partially hidden in deep folds of grass.

Her breath was momentarily knocked from her when

A sharp scream from somewhere close by drew Jeanine awake quickly. When her eyes focused, they widened in horror at the drama being played out before her eyes. Swallowing a wave of sickness she turned her eyes away quickly. But would she ever forget the sight of Cameron torturing Pale Dove's frail body with his own, savagely raping her?

She had to get loose. Oh, God, she had to get loose!

Jeanine's eyes widened in surprise when she worked with the ropes for only a moment and found that they slipped easily away from her wrists. Hope sprang forth inside her as she loosened the ropes from the rest of her body, her eyes on the shine of the knife so close to Pale Dove's hand. If she could only get to the knife. . . .

Stepping lithely away from the tree Jeanine moved toward Cameron, focusing her attention on the knife instead of the ravaging of poor Pale Dove's body. And just when Cameron's body trembled violently as his full lusts were being fulfilled, Jeanine circled her fingers fully about the handle of the knife.

As Cameron lay panting hard against Pale Dove, oblivious of Jeanine, his face burrowed against the tiny taper of Pale Dove's neck, Jeanine raised the knife above him, then plunged it into his back.

Cameron lurched with the impact of the knife, the sudden pain causing his vision to swim. With puzzlement etched across his face, he dropped on his side away from Pale Dove, uttering profanities, then became silent as his eyes slowly closed.

Pale Dove looked over at Jeanine through her tear-filled eyes. "Jeanine . . ." she cried, holding a hand out to her. "I . . . hurt . . . so. . . ."

Jeanine bit her lower lip in frustration, hurting *for* Pale Dove. Her gaze swept over her and saw bruises forming on Pale Dove's nude body and traces of Cameron's spent passion at the juncture of her thighs. And mixed with this was Pale Dove's blood.

"Pale Dove, I'm . . . so . . . sorry. . . ." she cried, drawing Pale Dove into her arms, gently rocking her.

"Pale Dove . . . saved . . . Jeanine?" Pale Dove whispered, her whole body a mass of trembles as she lay in Jeanine's arms. "I do *anything* for you. You my special friend."

Jeanine began to cry softly. She had not known the extent of Pale Dove's friendship for her. Perhaps Pale Dove would even *die* from the vicious attack! It was plain to see that Cameron Tyner had almost torn Pale Dove apart while raping her. She was so tiny. He was so *large*. And she was such a *child*. He was surely the devil himself, to be so cruel . . . so heartless!

Pale Dove's body seemed on fire with pain. Her vision was strangely doubling everything she looked at. But she was happy, for Jeanine was safe.

Jeanine's breath was stolen away when she saw Cameron Tyner stir and reach for his pistol though his whole back was drenched in his life's blood.

"You heathen bitch!" Cameron shouted, aiming the pistol at Jeanine. . . .

A loud swooshing sound tore through the air. Jeanine watched in wide-eyed disbelief as an arrow whizzed by her and swept into Cameron Tyner's bare chest. Cameron emitted a low gurgling sound as his eyes widened. He dropped the pistol to the ground and slumped over it, yet looked beyond where Jeanine and Pale Dove now clung to each other, seeing Lone Wolf as he rode into view on his masterful black stallion.

"I should've killed you when I had the chance at the jail," Cameron said between deep, painful pants. "You . . . damn . . . Injun. . . ."

Cameron's body jerked, his eyes grew wild, and then he gave in to death. . . .

Lone Wolf dismounted and ran to Pale Dove and eased her into this arms. "*Ah-nish-min-eh-way*?" he said softly, caressing Pale Dove's back. "Pale Dove. My Pale Dove."

"*Nay-mi-no-mun-gi*, I am fine," Pale Dove whispered. She gave Jeanine a sweet smile. "Jeanine alright. Pale Dove *save* Jeanine."

Then her body went limp in Lone Wolf's arms as she sank into a black void of unconsciousness. Lone Wolf placed her gently on the ground, reaching for her skirt to cover the marred body.

With a heavy heart and emotion-filled eyes, Lone Wolf turned to Jeanine. With a lunge she was in his arms, sobbing fiercely. "Thank God you came," she cried. "If only you could have come sooner. He . . . he . . . violated Pale Dove. He . . . hurt her, Lone Wolf. And she was only trying to help *me*. Lone Wolf, Cameron abducted me from your wigwam. He was going to rape me eventually, then probably *kill* me."

She looked down at Pale Dove. "Will she be alright, Lone Wolf?" she said, wiping her nose with the back of a hand. "She looks so . . . lifeless."

"This time Shaman required for healing," Lone Wolf growled. "We must return her to my village *quickly*."

Jeanine eased from his arms and buttoned her blouse, now knowing that Cameron had already had some fun with her while she had been unconscious. Her insides grew cold at the thought. She gave him an ugly stare, knowing that he would never harm anyone again.

Lone Wolf went to his horse and took a blanket from beneath his saddle. He took the blanket to Pale Dove and wrapped it gently about her. His eyes searched and found Cameron's white stallion. He nodded toward it. "You ride white man's horse. I take Pale Dove with me on *mine*," he softly commanded Jeanine.

Jeanine brushed her hair back from her face and moved quickly beside him to the horse as he carried Pale Dove to his. "Lone Wolf, how did you know to come looking for me?" she asked. "I thought you were to be with your father."

Lone Wolf held Pale Dove against him as he mounted his horse, then positioned her on his lap with her head resting against his chest. He gave Jeanine a slow stare. "I left long enough to come to you to say I was sorry for being so temperamental with you. I found you were gone from village without your horse *and* travel bag. I knew you surely were abducted,'' he said, then swung his horse around and galloped away in the direction of his village.

A sudden, sweet warmth flooded Jeanine's senses, helping to erase some of the ugliness that she had just witnessed. Lone Wolf had left his father's side to apologize to her! Apologies from him were rare. She felt honored to be a recipient of such a generous gesture. And this confirmed even more his feelings for her. Perhaps there was a chance for them, *after* all . . .

Without giving Cameron Tyner another look, she followed along behind Lone Wolf. When she saw Pale Dove still so lifeless she was swept into a world of worry all over again. The next several days would be hard for all concerned, but she would do all she could to help Pale Dove. It was Jeanine's turn to show loyalties, as Pale Dove had so proven hers.

Twenty-Five

One full week had passed since Pale Dove's brutal attack. Jeanine had taken over the responsibilities of doctoring her Uncle Fred while Pale Dove had returned to her parents' dwelling, healing slowly from her traumatic moments with Cameron Tyner. Jeanine's head bobbed as she sat beside her uncle, tired from the long hours of vigil at his side.

"Jeanine . . . ?"

Her head moving up in a jerk, Jeanine looked down at her uncle. He was now awake. He had spoken her name. He had been lingering somewhere between consciousness and sleep for the past several days and nights. First he worsened, then he would get better. It was as though Jeanine's mind was getting as disoriented as his, going in circles, it seemed, trying to keep up with the progress of both her uncle *and* Pale Dove.

"Uncle Fred?" Jeanine said, hope rising inside her when he revealed that he had enough strength to rise to a sitting position on his thick cushions of blankets and furs.

He was pale and gaunt, yet his eyes had a renewed sparkle in their depths. Soon Jeanine and her uncle would be going home, to Duluth.

Jeanine was torn with feeling over this. She did wish to return home to set things straight in her life *and* mind. Yet she did not want to leave Lone Wolf. She now knew that in her heart she had chosen him over everything else in life.

And because of Lone Wolf's intense feelings against Jeanine writing a book about the Chippewa, she had, after much thought and deliberation, decided that she was going to write it just for Lone Wolf, to give to him as a gift. If he ever wanted to share it with the world, it would be his decision to do so. Not Jeanine's.

She had yet to tell him of her decision. She wanted to wait until the book was in print, then give it to him as a surprise.

"Jeanine, your mind seems a million miles away," Fred grumbled, his fingers testing the length of the stubble of whiskers on his face. "Ain't you glad to see your Uncle Fred strong enough to sit up?"

Smoothing her hair back from her shoulders to hang in a satiny tumble of black down her back, Jeanine scooted closer to her uncle. She tucked her bare feet beneath the fullness of her skirt. The fringes of the sleeves of the Indian buckskin blouse that she had chosen to wear rippled and swayed as she reached a hand to her uncle's brow to check his temperature.

"You know I'm glad that you're showing improvement, Uncle Fred," Jeanine said, glad to find that his brow was cool to the touch. "Even that dreaded fever is gone. I think you're going to be as good as new real soon. For a while there I didn't know. . . ."

Fred looked down at the wound on his bare shoulder, glowering. "If that Injun squaw hadn't placed all those strange concoctions on my wound I'd have been well much quicker," he grumbled. "They damn well caused the infection. I'm damn lucky to be alive."

His eyebrows quickened upward, seeing scarcely a trace of a wound. "By jove, it's almost *gone,*" he exclaimed. "How . . . ?"

"That concoction you spoke so openly against is why the wound has healed so beautifully," Jeanine said, gingerly touching where his skin puckered so slightly. "Pale Dove instructed me from her bed just how to apply the other herbs to your wound that she hadn't had the chance to apply before her . . . her . . . attack. . . ."

Jeanine cast her eyes downward. She twined her fingers together on her lap, still unable to erase the rape scene from her mind. She told her uncle what happened in a few, horrifying words. "Uncle Fred, it was so horrible."

Fred's comforting hand touched Jeanine on the arm. He squeezed her arm affectionately. "I've been wrong about lots of things," he said thickly. "Cameron for one. I guess I wanted someone with a quick draw as my companion so bad I couldn't see farther than knowing that he was the best. And I *owed* him, Jeanine. It makes my blood turn cold to think that I could have been the cause for *you* getting raped by that sonofabitch. He even came close, didn't he?"

"Yes. If not for Pale Dove intervening, he would have raped me," Jeanine said thickly. "Instead, it was as though she offered herself to him, to take my *place*."

Her eyes lifted and met and held with Fred's. "She was so courageous, Uncle Fred," she murmured. "And she did it for *me*."

Fred nodded. He kicked a blanket aside, revealing his rumpled jeans, having refused to sleep without them. "As I said," he mumbled. "I've been wrong about a lot of things. Not only Cameron, but . . . but . . . also about the Chippewa Injuns. Damn, I hate to say it, but they are all a fine lot of people. Leastways, those I've become acquainted with."

"Does that include Lone Wolf?" Jeanine asked cautiously. "Do you now know that you were wrong about him . . . that he was accused wrongly of Silver Fox's murder?"

"Well, now, I didn't go so far as to say *that*," Fred grumbled, arching an eyebrow.

"Uncle Fred, he didn't do it," Jeanine said firmly. "Silver Fox . . . Giles . . . shot *himself*. I saw him toying with the gun right before he did it. I was there, ready to discuss the sale of his mother's paintings when he abruptly changed his mind about the sale and sent me away."

"Did you see Lone Wolf there?"

"No."

"Then how do you know he didn't do it?"

"Because he *said* he didn't. That's how."

"Why the hell was he there holdin' the gun like a guilty man? Huh? Tell me that, Jeanine."

Jeanine cast her eyes downward. "He hasn't told me."

"So you two keep secrets from one another, huh?"

Jeanine smiled sheepishly. "Yes, many," she said, nodding.

"Jeanine, just what are your feelings for that Injun?" Fred blurted, his eyes troubled.

"Uncle Fred, need I say?"

Fred looked away from her quickly. He clenched his fists at his sides, having to force himself not to say all that would be wrong at this time. It was apparent that Jeanine loved the Indian. With her stubborn nature there was not one thing that Fred could do about it. He would have to learn to live with it. But could he . . . ? He had hated Indians for so long. . . .

He turned his eyes back to Jeanine. "You do believe he's innocent, don't you?" he said hoarsely.

"I *know* he's innocent."

"Then, damn it, he's innocent," Fred said, almost choking on the words. "How could I believe otherwise? I have your word and he *did* save my life, didn't he?"

Jeanine again lowered her eyes. "I'm so sorry about shooting you," she murmured.

"I know, I know," Fred said, patting her hand. "If you

hadn't stopped me I would've shot Lone Wolf. I now know how wrong that would've been."

Jeanine's eyes widened in disbelief, her heart skipped a beat. "Do you really mean it, Uncle Fred?" she gasped.

"Don't I always say what I mean?" he growled. His eyes searched the wigwam. "Where the hell are my boots?"

Jeanine laughed softly. She placed a hand to his arm in an effort to dissuade him from rising from the bed. "Whoa there," she said. "You're not going anywhere just yet."

"I've taken up too much space in Pale Dove's home long enough," he grumbled, aware that his head began a slow spinning when he tried to rise. He reluctantly sank back down onto the blankets. "Damn, damn," he said, holding his face in his hands.

"Pale Dove won't be needing her wigwam for a while," Jeanine said softly. "She's going to be with her parents until she completely gets well. They may not even let her return, to live alone. They had only let her live in her own dwelling because she had seen her special vision given to her by her Great Spirit, Wenebojo, which made her look adult in her parents' eyes. Now she looks like a child again because she wasn't able to see to her own safety as she should have as an adult."

"That don't seem fair," Fred said, stretching back down on the blankets. He closed his eyes, now realizing just how weak he was.

"Well, maybe not, but perhaps it's best," Jeanine sighed. "She is so tiny and frail."

"Yeah. It's best," Fred grumbled, his gaze now directed at Jeanine. "There could be some Sioux Injuns out there. I know, personally, what they are capable of. Pale Dove wouldn't survive an attack by *them*."

Jeanine's eyes wavered. She now knew what he meant by such references to the Sioux. But he did not know that she knew. He had been talking out of his head when he had begun talking about his wife, and how she had died.

"Uncle Fred, I know. . . ." she said softly.

Fred's thick eyebrow lifted. "You know *what*?"

"About how Aunt Darla died."

Fred's cheeks grew pink with color. "How would you know that?" he said shallowly.

"Right after you were first brought to Pale Dove's dwelling you spoke in your . . . uh . . . sleep of how she died."

Fred turned his eyes away. "Lord," he said softly.

"I think I can understand why it was so hard for you to tell me about it," Jeanine said, placing a gentle hand on his arm. "It was such a horrible thing. I can even see why you would hate Indians so much. I'm sure I would have, also, had I experienced something so terrible."

Fred turned his face to her. "I will always hate the Sioux," Fred said thickly. "Always."

"Yes. I understand," Jeanine said, nodding. When he closed his eyes and emitted a quivering sigh, Jeanine could tell that he was in need of rest. "I'm going to leave you now, Uncle Fred. You must get your rest."

She didn't want to admit that she also needed rest. She had almost overtaxed her body, as well as her strength, these past several days. But now that her uncle was doing so well, she could sleep . . . she could rest much more peacefully.

But she knew that she would find Lone Wolf's wigwam lonesome and empty. He had sat vigil by his father's bedside almost steadily while she had been tending to her uncle. Word was that Lone Wolf's father might even be near death.

But she didn't know for sure. Lone Wolf hadn't taken her to his father, to introduce her to him. Lone Wolf had said that his father had the "shaking disease" . . . malaria. It was best that she did not see him in such a weakened state.

Lone Wolf had doubted whether his father should be introduced to *her*. Lone Wolf had not known for sure how his father would accept the knowledge that his son was totally . . . madly . . . in love with a white woman. There were many Indian maidens who wanted him as a husband.

"I want to start for home tomorrow," Fred said, grabbing Jeanine's hand almost desperately. "I've had enough of this sort of life. I need to be in Duluth. Hell, Jeanine, who's seein' to things while I'm away? You know everyone depends on me, don't you?"

"Uncle Fred, you can't rush things."

"I'm headin' home tomorrow. Even it I have to strap myself into the *saddle*, Jeanine. Now that's that."

He patted her hand, his lids heavy over his eyes, "Now go on about your business. I'm going to get a bit of shut-eye. I need all the strength I can muster up for the long trip ahead."

Jeanine shook her head in despair, yet smiled down at her uncle. He was becoming his old self, just as overbearing and bossy as usual. She was happy to see him this way again. Life would never be the same if her uncle were any different. Life would not be nearly as colorful!

Seeing that he was already dozing softly, Jeanine rose quietly to her feet and tiptoed from the wigwam. The twilight of night met her with its foggy mist rolling in from the lake, touching her all over with its dampness.

Shivering, she hugged herself with her arms, and hurried to Lone Wolf's wigwam. Removing her blouse, skirt, and moccasins, she draped a blanket about her shoulders and stretched out beside the fire on a thick layer of furs. Her eyes grew heavy and soon she was catapulted into the world of dreams.

Lone Wolf entered his wigwam. He at once saw Jeanine asleep beside the slow burning embers of the fire. He had felt neglectful of her these last several days, having spent most of his time since she had been there sitting with his ailing father.

But tonight Lone Wolf had needed Jeanine and the sort of comfort only she knew how to give him. His father was slipping away from him. Perhaps even at the next sunrise

Lone Wolf would not be only having to accept his father's death, but also the title of chief.

It would be then that decisions would have to be reached . . . whether or not to challenge Strong Hawk, to combine his and Lone Wolf's bands of Indians into one. If so, there could only be one chief. Which, in the end, would it be? Lone Wolf . . . or Strong Hawk . . . ?

Drawn to Jeanine, Lone Wolf knelt down over her. He once again cast thoughts of his brother aside and enjoyed Jeanine's loveliness before awakening her. Her facial features were so perfect, the color so pink. She was like a water lily, the angel of the lake . . . chaste and beautiful, amid the furs upon which she lay.

His gaze moved downward. Where the blanket that she was snuggled into draped open, it exposed the opulence of her satiny breasts, causing the fire to ignite in Lone Wolf's loins, as well as his heart.

The blood raced hot through his veins, oh, so hungering for her, wondering if she would understand the next several days ahead when he would have to pretend that she did not exist in his world of Chippewa. When his father's spirit began its long journey to the "hereafter," Lone Wolf would be fasting, alone. It would be at that time when he would draw strength for his duties ahead as chief, and for coping with the loss of a father who . . . in truth . . . was not his father at all.

Not wanting to think of anything but the moment, when he *could* be totally with Jeanine, Lone Wolf bent a soft kiss to her cheek. He smiled down at her when her thick veil of lashes began to flutter open. He smoothed the blanket from around her and began running his hands caressingly down her body, watching her eyes become inflamed with desire as she looked up at him.

When her body trembled beneath his continuing touches Lone Wolf knelt down over her and lowered his mouth to her lips. When she twined her arms about his neck, ardently returning the kiss, she became the only force behind his existence. For now there was her . . . only her. . . .

"It seems only right that you are here in my dwelling awaiting my return," Lone Wolf whispered, drawing his lips only a fraction away from hers. He looked down into her eyes, the reflection of the fire in them turning them golden. "It is perfect, my woman. So perfect."

Jeanine's thoughts returned to her uncle. She knew that he was determined to leave tomorrow. "I am glad you feel that way," she murmured. "But, Lone Wolf, I cannot stay. My uncle wants us to leave—*tomorrow* even."

"*Ay-uh,* it is best that you go," Lone Wolf said, finding the words hard to bear inside his heart. "But you can return soon, can you not?"

"You understand why I must go?" Jeanine asked, her eyes wide. She had thought he would argue with her, deny her the peace of mind required to leave at this time.

"It is not so much that I understand your leaving because of *you* wanting to leave," Lone Wolf said thickly. "It is because of duties ahead for Lone Wolf that I see that it is perhaps best for you not to be here. My father. He is quite ill. And my people. They will need Lone Wolf to draw courage from, when my father bids them farewell."

"He is no better?"

"No. I have only come to you tonight to seek comfort in your arms. Then I must return to my father. I am sorry I have not been able to be with you more these past several days. But you are an understanding woman. Are you not?"

"Yes, I understand. You have been a dutiful son these past several days," Jeanine murmured. She reached a hand to his copper cheek, always loving the touch of its smoothness. "I have been a dutiful niece. But, oh, how I have missed you, Lone Wolf."

He inhaled the sweetness of her skin as she pressed her lips gently against his. His body ached to have her satiny flesh become as one with his. There had already been too much talk. The moments with her were too precious to be wasted in mere talk.

"My woman, I have come to be with you now," he

said, cupping her breasts. "Let us be together. Totally. Let me show you just how much I do love you. Let me show you *now*."

It was now dark outside. The moon had shifted in the sky, reaching its silver light down through the smokehole in the ceiling. Jeanine watched Lone Wolf undress. First his golden chest caught the moonlight, and then his magnificent thighs, where at their juncture stood his magnificent man's strength, a copper, velvet sheath, ready to pleasure her.

A soft smile on his lips, Lone Wolf removed his moccasins and dropped them to the floor beside the bed of furs upon which Jeanine lay. He positioned himself atop her, shifting her body with his powerful hands, to fit into the shape of his.

"Love me, my woman," he whispered as she twined her arms about his neck. "Make the sun rise in my heart. Light the path of ecstasy inside me."

His eyes burned with passion as he looked upon her ruby lips. They were slightly parted, awaiting a kiss. His hands were tantalizing her as he skillfully played them along her flesh. He had memorized her pleasure points long ago.

Now unable to hold back any longer, he crushed his lips down upon hers and kissed her with an intensity never known to him before. A madness seemed to have engulfed him. He sought an excitement strong enough to drown out the worries of his father and all demands that awaited him as chief. Strong Hawk even became only a vague blur inside his mind.

Parting Jeanine's legs with his knee, he plunged himself deeply inside her and began his eager thrusts. He felt her respond with the upward arch of her hips, moving with him. He kissed her with a fierce, passionate hunger. She returned the kiss, her hands traveling over the expanse of his sleekly-muscled chest.

Jeanine writhed in response as soft moans repeatedly surfaced from inside her as she felt his largeness magnificently filling her. Her hands became still, her breath shallow. Her mind floated as pleasure spread through her body. Each of his thrusts sent a message of desire to her brain. His tongue was now flicking across one of her budded breasts; his hand cupping it flooded her senses with sensual warmth.

"Do you feel it?" Lone Wolf whispered, now moving his mouth to the lobe of her ear. "My woman, how I need you. Need me as much."

"Yes. As much," Jeanine sighed. She trembled with ecstasy as he lowered his mouth to her breast and hotly kissed it. "While with you all time and reason become lost to me. There is only you, Lone Wolf. Only you."

Lone Wolf cradled her closer and moved rhythmically inside her, feeling the desired pinnacle of release drawing near. He ran his fingers over the gentle curve of her thighs then placed them beneath her and locked her to him. The heat of his pleasure rose and scorched his insides.

Her body a river of sensations, Jeanine became overwhelmed by this that held her bondage, a prisoner of passion to this man of the golden copper skin and eyes of midnight black passion. His mouth searing hers with intensity left her breathless and trembling, her breasts pulsed.

A low moan escaped from Jeanine's lips as the quiet explosion of love flooded her insides with a delicious sweetness. She clung to Lone Wolf, feeling his release drawing near in the way his body would momentarily stiffen, then again he would move rhythmically into her.

Seductively, Jeanine swept her tongue between his lips. She clung to him as he kissed her long and hard. He then pressed his lips against her neck and emitted his husky groan of pleasure while filling her womb with his seed.

Breathless, their senses dazzled with the sexual excitement sought and found with one another, Lone Wolf slipped away from her and stretched out on his back.

Moving to his side, Jeanine began to trace a circle around a nipple of one of his breasts. "Lone Wolf, it was again beautiful," she sighed. She pressed her cheek against his heaving chest.

"*You* are beautiful," he said thickly, caressing her back, loving its softness, its splendidness.

He leaned up on an elbow to absorb the intoxication of her nearness because she soon would be gone. If he were sane he would not let her leave. But he knew the impossibility of her staying with him now, when time would not allow him to be with her in any capacity.

"You leave tomorrow," he said thickly. "Lone Wolf will worry about you. Lone Wolf sends many Braves to accompany your journey back to white man village."

Jeanine snuggled into his embrace. She sighed contentedly. "Do not worry about me, my love," she said softly. "All dangers are now gone. Cameron Tyner is dead. Thanks to you, the demon is dead."

Lone Wolf eased from her arms and rose to stand over her, drawing on his loincloth. "It is now time for Lone Wolf to return to duties of son," he said thickly, not wanting to think about what could have happened to his woman had he not gone in search of her after finding that she had been abducted. That Pale Dove had been viciously assaulted was enough to make him kill the evil white man over and over again in his mind!

Jeanine scurried to her feet and quickly dressed in the skirt and the fringed buckskin blouse that one of the women in the village had loaned her. "I will walk with you," she said softly, not asking him what had been bothering her. He had not once offered to introduce her to his father. Was it because he was ashamed of her? Or was it truly because his father was too ill? She would probably never know. But he had never known her parents. Wouldn't they need each other the more for such losses . . . ?

"I wish to go and see Pale Dove," she added quickly. "I think it will be best to say my good-byes tonight instead of tomorrow. Good-byes are so sad. . . ."

Lone Wolf drew her into his arms and held her close to him. "Do not speak as though those good-byes, will be forever," he said hoarsely. "You will return, will you not? Soon?"

"When you wish for me to return, you send for me," Jeanine said, placing her cheek against his chest. "You know that . . . I . . . will come."

Arm in arm they stepped out into the misty cool of night.

The smell of medicinal herbs hung heavy in the air, almost choking Jeanine. But she sat beside Pale Dove all the same, trying not to feel two sets of eyes on her, watching her. Pale Dove's parents sat beside one another on the other side of Pale Dove, as though guarding her from the harm that they feared another white person might cause. Would they ever even accept Jeanine as being more than just a white person? If all things worked out, she would be Lone Wolf's wife!

Pale Dove smiled up at Jeanine from her bed of blankets. "Pale Dove so glad that you came," she said softly.

"I would have come more often, Pale Dove, but I was taking care of Uncle Fred," Jeanine said in a soft apology. Her heart pained her at the sight of Pale Dove looking so gaunt . . . so poorly. "But you knew that my heart was with you every minute I was not here."

Pale Dove lifted trembling fingers from beneath her cover of blankets. She took Jeanine's hand and clung to it. "I have failed you," she said, her eyes wavering.

"How have you failed me?" Jeanine gasped, leaning down closer to Pale Dove.

"It was I who promised to look after your uncle," she said, remorse thick in her words. "I promised and I failed."

Jeanine lifted her free hand and brushed a stray lock of black hair from Pale Dove's brow. "How can you ever think that you failed me in any way?" she said thickly. "Pale Dove, if not for you I would probably now be dead. How can I ever repay you for coming to my rescue?

"You have repaid me. Over and over again," Pale Dove said, smiling up at Jeanine sweetly. "You are my *friend*."

"Yes. I am your friend," Jeanine said, almost choking with the need to cry. "Always and forever, Pale Dove."

"Thank you," Pale Dove said, tears sparkling in the corners of her eyes.

"But friends have to say good-bye," Jeanine said, hating having to.

"Good-bye?" Pale Dove said, her eyes widening.

"Tomorrow. My uncle wants to return to Duluth. I must go with him. He is not strong enough to travel alone."

"But you will return . . . ?"

"Yes. I will return."

"*O-nee-shee-shin,* good," Pale Dove said, sighing heavily. She turned her eyes to her mother. "*Gee-mah-mah?* You know the gift that I pointed out to you for Jeanine? Please give it to her now."

Jeanine looked in wonder from Pale Dove to Pale Dove's mother. Then she watched Pale Dove's mother rise and waddle her extreme weight to the far side of the wigwam. Her fringed dress was beautifully beaded and her coarse hair braided long and evenly down her back.

And when she returned and held out her hand with her offering to Jeanine, Jeanine gasped, so taken by the beautiful necklace of strung beads.

"Wampum beads now yours," Pale Dove said, leaning up on an elbow, pride in her eyes. "Pale Dove began making necklace shortly after meeting you. It was made especially for you, my special friend."

Jeanine had read enough about wampum to know that the word, the gift itself, was a sacred thing. It meant many things to Indians, ranging from treaties, to the ransom of a life. From friend to friend, it meant a total alliance.

She gazed down at the beaded necklace that she held between her outstretched hands with gratitude. It was easy to envision Pale Dove beside the fire the many evenings required to make such a thing of beauty. Each bead represented total friendship. Pale Dove had made the necklace from the valued purple spot in the clam shells. These dark-colored shells were regarded as the most valuable and one of them was worth four of the white beads, and the hardest to work with.

"How can I thank you for something so valuable?" Jeanine asked, gazing down at Pale Dove through misty eyes.

"Just return to my village, Pale Dove already misses you, Jeanine," Pale Dove said, sniffling as tears invaded her eyes.

Jeanine leaned down and fully embraced Pale Dove. "I will be back," she sobbed softly. "And I'll find you well. I know I'll find you well."

They clung to one another, their hearts beating as one.

Twenty-Six

Dressed in a brief loincloth, his face blackened with ash—that which was required of a son mourning the death of a great chieftain father—Lone Wolf rose from where he had been meditating and fasting for several days. With a deep sadness he looked down from the bluff on which he stood, looking over the domain that was not his. In the valley below he could see the peacefulness of his village where his people awaited his return, to begin acting out his role of chief. Smoke spiraled slowly from the smokeholes of the wigwams. A great outdoor fire was burning and had been kept burning throughout his absence, a beacon, reaching out to him both day and night.

It was time to go to his people. He was now their leader, now a great, powerful chief himself. All thoughts of his brother Chief Strong Hawk and his St. Croix Band of the Chippewa had been cast from his mind these past several days. Only now did he allow himself to think again of his brother, who was also chief. Lone Wolf was free now to go to Chief Strong Hawk and reveal the truth of their blood ties. There was no one to harm by such truths now that Chief White Cloud was dead. But Strong Hawk must be made to believe that Lone Wolf was not guilty of killing his brother. Perhaps Strong Hawk was even now making plans to avenge his brother's death. . . .

Ay-uh. The time was ripe for all truths! But first Lone Wolf must join his people. They must see that he would be a great chief! He must make them proud!

Going to a rippling brook only a few footsteps away, Lone Wolf knelt down onto a knee and splashed water on his face. He rubbed hard, then looked at his reflection in the water, having once again transformed himself into the man that he had been before his father had died. He was leaving his mourning behind him. Hopefully he would not be required to wear black ash on his face again for many, many sunrises! He had already lost too many he loved in his lifetime! A mother, two *fathers* . . .

He could not bear to think of any more losses. He was ready for the sunshine side to his life! He had much to look forward to. And soon!

In hasty steps he went to his stallion and swung himself up into his saddle, then began to descend from this high point of land that had heard his prayers . . . had shared his grief. He held his back proudly straight, not allowing himself to even think of the woman he loved!

Jeanine. Soon he would go for *her*. Life would soon be perfect, would it not? He would have his woman. He would find a way to settle this thing with his brother.

But nothing could ever take the place of his recent loss. "*Gee-bah-bah,*" he said, lowering his eyes. "My father, I do miss you so. You will forever be with me in thoughts and prayers. You will guide me in death, as you did in life. Lone Wolf *mee-gway-chee-wahn-dum,* thanks you, father, for being there, always being there, the most dutiful father, though in truth you were not my true father. But in love . . . in devotion . . . you were and will always be!"

His horse now galloping across a meadow of waving, green grass that stretched out into his village, Lone Wolf flicked his reins, anxious. Yet an insect hum, plus a crackling sound reverberating through the air behind him, made him grow suddenly tense.

With a jerk of the head he looked behind him into the distance. His insides grew numbly cold. Drawing his reins taut, causing his stallion to come to a shuddering halt, Lone Wolf looked upward incredulously. Suddenly the western sky had darkened, as it does before a storm. But what appeared to be a moving black cloud was not a cloud at all. Lone Wolf recognized this most dreaded sight to be billions of hungry locusts moving toward him and everything that lay in their paths.

"*Neen bay-mah-dis-i-gig*!" he half shouted, raising a threatening fist into the air. "My people's crops will be ruined! Our wild *mah-no-men*, rice, will be destroyed! When the winds turn blustery cold and the waters freeze over my people will starve!"

Spinning his horse around, he rode hard toward his village, leaning his body low over the flying mane of his stallion. Some locusts were already reaching him. As they hit the hardness of his body they snapped and crackled. He could feel them landing in and clinging to the coarseness of his shoulder-length, black hair.

He swatted and scraped them from his body. The battle ahead was going to be worse than any fought by the Chippewa since the many wars with the Sioux. These hungry locusts would be intent on destroying every plant in their path.

"They will take food from my people's mouths!" Lone Wolf cried, looking over his shoulder when he heard the hum and crackling sounds of the locusts growing louder. Many were already settling on plants. Everything in their paths would be stripped clean. And after this rush of locusts had passed on by, more would be expected.

Lone Wolf had been told by his father of the plague of 1873. That year the Chippewa had been robbed of all their supplies when they had been attacked by this same sort of flying insect.

"But Father also told me the methods to use the next time these pests threatened our people!" he mumbled to himself. "And Lone Wolf and his braves will try them all!"

Determined, he raced his stallion on toward his village. His mind was recalling his father's advice, even inventing new ways, to battle this terrible scourge that had come to this beautiful land of the Chippewa. . . .

Placing the last of her typed pages beside the typewriter in her office at the art museum, Jeanine sat back in the chair, smiling. She had gathered a lot of information on her journeys north, enough to give her book a good start.

But Jeanine still had the most important research to compile ahead of her. And that meant another journey north, to the St. Croix Band of the Chippewa, and she must get there and back before Lone Wolf sent for her.

She still didn't expect him to send for her for a while. Surely when one lost a chieftain father and then became chief himself, it would mean necessary time spent with his people. Once they were settled in with the business of life again with him as their leader, then Jeanine expected Lone Wolf to come for her. And she would go with him. This world that she had grown accustomed to was not important to her any longer. Only being with him was.

She was ready to be his wife. She could even endure living in the small spaces of his dwelling, if it meant being married to him. She would trade her love of freedom anytime for his kisses . . . his touches. . . .

Her cheeks flushing red with thoughts of being with Lone Wolf in the sensuous ways they had known together, Jeanine smiled awkwardly when her uncle suddenly entered her office.

"Hey, now," Fred said, sauntering over to her desk. "Did I catch you daydreamin', or what?"

He placed the palms of his hands on her desk and leancd

down into her face. "Thinkin' of the Injun, ain't you?" he said, his eyes gleaming.

"And if I were?" Jeanine tested, placing her hands on the pile of typed pages. "Would it matter, Uncle Fred?"

She looked him up and down, glad to see him as strong as before the accidental shooting. Since he had been so healthy before, it had made the healing much quicker. His cheeks were pink with color, his shoulders were squared beneath his dark suit.

"Bein' friends with the Injun is one thing," Fred grumbled, his face darkening into a frown. "But, missie, anything more ain't very smart. And knowin' that you spent all that time in the Injun's dwelling with him tells me only one thing."

"And that is . . . ?" Jeanine said shallowly, rising from behind her desk to get away from his close scrutiny. Her fingers toyed with the pleats of her checked taffeta dress with its dropped waist circled in burgundy satin. She wore black stockings and black shoes with ankle straps, and also a golden brooch with a heart-shaped locket hanging from it. Her breasts heaving where the dress trimmed with ruffles of lace, dipped low in front, revealing her anxiousness at the subject on which they were laboring.

"It don't take no expert to tell that you now want more than research from that Injun," Fred said, following Jeanine to a window.

She tensed, feeling him so near his breath was on the nape of her neck where the dark ringlets of her hair were tied back with a fashionable bow that matched her dress.

"Want?" she murmured, looking out to the busy thoroughfare that ran in front of the museum. Farther ahead, she could see the forest meeting the blue of the sky, both seeming to beckon to her. . . .

She turned around and faced Fred. "Uncle Fred, you already know that what I want is to be Lone Wolf's wife," she suddenly blurted, paling when she saw the pink of his cheeks turn crimson, "You seemed to have accepted it earlier. Why not now? You know that I love Lone Wolf. With all my heart I love him."

"You ain't that dumb," Fred said, jerking a cigar from his inside jacket pocket. He lit it and flipped the burned-out match into an ashtray on a table beside him.

He gestured with a hand toward her desk. "Marrying an Injun would take all of this away from you."

He half snickered, stepping on past her, to look out the window. "Naw. You're only joshin'. You love your freedom too much to be saddled with an Injun, livin' the life of an Injun *squaw.*"

He smiled crookedly as he gave her a half glance. "I can see you now. Cookin' over that firespace, carryin' a papoose on your back," he chuckled.

Again he looked from the window, shaking his head. "Yeah. You're only joshin' your uncle," he said thickly, wanting to believe that she was, yet truly knowing what she said was exactly how she felt. Before, when they had been at the Indian village, it had been easier for him to accept because he had thought that once she returned to civilization as she had always known it, she would soon forget this nonsense about the Injun.

Fred silently shook his head. He should have known better than to think that she would change her mind. Even in love she was as stubborn as a mule!

Jeanine placed a hand on his arm. "Uncle Fred, I *do* love him," she murmured, feeling him flinch. "Lone Wolf loves *me.* Uncle Fred, I would give my *life* for him. Knowing this, don't you understand that I will live however I have to live, just to *be* with him?"

She squeezed his arm affectionately. "Uncle Fred, you saw how kind . . . how generous the Chippewa were to you," she continued softly. "Can't you see how I could love one of them so easily? Please try to understand. Please . . ."

"Don't remind me of their generosity to me," he grumbled, never wanting to take sides with Indians, no matter that they had befriended him.

He gave her another half glance. "What's Lone Wolf think about this book you're plannin' to write about Injuns?"

he questioned, cocking an eyebrow. He puffed hard on his cigar, again looking from the window.

"He doesn't like it."

"See there? You've got problems with him and you ain't even married to him yet."

"There's no problem, Uncle Fred," Jeanine said flatly. She swung away from him and again sat down at her desk. "I plan to write the book, but only to give to Lone Wolf, to let him do with it as he sees fit."

Fred only half heard what she said. He grabbed his cigar from his mouth and leaned closer to the window. "Holy Jesus!" he gasped, paling.

Jeanine looked toward him quickly, then on past him, out the window. She rose slowly from behind her desk and went to the window so stand beside her uncle. "What *is* it, Uncle Fred?" she gasped. "The sky is dark, but what I see isn't clouds. What is it . . . ?"

Fred scratched his brow. "By Jove, it's locusts!" he growled. "It looks like it's going to be 1873 all over again."

"Locusts? You mentioned them before . . . your worry of them," Jeanine said in an almost whisper, straining her neck to get a closer look. "But if there are so many . . ."

"If there are so many it could be a disaster," Fred said, interrupting Jeanine. He yanked the cigar from between his lips, pondering over this newest duty as sheriff. How *was* he going to cope with a such a crisis? Back in '73, most agreed that only supernatural help could save the crops. Governor John Pillsbury had designated April 26 of that year as a statewide day of fasting and prayer for deliverance from the locusts.

"Like I told you before . . . most call the pests headin' our way grasshoppers," he said, smashing out his cigar in the ashtray. "But actually they are Rocky Mountain locusts, not native to this part of the country. The difference between locusts and grasshoppers is mainly that locusts have shorter antennae. But they damn well cause the same damage."

"Tell me more about what happened in 1873," Jeanine said, her mind now on Lone Wolf and what this could mean to *his* people. Their whole existence depended on their crops and their wild rice. If all of this were destroyed, how could his people survive the long, cold winter?

"After a wet spring that year, crops finally were growing well," he said. kneading his chin. "Then the damned locusts swept down upon Minnesota and destroyed every plant in their path."

Jeanine watched the dark shroud of locusts moving closer. Fred continued talking. "That ain't the half of it, though," he mumbled. "Locusts die at the end of the summer but the land they've ravaged is left infested with eggs that hatch the following spring to start the cycle anew."

"That means that next year . . . ?"

"Exactly . . ."

Fred spun around on his heel. "I've got to announce a town meeting," he said thickly. "Somethin' has got to be done and *fast*."

"Lone Wolf . . ." Jeanine said in a muted tone, but not too quiet for Fred not to have heard her. He stopped in mid-step and turned and glared at her.

"I hope I didn't hear right," he said, a deep frown creasing his brow. "You didn't say Lone Wolf, did you?"

Jeanine began to scamper about the room, arranging things on her desk, placing things inside her beaded purse. "I must go to him," she blurted. "He's going to need all the help he can get. His people's lives depend on it."

Fred took two long steps and clamped his fingers to her shoulders, stopping her. "Now you listen to me, young lady," he growled. "This time you listen good. You ain't goin' nowhere. The whole countryside will soon be swarmin' with those pests and everybody will be tryin' their damnedest to kill them. Fields will be set afire and all sorts of contraptions will be set up to either crush or trap the insects so their eggs can be destroyed. It won't be safe for you to be out gallivanting about. Do you understand?"

Jeanine stubbornly set her jaw, yet knew better than to

argue with him. But she would wait until he was fully occupied with his duties of sheriff and community leader; then, by damn, she *would* once again travel north. She would go to Lone Wolf. Again her journey to Chief Strong Hawk's village must be postponed. Would she ever get the information needed to finish her book? She was beginning to doubt it.

"Do you hear me, Jeanine?" Fred half shouted. "I don't like it one bit when you give me the silent treatment."

"I'm sorry," Jeanine said softly, easing away from him. "Please go on and see to your duties. I'll stay here. I've much to do."

"Then you're going to forget that foolishness about goin' to Lone Wolf?"

"For the moment," Jeanine said, nodding. The way he looked at her she knew that he understood the double meaning behind her statement of fact. He understood that nothing he could do would stop her from going to the man she loved. Nothing . . .

Fred's eyelids grew heavy over his eyes, he shook his head in disgust, then turned and left, mumbling something about Injuns going to be the death of her, also. Wasn't it enough that he had lost his wife because of Injuns? Now Jeanine . . . ?

She had also heard him say something to the effect that back in '73, some claimed the locust plague was a punishment for Minnesota's treatment of the Chippewa. But did his niece have to be the one to go to the Chippewa to make this wrong, right?

Jeanine went to the window and again stared up into the sky. The black cloud was growing closer . . . closer. It was surely already causing havoc up north, where Lone Wolf resided.

Twenty-Seven

The door to her office squeaking open behind her made Jeanine turn with a start. Her mouth went agape, her eyes widened in disbelief. "Judith? Judith McMahon?" she gasped, steadying herself by grasping onto the back of a chair. All these weeks her goal had been to get to the St. Croix Band of the Chippewa Indian village to meet with Judith, and suddenly she was *there,* in Jeanine's office. Why . . . ?

Jeanine's eyes swept over Judith and saw her unique loveliness as she remembered it from their first meeting. Her golden hair hung in a long braid down her back; she was attired in a beautifully-beaded, fringed doeskin dress and leggings. Her moccasins scarcely made a sound as she moved across the room toward Jeanine.

"Jeanine, how good it is to see you again," Judith said in a smooth, sweet voice, offering a hand of friendship.

Jeanine met Judith's approach and accepted the handshake, almost at a loss for words over Judith's sudden appearance. "As it is to see *you*," she murmured. Then she watched Judith go to the window to look into the sky. Jeanine knew that Judith was also worrying about what the locusts could do to the crops of the Chippewa. Why, even, was Judith not *with* the Chippewa?

Judith spun around, her blue eyes troubled. "There is so much I would like to say to you. There are so many questions I would like to ask about the book you are planning to write that Strong Hawk heard your uncle mention," she murmured. "But time does not allow it now. I must get to the point because my husband will need me very soon. The return of the locusts means only hardship ahead for my husband's people. I must be there, to *help*. I must return to my infant son who I have left behind with my husband's people because the journey to Duluth would have been too hard for him."

"Why have you come?" Jeanine said, so wanting to tell Judith that she had the same fears, except for a different Indian. Jeanine wanted so badly to share . . . to compare feelings with Judith. But even now with Judith there, it seemed the questions would *again* have to be postponed!

Judith moved around the room, pausing to look at each separate painting on the wall. "Danette Thomas, my mother-in-law, the wife of Gray Wolf, has made a decision to sell all of her paintings," she said hoarsely. She turned and faced Jeanine. "She has made a decision to sell everything . . . the Thomas Lumber Company . . . the mansion . . . the paintings . . . and return to live with the Chippewa. She wishes to leave her sadness in Duluth."

"And you wish to sell Danette's paintings to the art museum?" Jeanine asked, clasping her hands tightly behind her. She was finding it hard not to blurt out other questions that had been plaguing her for so long. Would she ever be given the chance? There was always something standing in the way, stopping her. . . .

"Yes, I have purposely come to Duluth to help Danette with the transactions," Judith said softly. "She is still grieving so over Silver Fox's death. It has been hard for her to understand how Silver Fox could . . . could . . ."

Judith placed a hand over her mouth and turned her back to Jeanine. Jeanine's heart skipped a beat. Had Judith almost said that Silver Fox had killed himself? How would she be *certain* of this? In most eyes Lone Wolf was still guilty!

With an anxious heart, Jeanine went to Judith. "What were you about to say?" she said, her voice cracking with emotion. Though her uncle had become convinced that Lone Wolf was innocent, there had never been any actual proof! Lone Wolf was still in danger of Strong Hawk avenging his brother's death, unless Strong Hawk also knew!

Judith's eyes were wide as she raised them to see the anxiousness in Jeanine's. "It is not easy to say," she murmured. "It was only today that we actually found *proof* of it."

"*What* proof?" Jeanine said in a strain. "Judith, *tell* me. Everyone still sees Lone Wolf as guilty. If you have proof that Silver Fox killed himself, everyone must be *told*."

"You speak so . . . so . . . devotedly of Lone Wolf," Judith stammered. "Why *do* you?"

"Judith, I love him, the same as you love Strong Hawk!" Jeanine said, pleading with her eyes. "I would do anything *for* him. Please tell me how you know about Silver Fox."

Judith's eyes misted with tears, moved by discovering that another white woman had become enamored of a handsome Indian brave. She understood, oh, so well, how this could have happened. Judith's own love for an Indian was special, oh, so very special! She swallowed hard, holding back the emotion swelling within and went back to the window. She felt that time was slipping away too quickly. Talk of love for an Indian would come later, for she did wish to share so much with Jeanine! But now there were too many unpleasantries standing in the way.

Judith turned and again faced Jeanine. "Danette was feeling low this morning," she blurted. "She picked up the family Bible to read a few verses and found stuck within the pages a note left there by Silver Fox.'' She placed a hand over her mouth. ''It was a *suicide* note,'' she uttered softly. ''Danette hadn't opened that Bible for consolation earlier. She also had one upstairs beside her bed. *That* was the one she turned to earlier for reading. *Not* the huge family Bible kept on a stand in the hallway of the mansion.''

Judith lowered her eyes. ''Lord, Silver Fox *killed* himself,'' she said, almost choking on the words.

Jeanine grabbed Judith's hand. ''The note,'' she said dryly. ''Where *is* it? Strong Hawk must be shown the note. He still thinks Lone Wolf killed Silver Fox. Judith, do you understand what that could mean?''

Judith raised her eyes slowly upward. ''Yes . . .'' she half whispered. ''Though Strong Hawk has not spoken openly of vengeance, being too caught up in mourning his brother, he *could* be planning now to avenge his brother's death, since the mourning period will soon be behind him.''

Jeanine swung away from Judith. ''Then we must go and tell Strong Hawk,'' she said, then stopped and again looked from the window, into the sky. ''Lord, how *can* we? I've never seen such a sight as those locusts!''

''That is even *more* the reason why Danette will want to sell everything,'' Judith said, stepping to Jeanine's side. ''The money could be used to buy supplies this coming winter for my husband's people. Surely the Indians' wild rice crops *will* be destroyed by the locusts!''

''I must go to Lone Wolf for *that* reason also,'' Jeanine said thickly. ''Perhaps I can help in some little way.''

Judith clasped onto Jeanine's hands. ''We could travel north together,'' she said softly. ''We could tell Strong Hawk that Lone Wolf did not kill Silver Fox. We could spread the news that there will be enough food for *all* of the Chippewa this winter. The money from Danette's sales could also benefit Lone Wolf's village.''

Jeanine's eyes widened into two pools of green. ''Danette would be that generous? That kind?'' she gasped.

"Danette will want to repay Lone Wolf for all of his misfortune brought on by her accusing him of Silver Fox's death. And she will also want to do this because she loves *all* the Chippewa, as do I, and I sense that even you feel the same" Judith said, smiling. "You will soon see why. You do plan to marry this man that you love, do you not?"

"Yes, oh, yes," Jeanine said in a sigh.

Judith nodded, then she saw the papers spread across Jeanine's desk. She went to them and began reading passages about the Chippewa.

Jeanine tensed, wondering if Judith would not want her to write such a book. When Judith turned to her and again smiled, Jeanine became filled with silent wonder.

"You are already writing a book about the Chippewa," she said, placing the typed pages back onto the desk.

"Do you mind that I have?" Jeanine dared to ask.

"I think it could benefit the Chippewa," Judith said, walking toward Jeanine. "Would you like to hear my ideas? I could tell you so much. While we travel north together I would have time to tell you perhaps all that you need to know."

Jeanine was taken aback by Judith's generosity. She could not believe this was happening. She had tried so hard to find ways to get information for her book and her lectures, and here it was, being handed to her . . . almost on a silver platter.

She was almost struck dumb by the realization.

"I would appreciate that. . . ." she finally said.

"Then shall we go to Danette's house so that you can price her paintings?" she said softly. "Then we can be free to go to our loved ones."

Jeanine grabbed her purse and followed Judith outside to her waiting buggy. Her insides were mushy and warm from what had transpired between her and this lovely woman. And it looked as though their future would be forever intertwined!

Jeanine's sudden feeling of security was robbed from

her when locusts began settling on her arms and in her hair. She cringed and began swatting them from her only for more to take their place. Lone Wolf! Gone off into the wilderness for his mission. Oh, how was he battling this plague?

She hurriedly climbed into her own buggy and began following Judith as they traveled up the steep streets of Duluth. . . .

While Danette stayed in her room, still in deep mourning for her beloved son, Jeanine dutifully followed Judith around Danette's mansion, yet her mind was drifting . . . worrying about Lone Wolf and the plague of locusts, and Strong Hawk not knowing that Lone Wolf was innocent!

Yet she had this chore to complete before going to Lone Wolf. It was important to secure the sales of the paintings in order to have the monies for the possible upcoming harsh winter for the Chippewa tribes. Hopefully, this delay wouldn't mean that Lone Wolf's life was in more danger. Though Jeanine now had the suicide note tucked neatly inside a pocket, Strong Hawk knew nothing of it!

Knowing that she must, she continued admiring the paintings, listing in a journal each of their descriptions and the price the art museum would be paying for each.

Then when she came to a portrait of Gray Wolf she stopped, stunned. It was as though she were looking at Lone Wolf! Everything about their facial features was the same . . . the same fathomless, dark eyes, the same square jaw, high cheekbones, and sensually full lips. Gray Wolf's coarse dark hair had been worn to the shoulders; the color of his skin had been the same beautiful copper color as Lone Wolf's!

"That is Gray Wolf. Wasn't my father-in-law so handsome?" Judith said. Seeing Gray Wolf's portrait made her miss Strong Hawk so terribly. This was one of the few times she had left her handsome husband to come to Duluth for business. She had been perfectly content to share her husband's life in his village. Very rarely had she become homesick for the white man's world!

"It's remarkable," Jeanine said, stepping closer to the painting. She studied the portrait even more closely. "Absolutely remarkable."

Judith smiled over at Jeanine warmly. "You like this painting better than the others?" she said softly. "Is this why you are so taken by it?"

"It *is* by far the most lovely of Danette's collection," Jeanine said, nodding. "But it is something else about the portrait . . . that . . . that draws my attention to it more."

Judith raised an eyebrow questioning. "Oh? And that is . . .?" she said, herself again studying the portrait.

"He so resembles someone else," Jeanine said, her gaze moving slowly to Judith. "Everything about this portrait so resembles someone *else*."

Judith laughed softly. She placed a hand on Jeanine's arm. "Oh, yes. You see the resemblance of my husband Strong Hawk in Gray Wolf's portrait," she said proudly. "It is only right that you should, since Gray Wolf was Strong Hawk's father."

Jeanine kneaded her brow and tilted her head, again marveling over the resemblance of the portrait. "Yes, I see so much of Strong Hawk in the portrait," she said in an almost whisper. "But . . . also . . . someone else . . ."

Judith twined her fingers together behind her back. "You speak of Giles . . .Silver Fox, my husband's twin?" she said shallowly.

Jeanine suddenly looked over at Judith. "No. It is Lone Wolf," she blurted. "When I look at the portrait of Gray Wolf, I see Lone Wolf."

Judith looked at Jeanine in wonder. "But how can that be?" she murmured.

Jeanine slowly moved her gaze back to the portrait. "I wonder . . ." she said softly, getting a strange feeling at the pit of her stomach. She was recalling Lone Wolf's obsession with Silver Fox and Strong Hawk. Was she beginning to guess why . . . ? Could Gray Wolf somehow be . . . ? Could Lone Wolf's mother have known Gray Wolf . . . ?

The sound of locusts hitting the window close to where

Judith and Jeanine were standing, now again silently studying the portrait, caused them both to look away, to glance toward the window.

"We must not delay our trip north any longer," Jeanine said, scrambling to the window. She drew the sheer curtain aside and peered outward and saw the locusts gathering on the lawn. "If Strong Hawk and Lone Wolf meet in the forest while battling the locusts . . ."

Jeanine turned and implored Judith with her eyes. "I have priced all of Danette's paintings," she said in a rush of words. "I can return the price list to the art museum and let someone else take charge of the actual sale. I hope you understand."

"Danette's lawyer can handle everything else from this end," Judith said.

"Are you saying . . . ?" Jeanine said, her voice anxious.

"Yes. I have done all I can here," she said thickly. "I am ready to return to my husband and his people. I am needed as never before."

Jeanine felt a sting of tears at the corners of her eyes, hardly believing the good fortune of having become acquainted with Judith all over again. She and Judith looked at each other for a moment, and quickly hugged.

Then they stepped apart. Jeanine went to the window and watched the locusts popping against it on the outside. She shuddered at the thought of them getting on her body. It would not only be uncomfortable traveling north under these circumstances, it would be dangerous. Jeanine was recalling her uncle talking about the many different ways that were used to try and stop the locusts. Traps . . . fires . . .

She swung around and gave Judith a questioning look, then they broke into a nervous, soft laugh together.

"Well, what are we waiting for?" Jeanine finally said. She tucked her journal beneath her right arm and headed for the door.

"Yes. Time is wasting," Judith said, accompanying Jeanine to the door, opening it for her. She swatted at locusts that began flying against her. "How soon will you be ready?"

"Soon," Jeanine said, flinching when a locust snapped against her face.

"I hope you have a veiled hat to wear on our journey north," Judith said, laughing softly as she continued to battle the onslaught of locusts.

"Several!" Jeanine shouted from across her shoulder as she rushed down the steps.

"And remember what I promised you!" Judith shouted back. "I will tell you all you need to know for your book while we are traveling. It will help take our minds off the locusts, don't you think?"

Jeanine stopped and turned to smile with gratitude at Judith. "My mind will absorb everything you tell me as though it were a sponge!" she said, then waved and boarded her carriage and headed for the art museum. Her heart beat anxiously. Life had its strange twists. But this time it was in her favor . . . !

But, oh, what of Lone Wolf? Would she be in *time* . . . ?

The sky was no longer black with locusts. They were now everywhere, *but* the sky. Trees and plants had been partially stripped bare of their leaves. Locusts were clinging to the stubble; some were on the ground, dead.

Weary from the several days of battling the insects, Lone Wolf rode ahead of his braves, surveying the damage to the vegetation. He had already traveled far and wide, trying everything imaginable to discourage the fresh onslaught of the locusts. Much land had already been burned. All sorts of contraptions had been made to drag over the land, to crush the insects.

But it was endless. Much land had not yet been reached by him and his braves. More fires had to be set. Many trenches had to be dug *for* the fires. Traps had to be placed in the ground, hoping that at least catching some of the locusts in these would be a way to stop them from laying the dreaded eggs that would hatch the next year and could begin the plague all over again.

Spying smoke just ahead through a break in the trees,

Lone Wolf raised an eyebrow. This fire had not been started by him or his Braves. They had yet to reach that area. So . . . who . . . ?

"*Ah-way-nish-ah-ow?*" he whispered to himself, then motioned with an upraised hand for his Braves to follow him as he sent his stallion into a hard gallop toward the smoke.

Riding tall and straight in the saddle, Lone Wolf's nose picked up the scent of the smoke as he drew closer to it. His trained ears picked up the sound of voices, one in particular, shouting out orders. Lone Wolf's heart skipped a beat. Though he had heard Strong Hawk's voice but once, he recognized it now, all the same. Had Strong Hawk traveled as far from his village? Were Lone Wolf and Strong Hawk going to meet halfway in their efforts to rid their land of the scourge of insects . . . ?

His shoulders squared, Lone Wolf traveled onward until he came to the opening in the trees that he had been riding toward. He drew his steed to a halt, the smoke now rising in great billows as it rolled toward him. He covered his mouth and nose with his hand to ward off the stench of the burning insects.

Then as the smoke separated, Lone Wolf caught his first sight of Strong Hawk, who stood instructing his braves to dig more trenches . . . build more fires . . .

Dismounting, Lone Wolf gave his reins to one of his own Braves to hold, then began walking toward his brother. When he reached him, they gave each other silent stares. Then Strong Hawk was the first to speak.

"We meet again, Lone Wolf," Strong Hawk said, wiping a smudge of ash from his chin, then scraping a clinging grasshopper from his loincloth. "But this time under much different circumstances."

"You battle the same demon as I," Lone Wolf said, stiffening when he saw a cold hate in the eyes of his brother, yet understanding such a hate. Strong Hawk still believed Lone Wolf was responsible for his twin brother's death. If not for the locust plague, Strong Hawk could even now be hunting Lone Wolf, to kill him! Lone Wolf could be challenging Strong Hawk for the title of chief of their combined tribes of Chippewa!

But, instead, Lone Wolf knew that Strong Hawk understood, as *he* did, that for the moment they must forget their differences. They must ride together and fight for the same cause for the sake of *their* people!

"You battle the pests in the same way Lone Wolf battles them," Lone Wolf said, gesturing with a hand toward the trenches. "I have left many trenches . . . many dead insects behind me."

"But the battle is only half won," Strong Hawk said solemnly.

"*Ay-uh,* yes," Lone Wolf said. "Only half won."

There was an added strained silence and then without any more words exchanged between them, both Lone Wolf and Strong Hawk moved to their respective horses. Together they joined in the fight against the locusts, casting aside all differences . . . until later.

Twenty-Eight

The trenches crisscrossed along the land where embers lay smouldering inside them on beds of gray ash. Lone Wolf and Strong Hawk rode away from these trenches, going to another section of land to dig more firebreaks and light more fires. For now, this particular section of land was already dealt with and they considered the insects dead, the fires out.

But the soft breeze continued to fan the dying embers, until sparks from them rose into the air and settled on a nearby pile of dead leaves. The orange glow of sparks spread, touching leaf after leaf with its teasing, dancing fingers. . . .

Jeanine's mare was moving in a slow, cautious canter through the forest. Alongside her, Judith rode straight-backed on an Appaloosa with its mottled skin, vertically striped hooves, and a dotted patch of white hair over the rump and loins.

It was hard to distinguish between the two travelers. Veils hid both Jeanine's and Judith's faces beneath them, and wide-brimmed sombreros were worn low over their brows. Long-sleeved plaid shirts and jeans covered the other vulnerable parts of their bodies.

Jeanine surveyed this land through which they traveled. Pines, the pillars of the forest, showed fewer signs of the locust damage than the other trees. The limbs of the maple and oak trees were a brown maze of resting locusts. The leaves were spotted with holes eaten through them. Many locusts lay dead and made ominous crunching noises beneath the horses' hooves.

Jeanine gave Judith a relieved smile, at last realizing that the worst of the swarming was over. "Finally," she sighed. "Now we can ride without swatting constantly at the pesky things."

"I hope the damage wasn't too severe at the Indian villages," Judith said, smoothing the veil up from her face, tucking it beneath her sombrero. "But if so, Strong Hawk's people . . . *my* people . . . will be happy to hear the good news that I bring them. The monies from the sales of Danette's paintings, business, and house will feed many a Chippewa on a cold, blustery day."

Jeanine lifted her own veil from her face, also tucking it beneath her sombrero. "When you talk of the Chippewa, sometimes you refer to them as *your* people," she said, closely scrutinizing Judith, again seeing her loveliness.

In Jeanine's mind's eye she could see Judith embracing a proud, handsome Chippewa, loving him as Jeanine loved Lone Wolf. It was good to know that Jeanine had something in common with this special lady. . . .

"Now that you're married to Strong Hawk, do you consider his people *yours*?" Jeanine added, hoping that she wasn't being too nosy.

Yet hadn't Judith already told her so much about the St. Croix Band of the Chippewa? Hadn't Judith told her that the first white woman, Lorinda O'Dell, had not gone willingly with Yellow Feather, but had been taken captive . . .

and then had fallen in love with him and had willingly stayed with him? Hadn't they had a beautiful son . . . Gray Wolf? And then hadn't Gray Wolf followed in his father's footsteps and himself chosen a white woman over all the Indian maidens of all the neighboring villages . . . ?

Judith had told her even so much more than that. She had told of the struggles with the Sioux and evil white men. She had explained the wild rice ceremony that was always celebrated when the moon became full in September when the rice was ready for harvesting. She had explained all the customs of the Chippewa.

Jeanine had not written any of this down, but inside her mind, as well as her heart, she remembered it all. She would always remember it. Soon it would be written into a book and presented to Lone Wolf. Hopefully, one day he would allow her to present it to a publisher so that the whole world would read of his special people. . . .

"My husband's people will always be my people," Judith said proudly. "I became as one *with* them after I became Strong Hawk's wife."

She gave Jeanine a warm smile. "My friend, you will one day call Lone Wolf's people *your* people. You will carry this proudly inside your heart. I can tell this. It is already written in your *eyes* when you speak the name Lone Wolf."

Jeanine smiled, then tensed, reminded of the suicide note in her pocket. She *must* reach Lone Wolf in time. She *must*! Thrusting her heels into Daisy's flanks, she rode onward quickly, again concentrating on her journey . . . a journey of the *heart*. There was a light undergrowth of saplings and fallen tree trunks, upturned roots, and a tangle of dead branches to work their way through. Quiet reigned in this, the early afternoon. The sunlight flickered its welcome beams of gold down through the treetops.

Jeanine and Judith had only recently passed through swampy glades. They had seen great bunches of cowslips, which they both had questioned aloud . . . were they to be called buttercups or water lilies?

It was uncomfortably humid. The atmosphere was suddenly becoming dull with a haze that could only be caused by fire. The air was pungent with its smoky dust swirling toward the two lone riders.

Jeanine tensed. She covered her mouth with a hand, coughing. There was much to dread in the forest when traveling though it. Fire was one of the most feared dangers. And as the smoke thickened, Jeanine knew that fire was *near*!"

"Judith, I don't like the looks of this!" Jeanine half shouted, again coughing. "Lord, Judith, what if we get trapped by fire?"

Judith edged her horse closer to Jeanine's "I'm sure there's nothing to fear," she tried to reassure her friend. "The fire is probably from the trench fires built by the Chippewa to kill the locusts. The smell of smoke is *promising*."

"Why promising?" Jeanine said, wiping tears from her eyes as the smoke stung them.

"Because we surely are close to where the Chippewa are digging the trenches. Perhaps even Strong Hawk or Lone Wolf is near," Judith said, coughing herself as the smoke grew denser. "Let's push our way through the wall of smoke. Hopefully we'll find our loved ones on the other side."

"And if you're wrong?" Jeanine said. She twined her reins more tightly around her fingers, now discovering that she had something else to dread. Daisy was snorting and shaking her head, spooked by the smoke.

"We must not think the worst!" Judith said, patting the thick mane of her horse. "Let's believe that *Wenebojo* is with us, guiding us."

"Lone Wolf has spoken often of his *Wenebojo*," Jeanine said softly. "It is the Great Spirit of the Chippewa, is it not?"

"Ay-uh, yes. And the Great Spirit has led me through many troubled times," Judith said, smiling. "He will *now,* also."

"Does that mean that you do not also pray to God?" Jeanine quietly tested, recalling that Danette had found Silver Fox's suicide note in her Bible, and Danette had surely become acquainted with the Indians' spiritual beliefs.

"I feel doubly blessed," Judith sighed. "I pray to God *and Wenebojo*."

Smiling, again feeling honored to now be a part of this special woman's life, Jeanine squared her shoulders and rode on alongside Judith.

But Jeanine's faith in what Judith had moments ago tried to reassure her of was faltering. The smoke was thicker. Daisy whinnied and jerked her head just as Jeanine heard a crackling sound not too far away. Almost as suddenly, she caught the glimmer of orange ahead, as flames were licking their way across the treetops.

"Fire!" Jeanine shouted, her pulse racing wildly as she quickly looked over at Judith. "Judith, the forest is on fire just ahead!"

Judith paled. She wheeled her horse to a stop and looked frantically all about her. She was becoming disoriented quickly. The smoke now surrounded them in a shroud of gray. "What shall . . . we . . . do . . .?" she gasped loudly.

"I know of a place where we can be safe from the fire!" Jeanine said, reining her mare to a halt beside Judith's. She was recalling the cavern that Lone Wolf had taken her to which, for only a short while, had been his hideout. "It can't be too far ahead. I was there only recently. I *know* we've been moving in its direction." Wiping her eyes, she peered more intensely about her. "It's to the left. I'm sure . . . it's to the left of us."

"But can we beat the fire?" Judith said, panic rising inside her. "It's . . . so . . . close. . . ."

"We *must*!" Jeanine shouted.

"*Ay-uh,* we must!" Judith said, tightening her fingers about her reins as her horse shook its mane with fright. "Go ahead. I'll follow along closely behind you."

"Stay close!"

"I will! Be careful, Jeanine!"

"I will!"

Slapping the reins, Jeanine urged Daisy onward. She leaned low over her horse and clung to her, all the while fighting the choking, irritating sting of the smoke that crept down her throat and up into her nose. Her eyes were watering, her vision blurred. Yet she continued, then winced when one of Daisy's hooves slipped while going over a deep trench on the ground.

"A trench!" Jeanine cried, looking over her shoulder at Judith. "It's surely one that was dug by one of Lone Wolf's or Strong Hawk's Braves. Perhaps they *are* close."

"I doubt it!" Judith shouted. "The fire! It must have started after they left the area! They wouldn't have allowed it to get so . . . out . . . of hand . . . !"

"Yes. I'm sure you're right," Jeanine said, her heart sinking as hope became less prominent in her mind.

She felt the clumsiness of Daisy's footing as another trench was found and conquered. "Watch out for the trenches!" Jeanine shouted from across her shoulder. But she knew that her warning had come too late, for Judith's response was a negative one. It came in the form of a mind-boggling scream.

Jeanine flinched when she heard a loud splat and the loud whinny from a horse. Before even turning back to see what had happened, she knew that Judith's horse had not made it over a trench. It had lost its footing and had fallen. She had to return to Judith! What if the horse had fallen *on* her . . . ?

Wheeling her mare around, Jeanine searched through the dense smoke. When she found the fallen horse, she quickly dismounted. She fell to her knees beside Judith, who lay unconscious on the ground a few feet away from her horse.

"Judith!" Jeanine cried softly. She placed her hand to Judith's throat, checking for a pulsebeat. She sighed with relief when she found one, then she looked around her frantically. She could see the fire eating away at the trees only a few yards away. She looked at Judith's horse. It lay panting hard, its leg twisted grotesquely beneath it.

"What . . . shall . . . I . . . do . . . ?" Jeanine whispered, feeling dizzy from her weakened, smoke-clogged lungs.

Then when a soft breeze made a tunnel in the smoke and she saw the familiar ground cover which another time had led downward into the safety of the cavern, she prayed a silent thank-you to God.

Rising to her feet, Jeanine began to drag Judith toward the cavern, but stopped and looked with wavering eyes toward Judith's horse. It would be inhumane to leave the horse to burn alive in the fire. Jeanine could urge her own horse to safety. But she couldn't do a thing to save Judith's lovely Appaloosa. There was only one thing to do. She must shoot it . . . !

Placing Judith easily to the ground, Jeanine rushed to Daisy and removed her rifle from its leather pouch. With shaking knees and trembling fingers, Jeanine aimed. The gunfire echoed around her, vibrating farther still, through the forest, and then again everything was quiet except for the popping and crackling of the flames which were moving closer . . . closer . . . closer. . . .

Jeanine wrapped the reins of her own horse around her arm and tied them snugly in a knot. And as she dragged Judith into the entranceway that led down into the cavern, Daisy followed dutifully.

Having discovered the fire raging out of control, Lone Wolf, Strong Hawk, and many Braves had circled around and had cut trees in the path of the fire, making a firebreak to stop it.

Perspiring, his fingers raw and bleeding from chopping with the axe, Lone Wolf stepped back and looked triumphantly at the large path of felled trees and cleared land, knowing that once the fire reached this point, it would lose its stamina and eventually go out.

Strong Hawk, breathing hard, went to Lone Wolf and

fiercely hugged him. *"Mee-ee-oo,"* he said hoarsely. "It is done. The locusts are stopped as is the *ish-sko-day*, fire!"

Lone Wolf was surprised by the sudden embrace, but reveled in this show of fondness by his brother. He returned the hug, thinking that perhaps now was the time to reveal the truth to Strong Hawk, while he had momentarily forgotten about Silver Fox. Wouldn't Strong Hawk be pleased to know that he had a brother who was now a great chief . . . ? Didn't Strong Hawk now understand that both could be chiefs of separate tribes? Anyone who fought the scourge of insects as valiantly as Strong Hawk *deserved* to be chief of the people for whom he had *done* this! Lone Wolf and Strong Hawk had battled side by side as brothers! They now hugged as brothers hugged!

Lone Wolf eased from Strong Hawk's embrace and looked into the depths of his brother's eyes with the command of his own. He placed a hand on Strong Hawk's corded shoulder. "Strong Hawk, there is so much that I would have to say to you," he began, but a sudden gunfire echoing through the forest at his left stole the thought of what he was going to say from his brain, replacing it with wonder.

"Who shoots firearm in forest?" Lone Wolf said, his hand moving quickly to the knife sheathed at his waist. "Who would be *in* forest at such a time as this?"

Strong Hawk and Lone Wolf exchanged quick glances, then mounted their horses and began riding in the direction of the sound, working their way through the thickness of the smoke, seeing the fire close by now, in the treetops.

"*Wee-weeb*!" Lone Wolf shouted. "Hurry, for the fire is too dangerously near! It will reach us before it reaches the firebreak!"

"We can't go much farther!" Strong Hawk shouted back, coughing as the smoke filled his lungs. "We must turn back. *Wi-yee-bah!* Soon!"

"Just a little farther!" Lone Wolf said, thundering his stallion onward. "Whoever fired the shot may be trapped!"

Together they rode through the light undergrowth of saplings and many fallen tree trunks . . . through the upturned roots and tangle of dead branches . . . and then Lone Wolf wheeled his horse to a stop when his stallion's hooves came within only a foot of a dead horse. His gaze searched and found the gunshot in its head and understood now why the shot had been fired. He glanced over at Strong Hawk as he moved to his side, then quickly dismounted and fell to his knees beside the dead horse.

Strong Hawk's heart raced as he ran his hands over the familiar contours of the Appaloosa horse. "Judith," he whispered. Then he looked up and frantically searched Lone Wolf's face with his eyes. "This is my wife's horse! Lone Wolf, it must have been my wife who shot her horse." His gaze settled on the twisted leg beneath the horse. "She had no choice. She *had* to shoot it." He began to look about him wildly. "This means that my wife is somewhere close *by*. She might be injured. The fire! She might even be wandering into the *fire*."

"What would your wife be doing here, at such a time?" Lone Wolf said, his insides growing cold with the thought.

"She would be coming because her heart would be heavy with *worry* over her *people*," Strong Hawk said thickly. "Worry over *my* people."

"Would she have traveled alone?" Lone Wolf dared to ask, not wanting to think of the fate of anyone alone in the wretchedness of the forest where fire was eating it away, one tree at a time.

"Perhaps . . ." Strong Hawk said rising to his feet. He swung himself up into this saddle. "We must find her. *Ah-szhee-gwah*!"

Lone Wolf placed a comforting hand on Strong Hawk's shoulder. "She cannot be far," he tried to reassure. "We heard the gunfire only moments ago. She could not get far."

His eyes moved to the entrance to the cavern. "If she found refuge in the cavern, she would be totally safe," he said, more to himself than to Strong Hawk. He nodded. "*Mah-bee-szhon*. Follow me."

Moving single file, Strong Hawk followed Lone Wolf through thick vegetation, then down . . . down . . . down . . .

Strong Hawk's eyes widened when he was led into a deep cavern, where at the far end he could see a soft ray of light. With his heart pounding against his ribs in his anxiousness, he still followed Lone Wolf. And when they reached the other side of the cavern, where it led to green vegetation and a meandering stream, his heart stopped, for beside the cool, blue stream was not only his wife, but also Lone Wolf's woman!

Lone Wolf blinked his eyes. He rubbed them with his knuckles, not believing what he was seeing. Was Jeanine an apparition? Or was she real? And was it not Strong Hawk's wife sitting beside her? How . . . ?

Quickly dismounting, Lone Wolf ran to Jeanine and grabbed her up into his arms and hugged her tightly. "My woman, you are safe," he said hoarsely. Then he held her away from him and looked into the green of her eyes, then twined his fingers through her tangled hair. "Why *are* you here? Did you know the foolishness of coming at such a time?"

"I am used to being called foolish by you," Jeanine said, laughing softly. She glanced down at Judith being hugged by her husband. Her insides grew warm, seeing Judith hugging him back. Judith had regained consciousness only moments after arriving to the other side of the cavern, where it hadn't even been touched by locusts, much less the fire.

Jeanine had felt that she had owed Judith a debt for Judith having been so kind and open to her . . . and now she felt as though that debt had been paid. Jeanine had saved Judith's life.

Then her heart skipped a heat. Lone Wolf and Strong Hawk were together! Strong Hawk hadn't killed Lone Wolf. Instead, it looked as though they had become friends.

Or was it only for *now*, when circumstances had thrown them together, forcing them to be comrades instead of enemies?

Lone Wolf's insides strangely quivered as he gazed at Judith. Jeanine had traveled with her from Duluth. For what purpose? Had she finally found a way to get information for her book? Or had she traveled with Judith to Chippewa country because she had been concerned about *Lone Wolf*?

He did not want to labor on the whys of things. At this moment he was just relieved that his woman was alright.

Placing an arm about Jeanine's waist, he began to lead her to her horse. "It is safe to return to my village now," he said flatly. "You will go with me. Strong Hawk's wife will go with him."

Jeanine stepped away from him. She placed a hand on his arm and stopped him. She could not allow Lone Wolf and Strong Hawk to go their separate ways until she had shown them both the suicide note. Strong Hawk must not have a reason to begin thinking about Lone Wolf as an enemy again, for he was *not*!

"Lone Wolf, let's not leave just yet," Jeanine said, slipping her hand inside the front pocket of her jeans to get the folded suicide note. "There is something I want to show Strong Hawk. It is written proof of your innocence. Strong Hawk will now know that you did not kill his brother."

While everyone looked on, quiet, Jeanine unfolded the note and read it aloud. She then watched Strong Hawk's expression reflect his many moods . . . discovery of the weakness of his brother Silver Fox . . . and discovery that the hate he had carried around inside his heart for Lone Wolf had been wrong.

Strong Hawk left Judith long enough to go to Lone Wolf. He placed one hand on Lone Wolf's shoulder, the other on Jeanine's. He looked from one to the other, his fathomless eyes dark, his expression warm. "My thanks to you both for many things," he said thickly. His gaze lingered on Jeanine. "You saved my wife's life. Strong Hawk will always remember that. *Ah-pah-nay.*"

A blush rose to Jeanine's cheeks. "I was glad to help your wife," she murmured. "She is special. So very special."

"*Ay-uh,* she is," Strong Hawk said, then went back to Judith and helped her onto his horse.

Lone Wolf framed Jeanine's face between his hands, smiled down at her, then grabbed her up into his arms and carried her to his horse and placed her in the saddle.

He swung himself up behind her and draped an arm about her waist, drawing her snugly against his hard frame and rode away with her. He had found himself a woman of many temperaments and virtues. She was like no other woman before. He became more intrigued with her each time he was with her.

This day he had battled locusts, fires, and torments of brothers, and had become victorious over them all! He even now had his woman with him again! This *was* a day of many victories!

Twenty-Nine

Beside the peaceful warmth of the fire, bathed and refreshed with blankets draped about their shoulders, Jeanine applied to Lone Wolf's raw fingers an application of herbs and water that Pale Dove had concocted.

"Pale Dove knows the art of medicine so well," Jeanine said, smoothing the medicine from one of Lone Wolf's fingers to another. "And I'm so glad she is well again."

"She is fortunate that her mother and father let her return to her private dwelling," Lone Wolf nodded. "She could have been forced to live as a captive in her parents' home for the remainder of her life. Without any Brave paying attention to her she would have become an isolated, aging squaw!"

"She is happy now?"

"*Ay-uh*. She is happy. She for the most part has forgotten the terrible ordeal in the forest with the white man and his vicious attack."

Not wanting to think about Cameron Tyner, Jeanine changed the subject. "You must have dug many trenches to cause your fingers to become so raw," she said, now placing the wooden bowl of herbal water aside. She returned Lone Wolf's gaze lovingly as his eyes burned into hers, setting her insides afire with want of him.

"Many were needed," Lone Wolf said, admiring, as many times before, the haunting image of her perfect features. "But it is now done and behind us." He leaned a kiss to the very tip of her nose. "My people . . . most of our crops . . . are safe, as are you, my woman. And are you not hungry? It has been a while since you have eaten."

Jeanine nodded. "Yes. Very," she murmured. She let the blanket drape more loosely about her shoulders as she freed her hands for drinking the broth that was simmering in a black kettle over the fire.

"One cup answers for two when shared by two in love," Lone Wolf said, offering a cup of broth to Jeanine. "Drink. It is good for your soul."

Jeanine smiled up at him warmly and accepted the cup. Watching him, adoring him, she drank several swallows, then offered it back to him. His eyes were locked with hers as he also drank from the cup. And when it was empty and placed aside, Lone Wolf reached a hand to Jeanine's cheek and touched it softly.

"You did not bring travel bag this time?" he asked thickly. "You did not bring journal? You came for only Lone Wolf?"

A nervous blush rose upward from Jeanine's neck, to her face. Though she had come this time out of fear for Lone Wolf's safety, she had also managed to get all that she needed for her book. But Lone Wolf need not know. Everything that Jeanine had found out was written inside her heart, not her journal. After the book was in print, *then* she would tell him how she had acquired the information.

There was no need to give him a reason to become angry with her all over again by telling him the full truth. Hadn't he evaded her questions over and over again, himself, about why he did what he did? Would she ever even know?

"No. I did not bring my journal," she said softly,

leaning her cheek into the palm of his hand, melting inside at his mere touch. "Only my heart, Lone Wolf. Only my heart."

Lone Wolf eased his hand away, then framed her face between each of his palms. His lashes lay heavy over his eyes as he studied her. "You were with Strong Hawk's wife," he said dryly. "Why *were* you?"

Jeanine swallowed hard, feeling vulnerable beneath his studious stare. "It was safer traveling in twos," she murmured.

"How was it that you knew of each other's plans to travel north?" he continued, his gaze locked with hers.

Jeanine placed her hands on his, covering them. Her eyes began to dance, having forgotten to tell him of Judith and Danette's generous plans to assist all Chippewa Indians in their time of need.

"Lone Wolf, wait until you hear," she said, moving to her knees before him. She was only half aware of the blanket creeping down from her shoulders.

"What do you speak of?" Lone Wolf asked, his eyebrows forking. He chuckled low, seeing her change of personality. Her moods were as changeable as a chameleon that had the skills of changing its color!

His gaze moved over her, her nudity tantalizing him, her skin gleaming like rich, warm satin beneath the glow of the fire.

Jeanine squirmed beneath his raking eyes, now quite aware of having lost the protective cover of the blanket. Lone Wolf's eyes were touching her, as though they were his hands, caressing her. She could feel the pulsebeat at the hollow of her throat pounding, sending a message of passion to her brain.

Yet she continued talking, though Lone Wolf's hands were now replacing the caress of his eyes, gingerly smoothing them across her shoulders, to now twine into her hair.

"Judith and her mother-in-law, Danette, are such generous women, Lone Wolf," Jeanine said, trembling as his hands now ran through her hair.

And then she tensed as he withdrew his hands and looked away from her, to look instead into the dancing flames of the fire. Feeling that she had touched a nerve, yet not knowing why, Jeanine crawled between him and the fire, placing herself in the line of his vision.

"What did I say that caused you to draw away from me?" she asked softly, reaching a hand to gently touch his cheek. Her eyes absorbed his handsome features of smooth copper skin, high cheekbones, his full face, oh, so sharply chiseled and masculine.

And then she recalled that it was Danette who had almost caused him to be hanged. "Oh, I see," she said, dropping her hand away from him. "You have not totally forgiven Danette, have you? You will hold anger for her inside your heart?"

Lone Wolf's jaw tightened. It would only require very few words to explain why Jeanine's words had built a momentary wall of tension between them. But he could not tell her, yet, that he did not consider Danette to be *that* generous. Had she not stolen Lone Wolf's true father? Had she not, in a sense, deprived Lone Wolf of knowing his father? If not for her, Lone Wolf's lovely mother would have more likely married Gray Wolf!

Then guilt washed through him. If not for Danette, Lone Wolf would not have had the opportunity of being raised by the wonderful Chippewa, Chief White Cloud!

As he was so often of late, he was torn with feelings. So torn . . .

"Lone Wolf, what is it?" Jeanine murmured, leaning up into his face, inhaling his warm, spicy fragrance, that which stirred many memories of him when she had been away from him, recalling his smell . . . his touch . . . his kisses. . . .

Lone Wolf looked away from her. Now *he* was the moody one, yet he could not seem to shake the feeling.

Jeanine curled up into Lone Wolf's arms, her lower lip formed into a pout. "Lone Wolf, you are shutting me out," she said in an almost whisper. "Is it always to be this way? From the very first you have shut me out. Will you always?"

With Jeanine so near, pressing her lovely face so close to his, her lips so tempting, Lone Wolf could not refrain from reaching out and fully consuming her. Gently kissing her, he eased her downward and spread her onto the blankets beside the fire. His hands swept down her spine, then even lower, enjoying the touch of her silken thighs.

A low moan spoke to him of Jeanine's pleasure as his fingers sought and found the triangle of floss where hidden beneath it was her bud of pleasure. Softly caressing her there, Lone Wolf trailed soft kisses from her lips, down the column of her throat, then teased the nipples of her breasts as his thumbs and forefingers urged them into hard peaks.

"*Gah-ween*, no," Lone Wolf said huskily, letting the blanket drop away from himself, his nudity now revealed to Jeanine's feasting eyes. "Lone Wolf not shut you out. Lone Wolf *love* you. Let our bodies become as one. One day soon our minds will do the same. Soon, my woman, I will reveal all my secrets to you. But it must be at the proper time. I have someone else to speak with first."

Jeanine sucked in her breath as Lone Wolf bent his lips to her breast and flicked his tongue around its hardened peak. "Lone Wolf, will I always take second place inside your heart?" she asked softly, wondering about this other person he would confide in, before her. "Who comes first, before *me*, with you?"

"My woman is jealous," Lone Wolf chuckled, his dark eyes gleaming. "That is part good . . . part *bad*."

He leaned down fully over her and swept his arms about her and drew her against him. "For now, I will only think about the *good* side of the jealousy," he said, hugging her to him.

Jeanine's eyes were hazy with passion as she looked up into the darkness of his when he leaned a fraction away from her. She placed her fingers to his lips and softly drew an invisible line about them.

"Take me now, Lone Wolf," she whispered. "Take me to paradise. Love me as never before, Lone Wolf. I love you, oh, so desperately love you."

Lone Wolf leaned into the yielding silk of her. Gently, he kissed her. His hands swept down the straight line of her back, to the curves of her buttocks. He drew her close and locked her to him, then sought entrance inside her.

"*Mah-bee-szhon*," he whispered against her cheek. "Let me fill your womb with my love seed. My woman . . . my woman . . ."

A sensuous tremor raced across Jeanine's flesh, realizing the full meaning of his words. A child. To have his child!

Placing her hands at the nape of his neck, she urged his face upward, then kissed him as their bodies gently tangled. And then Lone Wolf kissed her eyelids closed, then the tip of her nose, and then again her mouth, drawing from inside her a pleasurable sigh.

Jeanine trembled as a delicious warmth spun through her veins. She had again found Heaven in Lone Wolf's arms. She clung to him. Her cheek was pressed against his chest as he, too, began to shudder in total release, until he lay quietly, embracing her.

Spent, yet pleasingly, beautifully so, Jeanine crept from his arms, enabling her to look up into his eyes. "Is it wrong to love so much?" she sighed. "Is it fair that we have found such a love when so many never do?"

Lone Wolf sighed. He drew her back into his arms. "It is right," he said hoarsely. "Never question it. We are the lucky ones. Be proud. The Great Spirit, *Wenebojo,* has blessed us."

He leaned her away from him and placed a forefinger beneath her chin. "And because we are so blessed, I feel it is time to speak words of total togetherness between us," he added, his brow creased into a troubled frown. "We have waited much too long already to become man and wife. Do you also feel this, Jeanine?"

"Yes," Jeanine said, nodding her head. "But we must wait a while longer, Lone Wolf. I must return to Duluth, to set things right in my life there. And you said you have things to do. You have someone to speak with?"

Lone Wolf glanced away from her, then again into her

eyes. "*Ay-uh,* it is best we *both* set things right in our lives before sharing words of marriage between us," he said thickly. "You go your way. I go mine. Then we will come together and forever from that moment on follow only one path."

He drew her into his arms and hugged her fiercely. "You will return soon?" he said thickly.

"Yes. Soon."

"White woman who is married to Strong Hawk will return to Duluth with you?"

"Yes. She still has much to do to help Danette with all of the sales in progress."

"You are now friends with both Danette and Judith?"

"Yes."

"It happened quickly."

"Yes."

"How?"

Jeanine eased from his arms and drew the blanket up about her shoulders. She was feeling as though she were being pumped for answers. Again she wondered why he was so interested in the acquaintances of Chief Strong Hawk. Was this one thing she would never understand about him?

Yet hadn't he said that once they were married their paths would lead in the same direction? Surely then he would explain why his path led him so often to the family of Judith and Chief Strong Hawk!

Shaking her hair to hang long down her back, Jeanine studied Lone Wolf as she began explaining about Danette and Judith.

"As I began to tell you earlier, Danette and Judith are quite generous ladies," she said softly. "Lone Wolf, Danette is going to sell her business in Duluth, her house, *and* her prized possessions . . . paintings painted by *her*, to gather up enough money to help the Chippewa cause. She is even going to offer to share this money with *your* band of Chippewa. Judith is helping to supervise all of these sales. You see, there is not a stingy bone in either of their bodies. It is very easy to become fond of them both. They are friends I will always value. And perhaps even soon *you* will share such feelings."

"Danette and Judith are planning to offer my people assistance?" Lone Wolf said in a low gasp. He saw no reason not to like Judith. But was he going to be forced to like Danette, the woman who was of his mother's sad past? Yet how could he not? She *did* now seem to represent everything good. More and more he was understanding why his true father, Gray Wolf, had fallen so in love with this white woman and also why Strong Hawk had married Judith. It was not only their fair skin that had blinded him, it was their kind hearts, as well!

"You will accept Danette and Judith's help, Lone Wolf?"

"Lone Wolf will see," he said, stubbornly lifting his chin. "Lone Wolf will see . . ."

He drew on his loincloth, then placed a heavily beaded headband about his coarse, black hair.

Jeanine watched him apprehensively. "Where are you going?" she dared to ask.

Lone Wolf grabbed Jeanine's shirt and jeans and thrust them into her arms. "We must hasten with what is required of us to bring the time we will be totally together more quickly to us," he said thickly. "You dress. Then I will instruct many Braves to see that you return safely to Duluth. Lone Wolf give you enough sunrises to set your life into order then Braves return, to bring you back to me. Do you understand?"

"But, Lone Wolf, I only arrived . . ."

"You strong white woman. You will withstand the struggles of long journey," he said stubbornly.

Then his mood lightened. He drew her into his embrace. "But Lone Wolf will feel empty until you return," he said in a whisper. "Without you, *life* is empty. Is it the same for you, without Lone Wolf?"

Jeanine had so often heard the way he said yes in Chippewa and practiced saying it, for she knew that once she returned, she must learn the complete language, to be able to communicate with his people, alongside him.

"*Ay-uh,*" she murmured. "Since I first became aware of my feelings for you I have felt such an emptiness when not with you. Even when you held me captive I knew that was the way it would be when we were to say our first good-bye."

"Do you not know that when you return, you will again be my captive?" Lone Wolf said, looking down into the crisp green of her eyes. "My woman, how could I ever let you leave my eyesight again? I must confess, though, something to *you*."

"And that is?"

"Lone Wolf has become a captive."

"A . . . captive . . . ?"

"*Ay-uh. Your* captive."

His words touched her with a sweet warmth. She twined her arms about his neck and kissed him passionately . . . devotedly.

"You were such a brave woman," he said, drawing his lips momentarily from hers.

"Brave . . . ?" she asked, looking up into his eyes of fire.

"You saved Strong Hawk's wife," he said thickly. "You saved Judith."

Jeanine laughed softly. "Well, yes . . ." she murmured. "I guess I *did*."

"My Braves will accompany you to Chief Strong Hawk's village to get Judith for your joint journey south so that it will not be necessary for you to be as brave again," Lone Wolf grumbled. "Never again will you travel the forest alone. Never!"

A sudden feeling of uneasiness was swimming through Jeanine's veins. Suddenly Lone Wolf was sounding so possessive . . . *too* possessive? Jeanine had always treasured her freedom. Could she truly give it all up so easily?

Yet when Lone Wolf again swept her lips to his and kissed her oh, so sweetly . . . oh, so gently . . . she knew that she was ready to accept losing anything, in exchange for him.

Thirty

Stretching her arms over her head, Jeanine yawned, causing the sleeves of her cotton shirt to inch up her arms from where they had been already casually rolled to her elbows.

Then she lowered her arms and wiped sleep from her eyes as she looked down at the stack of typed pages beside her Remington typewriter. Finally. She was finished. Since she had returned home from Lone Wolf's village this last time she had spent as much available time as possible typing.

And now, besides preparing herself for her return journey to Lone Wolf, to become his wife, she had the Chippewa Indian book written. It wasn't as long as she had hoped. But it was enough to get her feelings . . . her insights . . . on paper.

Heavy footsteps entering her office at the art museum drew Jeanine around. She smiled warmly at her uncle, then went and hugged him heartily.

"Well. I think I'll leave and make another entrance so I

can get a second hug as nice as this one,'' Fred chuckled, patting Jeanine fondly on the back as he also embraced her. ''Are you already missin' ol' Uncle Fred, Jeanine? Maybe you've even changed your mind and ain't going? Huh?''

Jeanine eased from his arms and looked almost shyly up into his eyes, touched when she saw a mistiness in them. He *was* going to miss her. That moved her almost to tears. But she didn't want to behave as less than the woman she had become since having found a man she had shared so much with.

''Nothing could keep me here, Uncle Fred,'' Jeanine said softly. ''And thank you for at least *half* understanding. I had expected for you to have fits when I told you that I was going to return to Lone Wolf to become his wife.''

Fred withdrew a cigar from his coat pocket and thrust it between his lips. Scratching a thumbnail on the head of a match, the match burst into golden flame. ''I learned long ago that once you set your mind to something it would take lockin' you up in my jail to keep you from doing it,'' he said, lighting the cigar. ''But that don't mean that I have to like the prospect of havin' a damn Injun as a nephew.''

Jeanine took Fred's hands and squeezed them affectionately. ''Now, Uncle Fred, admit that you like Lone Wolf,'' she teased. Her eyes sparkled. ''Did he give you any reason not to like him?''

''He's an Injun,'' Fred growled, yanking his hands free. ''That's reason enough in *my* book.''

Jeanine shook her head disgustedly, then swirled her fully gathered skirt around and went to sink down into the chair behind her desk. She ran her hands over the top of the desk, knowing that this would be the last time she would be sitting behind it. After today she would no longer hold the proud title of art curator. She was exchanging that love for the proud title of *wife*.

She picked up the stack of typed pages and held them

out for her uncle to see. "It's finished," she said, smiling up at him. "Will you do as I asked, Uncle Fred? Will you see that it is printed, then bring it to me at Lone Wolf's village so that I can present it to him? It would mean a lot to me. You can even stop by and see Pale Dove. You know how fond you've become of her, though I know you won't confess *to* such a liking."

"Harumph," Fred said, settling down into a chair opposite Jeanine's desk.

"Well? Will you?" Jeanine persisted, stubbornly placing her manuscript close to Fred's hand, where his fingers were nervously drumming on the top of the desk.

"I said I would, didn't I?" Fred grumbled, cocking an eyebrow as he gave Jeanine an annoyed glance.

Then he leaned across the desk, the green of his eyes darker as he glowered over at her. "Tell me. What do you plan to do all day at that Injun village?" he drawled. "I tell *you* one thing. I ain't plannin' to sell your house. I bet you'll be back there before winter's over. How could you even consider livin' in a wigwam? You're used to space, Jeanine." He flailed a hand in the air. "Space!"

Jeanine settled back into the plushness of the chair, not wanting to admit to having had doubts, herself. "I'll be with Lone Wolf," she said dryly. "That's all that matters."

Then she rose from the chair and went to the window to peer from it. "Judith McMahon has a house at Strong Hawk's village," she murmured. "Perhaps, in time, Lone Wolf will build me one in *his* village."

"Until then? What do you plan to do with your time?" Fred said, rising from the chair to saunter over and stand beside her. "Do squaw chores all day? Or what?"

Jeanine turned on her heel and looked at her typewriter. She then gave Fred a mischievous smile. "Uncle Fred, when you bring my printed book, perhaps you can also tuck away my typewriter in your saddle bag," she said, now turning to face him. "After Lone Wolf sees the book in print and knows that there is only one copy, and that it will be his, surely he won't fuss at me when I tell him that

I want to spend some of my spare time writing. I have many books to write. He surely won't deny me this. I even plan to spend some of my spare time teaching the children of the village how to read and write."

She placed a hand on Fred's arm. "So you see? I've much to do besides being a wife," she said anxiously. "I plan to use my time wisely. I'm very anxious about my plans, Uncle Fred."

"Yeah. If your Injun husband will *allow* it," Fred grumbled.

"He'll allow it," Jeanine said, smiling.

The canoe rode gracefully through the water as light as a cork. The bark of the vessel was the most beautiful Strong Hawk could have found for his masterful craft. It had been generously made, complete with the rind of one birch tree, and ingeniously shaped and sewn together with the roots of the *Wat-tap,* tamarack, making it water-tight. It leaned and dodged about under the skillful balance of both Strong Hawk and Lone Wolf, moving among the green, tall and swaying wild rice plants, inspecting them.

The wild rice beds had not been fully damaged. Strong Hawk had left many Braves behind to stand guard to keep fires built, to smoke away any locusts that even looked as though they might draw near the precious waving, green plants that grew out of the water, the *king* of *all* plants to the Chippewa. Lone Wolf had done the same in *his* village.

"We are lucky this time that the locusts didn't do more damage," Strong Hawk said, placing a paddle on his lap as he turned to face Lone Wolf. "The wild rice has been spared in my village of Chippewa. My Braves smoked the plants quite well. The insects moved to other less valuable plants."

"It is the same for the white rice plants of my village," Lone Wolf said, squaring his shoulders as he also placed the paddle aside to enjoy this time alone with his brother.

He had come to Strong Hawk, showing concern for how the plague had affected Strong Hawk's people, yet knowing deep inside himself that though his concern was genuine, there was another reason for wanting to be with Strong Hawk in such a way. This was the best of opportunities to tell his brother the full truth.

Yet Lone Wolf had not yet had the courage to bring himself to tell Strong Hawk. They had first traveled side by side on their steeds, inspecting the land. Now they shared a canoe.

But still Lone Wolf could not tell Strong Hawk, though he had waited seemingly forever for such a moment. They had formed such a close friendship! What if Strong Hawk would not understand or accept the fact that Lone Wolf was a true brother . . . that Gray Wolf had fathered them both? Perhaps Strong Hawk, in his frustration of knowing this about his great, late father, would even banish Lone Wolf forever from his village! Perhaps full warfare between their people would erupt to determine who should rule their common tribe.

"We must have a celebration of victory over the insects!" Strong Hawk said, interrupting Lone Wolf's thoughts. "*Mah-bee-szhon.* Strong Hawk will host the celebration. Your people and my people will become as one!"

Strong Hawk's copper skin gleamed beneath the midday sun. His eyes were black as the darkest nights as they searched Lone Wolf's face, that which so resembled his own . . . even Strong Hawk's father, Gray Wolf! When looking upon Lone Wolf's face it was as though looking at himself in the mirror of the lake. Was it destiny that these two who so resembled each other should become such close friends?

It was as though Lone Wolf had become a link which had been missing in Strong Hawk's life, and he wondered, day and night, about this. Never before had Strong Hawk had such a friend, and this was a newfound friend!

Lone Wolf's eyebrows raised, he kneaded his chin. "A celebration?" he said, contemplating such a celebration with a brother he now so admired . . . so loved. "*Ay-uh.*

A celebration. My people will gladly come. And I shall bring my woman who will soon be my wife. I shall bring Pale Dove.'' He chuckled low, beneath his breath. ''Perhaps you have a young Brave who needs a child budding into a woman? Pale Dove could be some Brave's queen!''

''This Pale Dove that you speak so fondly of. Is she your sister?'' Strong Hawk asked, leaning closer to Lone Wolf. ''Do you even have brothers to bring to the celebration?''

A dark shadow passed across Lone Wolf's face as his smile turned into a frown. Now! Would there ever be a better time than now to tell the truth?

Yet something deep inside his heart cautioned him against it. Strong Hawk was a true, dedicated friend. Perhaps his being a friend had better advantages than being a *brother*!

But Lone Wolf had for so long held this truth locked inside his heart. How could he go another day without telling someone? He would not want to keep such a truth locked away as long as his mother had.

In his mind's eye the lovely, sweet face of Jeanine formed. It was as though *Wenebojo* had placed her likeness there, for him to think about, for a purpose!

Then a silent smile flashed across his lips. She would be the one in which to confide! Ah, how perfect it would be. She would finally know the whys of everything . . . why he had abducted her . . . why he was so fascinated by Chief Strong Hawk.

Perhaps later, in time, he would take Strong Hawk into his confidence. But not now. Not now when such a revelation could wound a budding relationship beyond repair.

Lone Wolf nervously cleared his throat. ''*Gah-ween,* no,'' he murmured low, commanding his eyes not to waver as he found Strong Hawk so closely scrutinizing him while awaiting an answer. ''Pale Dove is not my sister. Nor do I have brothers. My *gee-mah-mah* was quite frail. One child was all that her body would allow.''

Strong Hawk leaned and clasped his hands firmly onto Lone Wolf's shoulders. ''Lone Wolf, you no longer are without a brother,'' he said, smiling broadly. ''*I* will proudly be your brother! You will be *mine*. I have missed having a brother!''

Lone Wolf's eyes widened. His heart was beating as though there were many drums inside him. He was in awe of how things had turned around, definitely in his favor. No matter how he looked at it, he could now claim his brother as his own, without even having to reveal the truth *to* his brother. It was perfect.

''*Ay-uh, gee-gee-kee-wayn-zee,* brothers,'' Lone Wolf said thickly. ''Lone Wolf is *mee-nah-day-nee-mo,* proud to be your brother! *Mee-gway-chee-wahn-dum.*''

He placed his hands to Strong Hawk's shoulders. A keen feeling of peace was flowing through his veins. He was, ah, so *gee-mee-nwayn-dum,* happy.

Thirty-One

The sun was a great, ruddy orb sinking behind the pine woods in the west. The sky above it was flushed with a rosy color that faded into saffron and light yellow, and then into an almost soft, velveteen blue. The sound of singing and drums marked the victory celebration. Squirrels and the hindquarters of many deer were roasting over the great outdoor fire, around which sat the two joined tribes of Chippewa.

On a fur-covered, raised platform in the most prominent point of this circle, Chief Lone Wolf and Jeanine sat side by side, where to the right side of them were Chief Strong Hawk, his wife, Judith, his mother, Danette, and even Judith and Strong Hawk's child, Flying Eagle, who lay snugly wrapped in blankets on his cottonwood cradle board.

Pale Dove looked up adoringly from where she sat across from the platform, flanked by her mother and father.

Six drummers moved inside the immense circle of Chippewa and positioned themselves around a huge drum. As they began beating a continuing "tom-tom-tom-tom," lusty throats shouted and wailed the songs that belonged to each of the tribes. The sound was a strange mixture of a wailing coyote chorus and the minor music of a storm-brewing wind.

And after a while, this was silenced by the appearance of two young Braves entering the circle to stand before Chief Strong Hawk and Chief Lone Wolf. One was carrying a long-stemmed pipe decorated with duck feathers, its bowl that of a true calumet made from a stone, catlinite. The bowl was fitted with a long stem. It was a pipe for giving reverence, sacred in the eyes of all Chippewa.

The other lad was carrying a stone bowl of coals with which to kindle the pipe. Moving to his haunches he held the bowl of coals before him, then offered it first to the Heavens, and then to all the spirits, with an invocation for them to witness the celebration of victory.

The lad then placed this bowl of coals beside Chief Strong Hawk and left while the other lad reverently handed the pipe to him. He didn't promptly leave. Instead, he removed two leather pouches from his waistband and knelt down beside Strong Hawk. He mixed tobacco and l'herbe on a slab of stone, chopping it fine, then filled the pipe with this mixture as Strong Hawk held it out before him.

"*Ho, ho, oneegishin, oneegishin,*" Strong Hawk said in what sounded like a grunt, a comment of approval as the lad lifted the bowl of hot coals toward him.

Chief Strong Hawk lighted his pipe, inhaling deeply, puffing on it. He then took it from his mouth and raised it out beyond his eyes, blowing smoke first to the ground, presenting it to the earth, then blew smoke upward, presenting it to the sky, then turned the pipe to the four corners of the compass for the favors of the spirits.

Bringing the pipe downward, holding it before him, he nodded toward the waiting lad. "*Nin-mamoi-awe,* thank you," he added. "You may now go. Go with love, my young Brave."

The lad smiled up at Chief Strong Hawk warmly and moved backward, then turned on his heel and left.

Strong Hawk passed the pipe to Lone Wolf. "With this pipe, we seal our people's friendship, my brother."

Square-shouldered and proud, Lone Wolf nodded a silent thank-you to Strong Hawk. When he received the pipe he took it and smoked a few whiffs. As he blew the smoke into the air, he passed the pipe back to Strong Hawk. Strong Hawk grasped the stem with both of his hands, palms down, spreading and crooking his fingers, almost seizing, pouncing upon it, a near imitation of the way of the bear, a sign that he was the most powerful between these two chiefs present.

Lone Wolf smiled to himself, accepting Strong Hawk's silent declaration for now, for it would not be right to challenge Strong Hawk at this time when Lone Wolf and his people had so graciously been invited to join in the victory celebration in Strong Hawk's village.

But one day he would challenge Strong Hawk in games that were played between brothers. *Then,* the truly most powerful would be discovered.

For now, Lone Wolf, was content. His heart was filled with the beauty of the moment. Such peace of mind made him feel the power and love of *Wenebojo*, the Great Spirit. He had not blessed Lone Wolf, once, but many times over.

Placing an arm about Jeanine he drew her closer, feeling a trembling in her hand as she pressed it into his.

Jeanine looked up into Lone Wolf's eyes, adoringly, then looked at the way he was attired. It was almost identical in appearance to Strong Hawk. He wore a full Indian headdress of many beautifully dyed feathers. His fringed shirt and leggings were decorated, wondrously with beads and porcupine quills of every color, size, and shape. He looked dignified, proud, and immensely happy.

And she knew that she wasn't the only cause of such a radiance on Lone Wolf's handsome copper face. Again she saw it in his eyes when he looked at Strong Hawk. There was something unspoken between them. Perhaps one day she would know what. For now she was just content to be a part of this ceremony, knowing that tomorrow, even, there would be cause for another. She would officially become Lone Wolf's wife. She beamed with the thought.

She looked past Lone Wolf and over at Judith, who was dressed in a lovely doeskin dress and whose golden hair was braided to hang long down her back. Judith sat straight-backed, her face a mask of happiness.

And then Jeanine looked on past Judith, at Danette. She was also dressed in Indian attire. Her eyes were drawn back to Judith who was looking her way, smiling. Jeanine understood the meaning behind the smile. Judith approved of Jeanine's Indian dress and fringed leggings. Jeanine was already one of them without the marriage ceremony to make if official. She already felt accepted. Totally accepted!

When the drums began another steady rhythm of beats, Jeanine watched as dancers began to form in the immense circle. It was a dance of young Braves, Braves perhaps the same age as Pale Dove.

Jeanine glanced down at Pale Dove, seeing that she was in awe of one dancer in particular.

The young Brave, Brave Cloud, stood tall and lean, attired in only a loincloth and attached to an ornamental sash was a tail, extending nearly to the ground, made of the choicest arrangements of quills and feathers.

Brave Cloud began to dance to the rhythm of the beat of the drums along with the other young Braves. At intervals they stopped and one of them stepped into the ring and vociferated as loudly as possible with the most significant of gesticulations the feat of bravery which he had performed during his life.

Brave Cloud stepped into the ring and began going through all the motions and gestures that he had used while shooting a bear with his bow and arrow. At the end of his boasting, all the other Braves assented to the truth of his story and spoke in guttural tones of "waugh," and the dance again commenced. At the next interval another made his boast, while the one who had already performed would drop out of the circle.

Having seen the wide, doeful eyes of Pale Dove watching him, Brave Cloud went to her and offered her a hand, to invite her to rise and leave the celebration with him.

Her heart faltering, having never before been paid any attention by a handsome Brave, Pale Dove recoiled, blushing. But as Brave Cloud persisted to motion with his hand for her to take it, Pale Dove slowly raised her hand to his and when he touched her, she felt the strangest of sensations stirring around at the pit of her stomach.

Getting a nod of approval from her parents, she limped away from the circle of Indians with Brave Cloud. Pride was shining in her eyes when she realized that her crooked back had not caused him to look at her with pity. Somehow he had chosen her out of the crowd of many beautiful maidens. She would not linger on the wonder of this. She would let herself feel the pleasure *of* his attention.

Jeanine watched, wide-eyed, as Pale Dove left with the handsome, young Brave. Then something drew her eyes around, catching smug smiles being exchanged between Lone Wolf and Strong Hawk. And then she heard their exchanged whispers. . . .

"Did I not choose the right Brave for your special friend?" Strong Hawk whispered to Lone Wolf. "It did not take much coaxing. Just one of my best bows and quivers of arrows."

"*Ay-uh.* Lone Wolf approves," Lone Wolf whispered back. "Pale Dove could not have looked more pleased."

"The truth is," Strong Hawk again whispered, "Brave Cloud confessed only moments before the celebration began that he thought Pale Dove quite pretty. He looked past her crooked back. You see, his mother had the same affliction. He understands sorrow brought on *by* such afflictions. He will make Pale Dove happy, Lone Wolf. He will make her a good *husband.*"

Lone Wolf nodded, then smiled down at Jeanine, realizing that she had just eavesdropped and had discovered schemes between friends.

"Lone Wolf, what if Brave Cloud hadn't treated Pale Dove so grandly?" Jeanine softly scolded.

"The Great Spirit, *Wenebojo*, would not have allowed anything but the way it happened between the two adult children," he said. He took her hand and squeezed it affectionately. "Just the same as how the Great Spirit saw to it that everything worked out so perfectly for *us*."

Jeanine smiled up at him adoringly. Lone Wolf's gaze swept over her. He again saw the demure display of her creamy skin where the doeskin dress parted at the slim column of her throat. No one had coaxed him with special gifts to claim *her*. His heart had led him into wanting . . . loving her. And it would be forever . . . *ay-uh,* forever . . .

The celebration continued, on into the night. Much joy was exchanged between the two bands of Chippewa. Much drink and food was shared, and much . . . much love and understanding. And when they said good-bye, it was only for a while, for these two bands of Indians would forever be as one. Their chiefs were now the greatest of friends, even closer than most brothers.

Several weeks had passed. Jeanine was content in her new role of wife. But she had begun worrying about her Uncle Fred. He had not yet arrived with the bound book. Had he gone back on his word? Was he not going to bring it to her after all? Was he going to stay away from her because of his past feelings for Indians?

Full of concern over this worry, Jeanine tried to busy herself with her chores.

Grumbling beneath her breath, Jeanine dressed in a soft buckskin skirt and blouse, with her hair braided and hanging long down her back, continued dressing skins. She had removed some skins from where they had been immersed for a few days under a lye made from ashes and water until the hair could be removed. She had spread them out on the ground on a frame, with stakes driven through the edges into the earth, where they were to now remain for several days with the brains of the elk spread upon them.

Holding onto the small of her back, she rose from the ground, then tensed when she heard the sound of a horse approaching. Just as Lone Wolf stepped to her side beside their wigwam Fred came into view, his saddlebags bulging on each side of his horse.

Jeanine began to run to him, her heart beating anxiously. "Uncle Fred!" she shouted, waving her hand. "I didn't think you would ever come!"

Fred reined his horse beside Jeanine, then dismounted. Lone Wolf moved tall and straight to Jeanine's side. He reached a hand of friendship to Fred. "Welcome," he said warmly. "You have come to see how your niece is faring in the capacity of wife?"

Fred slapped his hand into Lone Wolf's. "Well, I guess you could say that," he grumbled.

Jeanine's eyes were dancing. "Did you bring it, Uncle Fred?" she said almost hoarsely.

Fred swung away from Lone Wolf and went to his saddlebag and opened it. "Said I would, didn't I?" he grumbled. He reached inside the saddlebag and found the bound book, then presented it to Jeanine. "Cost a bundle, but here it is."

Jeanine's hands were trembling as she grasped onto the book. She felt Lone Wolf's eyes of fire on her as she opened the book and looked at the printed words. Then her gaze moved to Lone Wolf as she handed the book to him.

"It's yours," she said softly. "No one else will have a copy. Only you. If you ever decide to let the world see it, it will be your decision. Not mine."

Lone Wolf's eyes widened. He took the book and slowly opened it, seeing the printed pages. "This book tells of the Chippewa?" he said quietly.

"*Ay-uh*," Jeanine said, tears near. "It speaks the truth of your people. The beautiful truth."

Lone Wolf frowned as he looked up at Jeanine. "You know that I did not wish that you do this," he said, yet holding the book between his hands as though it were a sacred thing.

"I know. But since it is a gift to only you, I thought you would not mind. Do you? So terribly?"

A slow smiled erased his frown. *"Gah-ween,"* he chuckled. "No. Lone Wolf not mind. This is the first book Lone Wolf ever owns. And my woman *wrote* it, It is a special gift . . . a gift given to me from the heart."

Jeanine eased into Lone Wolf's arms and hugged him as Fred stepped away from them and began unloading the rest of the things from his saddlebag. When Lone Wolf saw the typewriter as Fred placed it on the ground, he eased away from Jeanine and went to stoop to his haunches, to marvel at it.

"It is a typewriter," Jeanine dared to say, as she crept to Lone Wolf's side. "It has a strange sort of magic. It has the skills to place words on paper. I would like to show all the children of your village such magic. May I, Lone Wolf?"

Lone Wolf moved a hand slowly to the typewriter and touched it. He flinched when the keys were cold to his fingertips. Then he smiled up at Jeanine. "You bring magic to my people?" he said. "Pale Dove will be jealous."

Jeanine sighed a breath of relief and fell to her knees beside Lone Wolf, knowing that he had accepted even the typewriter. "I don't think so," she softly laughed. "I don't think so."

Placing an arm about Lone Wolf's waist, she snuggled against him. Everything was wonderfully sweet between them, except that he still hadn't told her why she at first had been taken captive by him. But it somehow didn't even matter to her any longer. She was glad that he had. Had he not she would never have known the joy she knew today . . .

Thirty-Two

The fire in the firespace had died to only glowing embers, shadowing two figures stretched out on a thick bed of furs beside it. Lone Wolf's eyes swept over Jeanine in a silent message only she knew how to interpret. Twining her arms about his neck she urged his mouth downward and touched her lips to his in a soft, sweet kiss, his body now fusing with hers as he gently entered her with easy strokes.

As his lean, sinewy buttocks moved, Jeanine felt herself growing languorous as the usual pleasant current of warmth began to blossom inside her. His hands crept to her breasts. His tongue coaxed her lips apart. A tremor went through Jeanine's body as his strokes speeded, deeper . . . deeper, as she responded in a matching rhythmic movement. She clung and rocked with him in their beauty of joined bodies.

Lone Wolf's lips lowered and skillfully teased Jeanine's taut breasts. His mouth was soft and passionate, yet his hands were as though hot coals, spreading heated flames wherever he touched her anew as he searched and found her every sensitive pleasure point.

And then the pressures building inside Jeanine exploded, dissolving into a delicious warmth, spreading . . . spreading . . .

Lone Wolf felt the drugged passion he always discovered when making love with his woman. Her answering heat and excitement fired him onward. He cupped her swelling breasts, marveling again at their utter softness. The heat in his loins was rising . . . rising . . .

And then he heard her soft sigh and felt her body warmth as she arched her body more fully into his. And as she shuddered with intense release, so did Lone Wolf. His lips bore down upon Jeanine's. His fingers dug into the flesh of her buttocks as his body violently trembled into hers. And then it was too soon over. Their bodies became quiet against the other. Lone Wolf's kiss became soft, less demanding.

And then he raised his lips away, his eyes dark with spent passion as he looked down at her. Jeanine could feel her body turning to liquid beneath his raputurous gaze. She laughed softly and ran a forefinger across his sensual lips.

"Are you memorizing me, Lone Wolf?" she half giggled. "Oh, how you are studying me! It is no longer necessary, you know, to imbed so deeply inside your heart remembrances of how I look. I am yours. Totally yours. I shall never leave you again, Lone Wolf. Never."

Lone Wolf rose to a sitting position and drew her up beside him, cradling her against him. "You no longer question me why I took you captive," he said, his eyes watching the coals of the fire as some would suddenly glow orange as though a light had been lit beneath them, and then again slowly fade away into gray ash.

"It is no longer important to me to know why," Jeanine said in a low whisper. She cuddled closer to him and peacefully closed her eyes. "That you *did* was a blessing to me. Had you not I would still be in Duluth, chasing dreams that did not include you. Oh, how shallow my life was before I met you."

"*Ah-szhee-gwah?*" Lone Wolf said thickly. He turned his eyes to hers and looked into their green depths.

Proud of her growing knowledge of the Chippewa language, Jeanine smiled up at Lone Wolf as she answered. "You ask how I feel now?" she murmured. "You know. I've showed you in so many ways how I feel about being here with you."

Lone Wolf's face shadowed with a sudden frown. "Though you do not ask questions you asked so many times before, I have a need to tell you so much," he said. He placed a forefinger to her chin and lifted her face more fully to his. "Now is the time."

"Why now? Why have you waited so long?" Jeanine asked, scooting so that she would be directly in his line of vision.

"It was my worry of what you were going to write in your book of Chippewa," he said in a low grumble. "It would not have been best that you know full truths about Lone Wolf and Strong Hawk. You could have written much that must never be known by my people, *nor* Strong Hawk's people."

Jeanine's pulse raced, hearing so much in his words, seeing so much in his eyes. What did he mean? What could she have discovered that he did not want in her book? Why did his concern also included Strong Hawk? Was she going to finally know why Lone Wolf was fascinated with . . . had even become such close friends with . . . Strong Hawk?

"How . . . do . . . you mean . . . ?" she asked, an air of caution in her voice. She did not want to frighten him into again choosing not to tell her. Now that her intrigue was again aroused, she did not know if she could bear not knowing!

Lone Wolf took both her hands in his, looking heavy-lashedly into her eyes. "The story is not a happy one," he said thickly. "A story which began with my mother . . ."

Without hesitating, Lone Wolf explained about his mother's love affair with Gray Wolf . . . of how he had discovered that he had brothers . . . and of his deep desire to claim Strong Hawk as his brother, but how he had decided that for all concerned, it was best to only share the secret with Jeanine. . . .

Touched and saddened at the same time, Jeanine moved into Lone Wolf's arms and hugged him tightly. "I feel so honored that you have chosen to share your secret with me," she sighed, pressing her cheek against his powerful, sleek chest. "Thank you, Lone Wolf. Thank you for trusting me so much."

Locking his arms about her, nestling his nose into the sweet scent of her hair, Lone Wolf sighed deeply. "My mother kept the secret locked inside her heart until just before she died," he said hoarsely. "I could not do this. The truth has eaten away at my insides since my discovery of it. My woman, it could not have been locked away inside my heart. It would have slowly eaten *it* away, had I left it."

Then he leaned her away from him, yet keeping her under the command of his dark eyes. "It was because of the truths told to me that Lone Wolf took you captive," he said, watching her half flinch at the word "captive."

"But . . . *why* . . . ?" Jeanine half gasped.

"Lone Wolf had to *test* you," he said softly.

"Test me? Lone Wolf, *why*?"

"To understand why my true father, Gray Wolf, chose a white woman over my Chippewa *mother* and to understand why my brother Strong Hawk also chose a white woman to be his wife."

"And did I fail any of those tests . . . ?"

Lone Wolf drew her gently into his arms. "My woman, only a few," he said, chuckling low.

Jeanine splayed her fingers against his chest. She looked up into his eyes and saw them gleaming with amusement. "A few?" she softly laughed. "Which ones did I *pass*?"

"Does it matter? Lone Wolf made you his *wife*, did he not?"

"Then I must have passed more than I failed? Right?"

"*Ay-uh.*"

Settling back into his embrace, Jeanine twined her arms about his thick chest and back. "I'm so glad," she sighed.

A blinking, soft yellow on the far dark side of the wigwam drew Lone Wolf's attention. He slipped from Jeanine's embrace and crept toward it.

Jeanine turned and watched him. Lone Wolf was moving as stealthily as a cat. "What are you doing?" she whispered.

"A firefly. It has become lost. I must return it outside so that it can find an appropriate lover," Lone Wolf said. He scooped the firefly up into his hand and cupped his fingers lightly about it.

He turned to Jeanine. "Open the entrance flap," he urged. "Watch the firefly as I release it."

Moving on her knees to the entrance flap, Jeanine lifted it. As Lone Wolf moved to her side and released the firefly she watched along with him as it flew away, toward the tall, swaying grasses which edged the forest. Though it was a dark summer night, it was not as dark as Jeanine had anticipated. The moon was casting shadows. The stars were twinkling. Campfires danced throughout the Chippewa village, and fireflies glowed in abundance.

"Love was not only in our dwelling tonight," Lone Wolf said, easing an arm about Jeanine's waist. "Romance is in the air outside also. The courtship rituals are in progress among the fireflies. Watch how the adult male fireflies periodically flash their yellow body lights. They are announcing to the females that they are there. The females have climbed to the tops of the grass and when one of these gentlemen callers comes closer to her she flashes her response, letting him know that she knows he is there. The male will then follow the female until he is directly above her, then will drop out of the air and into her six waiting arms."

"How lovely a tale," Jeanine said, smiling up at Lone Wolf. "From now on, on summer nights, when I gaze into the darkness, I will know that with every little light that shines golden, romance is in the air."

"Summer nights are not required to bring romance into our dwelling," Lone Wolf said, closing the entrance flap. His palms began moving seductively over Jeanine's yielding body. "My woman, every night, through snows . . . rains . . . and gentle breezes . . . we will be together. No more tests are required of *either* of us. Is this so?"

"*Ay-uh*, it is so," Jeanine murmured, his hands turning her wild and weak.

He then kissed Jeanine with a fierce, possessive passion, causing an incredible sweetness to sweep through her. She was no longer a captive, yet . . . wasn't she . . . ? Totally . . . ?

She would have it no other way. . . .

Dear Reader:

It is my sincere hope that you have enjoyed reading SAVAGE SPLENDOR. SAVAGE WHISPER, my next Indian romance published by The Berkley Publishing Group, will transport you to the intriguing world of the Kiowa Indians!

I would be delighted to hear from you all and I will respond to all letters received!

Best Wishes,
CASSIE EDWARDS
R #3, Box 60
Mattoon, Illinois 61938